The Economics of
Agricultural Policy

BY THE SAME AUTHOR

The Economics of Agricultural Land Tenure
The Social Economy of West Germany
Housing and Land Policies in West Germany and Britain
Urban Land Economics: Principles and Policy
Second Thoughts on Regional Policy
Regional Policy for Ever?
(with Peter Randall and E. G. West)
Maritime Industry and Port Development in South Wales
(with Peter Randall)

Graham Hallett

The Economics of Agricultural Policy

Second Edition

BASIL BLACKWELL · OXFORD

© Basil Blackwell 1968, 1981

First edition 1968
Second edition 1981

Basil Blackwell Publisher
5 Alfred Street
Oxford OX1 4HB
England

British Library Cataloguing in Publication Data

Hallett, Graham
   The economics of agricultural policy.
   1. Agriculture and state
   2. Agriculture—Economic aspects
   I. Title
   338.1'8   HD1415

   ISBN 0-631-12493-4
   ISBN 0-631-12503-5 Pbk

Typeset by Preface Ltd, Salisbury, Wilts.
Printed in Great Britain by Book Plan, Worcester

To Veronica, Alison and Isabel

Contents

CONTENTS

Preface to the Second Edition

This book was first published in 1968, and has remained in print ever since. At the end of 1979, it was decided to produce a completely new, revised edition. In Parts I and II, which deal with general principles and their quantification, I have retained the original framework and most of the original text, although bringing statistics up to date. I have extensively re-written Part III, which deals with policy, and have added two new chapters on the problems of food and agriculture in the 'Third World', which were discussed rather briefly in the first edition.

I originally wrote this book because, at the time—apart from some excellent but insular American books—there was no book which satisfactorily guided students from basic economic principles, through empirical work, to an examination of national and international agricultural policy. The continuing sales in many countries have encouraged me to think that it has fulfilled this role. On reading a text which I completed thirteen years ago, I was encouraged to find that, although some parts had begun to date, nothing in it had been disproved by events, and the basic analysis was still applicable; this is not always the case in economics.

'Agricultural economics', in the UK and some other countries, is a specialised field, organisationally separate from 'economics'—a separation which has not, perhaps, raised the intellectual calibre of 'agricultural economics' or increased the knowledgeability of economists' forays into agricultural matters. After writing this book I ceased to be an 'agricultural economist' and devoted myself primarily to urban and regional policy, which is in fact closely linked to agricultural policy in the broad sense. In my subsequent books I have attempted to build up a body of economic analysis of urban policy, similar in its middlebrow, eclectic style, to my previous work on agricultural policy, but it has been a lonely and often discouraging undertaking, as I find myself in something of a professional limbo. The Professor of Agricultural Economics at one of Great Britain's most famous universities once told me, 'The only doubt we have about you, Hallett, is that you are inclined to be academic; we don't want that sort of thing here.' (To my shame, I denied the accusation, but it was a 'moment of truth'.) On the other hand, advanced economists would not consider what I write to be economics at all. But is 'advanced economics' of much *use*? After the 'nonsense on stilts' of cost–benefit analysis, the harm done by the most fashionable kind of development economics to developing countries, and the feet of clay of many a 'sophisticated' economic model (not to mention the increasing 'show-biz' element in economics), even well-wishers have begun to have doubts about the present state of the subject, and to sympathise with the plea by the 'Think Tank' pioneer Lord Rothschild, 'God spare us of these academic economists' (letter to *The Financial Times*, 10 October 1979).

I believe that economic analysis can be valuable and even essential, but only if it becomes again what it was for Mill, Marshall or Keynes—a blend of simple theory and practical knowledge, with a historical and an international dimension, practised by people who have the broad culture needed to see economics in context, and who seek, in the words of the motto of the London School of Economics, 'To understand the causes of things' and to convey this understanding to others as clearly and simply as possible. During my 'agricultural period' at Aberystwyth and Göttingen, I had the privilege of knowing several economists in this tradition.

The need for a modern 'political economy' applies, I suggest, to both agricultural and urban economics, which are best studied with some reference to each other, since the problems of the city and the countryside are closely related, although in different ways in different countries and at different times. In the 'developing' countries, rural development has to take into account the problems of the exploding cities; in the 'developed' countries, agricultural policy has to deal with the problems of land which is no longer needed for agriculture, but which has to be managed in the interest of a primarily urban population.

Given this close connection between urban and rural problems, it is unfortunate that there has recently been little interest, in 'land economics', in the sense of the study of the theoretical and institutional aspects of all types of land use envisaged by the pre-War Wisconsin School. This school had a breadth of vision, and a blend of theory and practice, singularly lacking in much of the over-specialised academic work of recent years. The problems of a shrinking Earth call for a comprehensive approach to rural and urban development. I hope that this revised edition of my textbook on agricultural policy, together with its counterpart *Urban Land Economics: Principles and Policy*, will prove useful to students and teachers in an important field of study.

Graham Hallett
University College, Cardiff

Acknowledgements

The author is deeply indebted to Mr David Patchett, who up-dated a great deal of statistical material for this edition, and also the library staff of the Institute of Agricultural Economics, Oxford. He is grateful to The Economist Newspaper Ltd for permission to quote from 'The 35,000 villages that know growth works', *Economist*, 14 July 1979 and 'The Poor World's Cities', *Economist*, 6 December 1969.

PART I

The Theory of Supply and Demand applied to Agriculture

CHAPTER ONE

Introduction: The Background to Agricultural Policy

The Market Economy and the Planned Economy

To adapt a classification of general economic problems given by an American economist, we may say that there are three basic agricultural problems underlying all the complex issues discussed in subsequent chapters:

(1) What quantities of the various agricultural commodities should be produced? (The product mix)
(2) What production methods should be employed; e.g. small farms or 'factory farms', extensive or intensive cultivation, machines or muscle power? (Resource combination)
(3) How is the national income to be divided between those engaged in farming and those engaged in other occupations? (Income distribution)

These three problems are common to all economies, but they are answered in different ways in three main groupings into which economic systems can be divided. In a *traditional society*, custom is the main determinant of what is produced and of the methods employed. A large proportion of the food produced is for the farmer's own family, and methods of production are little influenced by scientific techniques or market forces. A farmer's life in such a society is hard and, although he may eat well when there is a good harvest, in bad years he may come near to starvation. This type of subsistence farming is still widespread in Asia and Africa.

In a *centrally planned economy* on the other hand, the production of the various commodities, the methods employed, and the distribution of income are determined by a central body. Examples of this type of economic system—or at least approximations to it—are to be found in wartime economies and today in Communist countries. In the Soviet Union, for example, production targets for the various agricultural products are laid down nationally, then divided up among smaller administrative areas, until finally the production quotas for each farm are fixed. At least that is the theory. In practice, a considerable margin has to be left for a semi-offical 'grey' market.

In a *market economy* it is the interaction of prices, costs, profits which determines what is produced, how it is produced, and how the rewards are distributed. The *entrepreneur*—whether he is a farmer or a textile manufacturer—is faced by a pattern of prices for inputs and outputs, which in the farmer's case means, on the one hand, wages, fertilisers, machinery, land etc., and on the other hand cereals, beef, milk etc. The technical relations between input and output, and the prevailing pattern of resource and product prices determine the most profitable combination of inputs and outputs. The difference between the cost of inputs and outputs represénts the reward of the *entrepreneur* for his labour, capital and management. The consumer is also faced with a pattern of prices—for foodstuffs and other goods—and makes his purchases according to his tastes and income, in the light of the prices of the various goods available. It is going too far to suggest, as Professor Galbraith has done,[2] that firms, by means of advertising, can today so manipulate demand as to make the public buy whatever they wish to sell. In recent years producers of milk, coal and linen—to give only a few examples—must have wished it were as easy as that. Thus production is—in spite of inefficiencies and frictions—in the last resort determined by the wishes of consumers. Such an economic system is not 'unplanned', in the sense of chaotic; it is rather guided by the plans of innumerable consumers and producers.

A pure market economy, however, is as much an abstraction as a pure centrally planned economy, since most modern economies contain elements of both. The nations of Western Europe and North America are today 'mixed' economies in which the state frequently intervenes to modify the workings of the market, both in agriculture and other fields. In some cases, this is done through the price system, without directly interfering with production. By imposing a tariff on imported wheat, for example, a Government can maintain a higher level of wheat prices than would otherwise have prevailed. If farmers remain free to plan their production in the most profitable way, this will (other things being equal!) lead to the extension of the wheat acreage. But the state can also intervene directly in the production process by, for example, setting quotas for the acreage of wheat farmers are allowed to grow.

'Centrally planned economy' and 'market economy' are therefore limiting cases which in a pure form are rarely found in the real world. In practice, it is a question of different 'mixes' of the two systems, and of different sub-systems within each. A marketing system, for example, in which producer-controlled cooperatives play an important role is different from one in which illiterate, debt-ridden farmers face well-organised dealers. Similarly, the South American 'estancia' system (described by Marxist writers as 'capitalist' although it can equally be described as 'feudal'³) is different from the North American farm system. Nor is the distinction between a centrally planned and a market economy synonymous with that between public and private ownership. Economists have developed ideas for a 'socialist market economy' and some of the communist countries have begun to undertake experiments on these lines.⁴

Free Trade and Protection
A further distinction is that between 'free trade' and 'protection'. Free (international) trade implies an unrestricted flow of goods across national frontiers, whereas protection implies that imports are subject to tariffs, levies, or physical restrictions in order to reduce their competition with home products. The traditional form of protection was import tariffs, which—provided they were not prohibitively high—reduced rather than excluded foreign competition. Since the 1930s, however, in the field of agriculture, methods such as quotas, variable

import levies and subsidies have increasingly been employed, which exclude foreign competition far more drastically than tariffs.

In a centrally planned economy, on the other hand, it is difficult to tell to what extent a protective policy is being followed, since all foreign trade is the hands of state monopolies. Nevertheless, the planning authority still has to decide the allocations of resources between industries, which in a market economy are solved more or less automatically by the price system. The Russian authorities, for example, have in recent years had to weigh up the relative advantages of growing more wheat at home and importing it in exchange for exports of other products.

The Objectives of Agricultural Policy

Agricultural policy, like any other aspect of economic policy, depends in the last resort on certain political objectives. One objective in the past has been to maintain the maximum number of persons engaged in agriculture, either because the farm population was regarded as a source of courageous and unquestioning infantrymen in time of war, and a stabilising and 'reliable' force in society in time of peace, or because the country was considered to provide better living conditions than the town. A second objective has frequently been to maintain a certain degree of self-sufficiency in food, either because of the risk of war, or of a curtailment of imported supplies for other reasons, or because of balance-of-payments difficulties. A third objective, which in developed countries in recent years tended to become the most important, has been to maintain the incomes of the farming community and improve the efficiency of agricultural production and marketing.

The last type of objective arises because of defects in the working of the market economy in the field of agriculture. Taking the three basic economic problems—product mix, resource combination, and income distribution—the market economy works well for the first, less well for the second, and often rather badly for the third. It causes the type of agricultural produce desired by the consumer to be produced, but it does not always cause them to be produced efficiently, nor does it result in an acceptable distribution between the agricultural and non-agricultural sectors. Marketing and production methods sometimes lag behind requirements of the time and, in the absence of intervention, farmers are subject to low and fluctuating incomes. In developed countries such as those of Western Europe and North America, there is a tendency for rapid technical advance to cause production to rise faster than demand, which leads to low prices and incomes. At the same time, the biological nature of agriculture leads to unplanned fluctuations in production which cause sharp fluctuations in prices, and hence in farmers' incomes. In many developing countries, on the other hand, the problem if one of agriculture production lagging behind requirements.

Types of Agricultural Policy
Government policies towards agriculture, which can be divided into three main groups:

(a) Price Policies;
(b) Structural Policies;
(c) Marketing Policies.

Agricultural price policy is concerned with the prices which the farmer receives for his products (the farm-gate price) and the prices at other stages in the distributive chain. The objectives of price policy can be varied and often mixed. We can distinguish the aims of (a) stabilisation, (b) raising (or occasionally lowering) farm incomes, (c) holding down retail prices in the interest of consumers. For reasons discussed below, the prices of agricultural products can fluctuate greatly, causing large fluctuations in the incomes of farmers or, in the case of countries heavily dependent on one export crop, in foreign exchange earnings. These fluctuations can go beyond those which serve an economic purpose, and some measure of stabilisation—if it can be obtained at a tolerable cost—may be desirable. However, 'stabilising' prices is frequently used as a euphemism for 'raising'. Prices are often raised as a means of raising farm incomes: price support, however, is not always an efficient means of attaining this objective since (in developed countries) it can stimulate excessive production and delay structural change. In some developing countries, the aim of price policy is to hold down retail prices in the interests of urban consumers, which can sometimes limit the growth of agricultural output. This policy has been criticised as one aspect of an unfortunate 'urban bias' in developing countries (see Chapter 14). An early example was the policy adopted in the 1950s by the Argentinian President Juan Peron of holding down meat prices, which was influenced by the fact that the agricultural landowners were his political opponents. The policy eventually brought about meat shortages in one of the agriculturally most favoured countries in the world.

Agricultural price policies can be pursued either nationally or internationally. National policies have used many methods, such as tariffs or variable levies on imports, import quotas, subsidies, support buying, production control, statutory marketing organisations, and various combinations of these. Policies of this type, which are generally protectionist in their effect, are not confined to agricultural products: many countries give protection to manufacturing industries. In most developed countries today, however, the protection given to agriculture is more comprehensive than that given to most industries. International price polices, up to the present, have consisted mainly of the 'international commodity agreements' which, from the 1920s to the present day, and with very varying degrees of success, have been negotiated for products such as wheat, rubber, tea, coffee, and sugar. There has in recent years been a revived interest in these international commodity agreements, which have been seen as a means of reconciling conflicts of interest—e.g. between exporting and importing countries—caused by divergent national policies (see Chapter 16).

National policies for maintaining farm incomes date from the late nineteenth century in Continental European countries such as Germany and France, and from 1931 in the United Kingdom. Since 1945, however, many countries have passed laws specifying the objectives of agricultural policy. In the British Agriculture Act of 1947 the aim (Pt. 1, Section 1) is stated to be 'a stable and efficient agricultural industry capable of producing such part of the nation's food as in the national interest it is desirable to produce in the United Kingdom, and of producing it at minimum prices consistent with proper remuneration and living conditions for farmers and workers in agriculture and an adequate return on capital invested in the industry' (an unexceptionable criterion which would permit almost any policy). The West German Agriculture Act of 1955 states 'In order to ensure that agriculture participates in the progressive development of the German economy and that the population obtains the best possible supply of foodstuffs, all the means of economic and agricultural policy—are to be used to compensate agriculture for its physical and economic disadvantages compared with other occupations, and to enable it to increase its productivity.'[5]

Some countries lay down more specific objectives for agricultural price policy. The Swiss Agriculture Act of 1952 states that prices should be designed to cover the average costs of 'properly managed farms under normal conditions', whereas Sweden goes into more detail and relates prices to the costs of properly managed farms of a middle sized group (25 to 50 acres of arable land). The United States has adopted prices in a historical period as the basis of its agricultural pricing; namely the relation between agricultural and industrial prices in the period 1910–1914. In practice, however, this concept of maintaining the 'parity' between agricultural and industrial prices which existed before the First World War—which is open to a great many theoretical objections—has been largely abandoned.

Structural policies are those designed to improve the structure of agricultural production, i.e. the size, layout, and equipment of farms, as well as the rural 'infrastructure'—electricity and water supplies, educational and advisory services and, in a broad sense, social facilities in the countryside. Similar structural policies are not unknown in other industries. The concentration of the Lancashire cotton industry into fewer and larger firms, for example, has been actively encouraged by British governments since the 1920s. Nevertheless, in most industries the process of adjustment to new circumstances is brought about solely or mainly by economic pressures. In agriculture, the process is unusually slow and difficult, partly because of the 'family business' nature of farming, and partly because most farming operations require the use of a large area of land. Once a pattern of farms has been established, it tends to be extremely resistant to change, even when it is quite clear that a change in layout would be desirable.

Marketing policies are concerned with changes in the distributive chain between farmer and consumer. The objective here may be to strengthen the farmers' bargaining position by, for example, encouraging the development of producer-controlled marketing organisations; or to improve hygiene or quality; or to reduce the costs of marketing. The costs of marketing, i.e. the size of the distributive margin, has always been a subject of criticism, and there is often a (quite unjustified) tendency to regard distributive and processing costs as somehow less legitimate than production costs. In general, however, improvements in the efficiency of food retailing, wholesaling and processing have not lagged behind improvements in efficiency in other sectors of the economy (see Chapter 9).

Developing countries tend to have systems of food distribution which are inefficient compared with those in the developed countries of North-West Europe and North America. These developed countries have distributive systems which rely mainly on the competitive process. In some cases, however, the state has found it necessary to intervene, either to replace competition—as has frequently been done in the arrangements for collecting milk from farms—or to direct it—as when sales of livestock or vegetables are permitted only at certain markets. The distinction between price and marketing policy is in practice not always clearcut, since organisations with distributive functions, such as certain British Agricultural Marketing Boards, are also used to implement price policies. It is important, however, to distinguish in principle between policies designed to raise prices—usually by in some way restricting supply—and those designed to improve the efficiency of marketing.

Development of Economic Policy and Doctrine

Agricultural policy cannot be regarded completely in isolation from general economic policy. The present 'mixed' economic systems in the countries of Western Europe (which in spite of national differences have a great deal in common) are the result of a historical development, in which various forms of economic system have succeeded one another.[6] In this development, the current economic doctrine has partly influenced, partly reflected, the prevailing system. At the beginning of the modern era, in the seventeenth and eighteenth centuries, the prevailing doctrine in most European countries was *Mercantilism*. This doctrine advocated a strong state control of the economy with the aim, among other things, of building up home industries. A number of policies of this period have a very modern air about them. For example, in England the Corn Laws protected wheat growing by means of an import levy. When harvests were poor, and prices correspondingly high, the levy was removed; when prices were low, exports were subsidised. The market regulations for cereals introduced in 1962 in the European Economic Community rest on the same principle! Not without justification do some liberal economists speak of a modern 'neo-mercantilism'. Mercantilism, however, often favoured industry at the expense of agriculture, and as a reaction there arose in France in the late eighteenth century the doctrine of the *Physiocrats*, who regarded agriculture as the sole 'productive' occupation. Other economic activities, and especially trade, were regarded as 'unproductive', an outlook utterly rejected by modern economics, but still to be discerned in some controversies on agricultural policy.

With the beginning of the Industrial Revolution, the doctrines of economic Liberalism and Free Trade were adopted enthusiastically in Great Britain and, more reservedly, in other countries. Between the repeal of the Corn Laws in Great Britain in 1846 and the imposition of tariffs on cereals by Germany in 1879 there were three decades in which international trade was almost completely free, and the economic activity of the state reduced to a minimum. According to liberal economists, the general good was best served when consumers could obtain their requirements, both of foodstuffs and manufactured articles, in the cheapest market, whether at home or abroad. Hence they opposed restrictions on international trade (with some qualifications regarding national defence) and state intervention in the market process.

This theory of *laissez faire* was opposed by the German

economist *Friedrich List* (1789–1846). He emphasised the need of an 'infant industry' in one country for protection against established foreign industries, and the responsibility of the state for the building up of the industrial 'infrastructure'. These ideas came to fruition towards the end of the nineteenth century, when Germany introduced import tariffs for manufactured products and foodstuffs. Ironically enough, List himself had advocated free trade for agriculture, on the grounds that it was already present in all countries, and did not need to be built up.

The depression of the 1930s introduced a new phase in the economic policy—and especially the agricultural policy—of most Western countries. With the exception of Great Britain, many countries had already introduced protectionist agricultural policies, but these consisted merely of tariffs on imports. The depression led to far reaching intervention by the state in agricultural marketing and production, even in countries with such liberal traditions as Great Britain and the United States. Imports of agricultural products were strictly controlled by means of state trading monopolies, import quotas and levies; exports were often subsidised. On the home market, prices were maintained through support buying by state agencies, subsidies, and sometimes regulations compelling manufacturers to use a certain proportion of home-grown produce. Agricultural production was sometimes controlled by means of acreage quotas.

During the 1939–45 War, rationing and state control of food marketing was imposed, and continued for some time after the War. It was continued for an exceptionally long time in Great Britain, where rationing by allocation was considered more equitable than 'rationing by the purse'. In 1954, however, rationing was ended, and trade in foodstuffs handed back to private firms, in some cases acting under the control of marketing boards. British agriculture continued to be protected, however, mainly by means of 'deficiency payments' which made up the difference between a guaranteed price and the current market price.

The change, in the mid-1950s, from a completely state-controlled 'siege economy' in foodstuffs to a free market (supported by deficiency payments) was one of the success stories of British post-War economic history—in spite of the dire warnings of those who opposed the change. Consumers gained much greater freedom of choice, and producers learnt to produce for market requirement. (The point is worth making at a time when a 'siege economy' is once more gaining favour—as evidence by the British Labour Party's support for import controls and hostility to the European Economic Community (EEC), the EEC's own un-neighbourly agricultural policy, and the protectionist trend of US policy.)

However, the successful working of this combination of free marketing and deficiency payments was aided by the current situation; the UK was at the time a large net importer of most agricultural products, and the world market was still moving from post-War scarcity to surplus. As conditions eased on the world market, it became clear that the deficiency payments scheme represented a, for the Exchequer, dangerously open-ended guarantee; a fall in the market price could lead to a sharp unbudgeted rise in subsidy payments. Attempts began to be made to put a 'floor' on market prices by introducing import quotas, or by imposing a levy on imports if the price fell below a minimum level. Between 1962 and 1964, schemes on these lines were introduced for butter, bacon, and cereals.

British policy experienced a more radical change when it joined the European Economic Community in 1972, and gradually changed over to the Community systems. The original Community members had always relied more on import tariffs and controls than on deficiency payments to support prices, and the Common Agricultural Policy developed in the 1960s was based mainly on import levies and intervention buying. However, national or Community deficiency payments are made for some products and—given the increasing questioning of the Common Agricultural Policy—it is quite possible that deficiency payments, or some other kinds of subsidies, will play a more important role in the future.

Price Analysis under Different Agricultural Policies
Most countries possess a variety of types of agricultural price formation. There are products the price of which is fixed by the state, and the marketing of which is tightly

controlled by a monopolistic organisation. This situation is common in 'centrally planned' economies but a very similar situation prevails for the marketing of milk in the UK. There are products for which there is virtually no state intervention. There are products for which the market price is maintained by import levies and intervention buying. There are products for which the producer price is maintained by deficiency payments.

The process of price formation in all these different types of situation can be clarified with the help of the various analytical concepts discussed in subsequent chapters. The analysis may begin with a free market, in order to explain certain general principles, but the policies of state agencies and marketing boards can be examined with the same analytical tools. A particularly well developed section of agricultural price analysis is demand analysis, which has been developed empirically as well as theoretically. Demand analysis uses statistical techniques to estimate the relationship between the *per capita* consumption of a particular foodstuff, its price and consumers' incomes. These relationships—price and income elasticities—can be used, in conjunction with estimates of future population, to calculate future consumption. There are naturally so many variables, which can vary in an unexpected way, that any such projection is always subject to a wide margin of error. It is nevertheless better to have certain rationally based assumptions on which to plan, than to be completely in the dark about future developments. Economic analysis can therefore make a significant contribution to an understanding of the factors which influence agricultural prices, and of the likely results of governmental policies. But it cannot by itself decide what policies should be adopted; this is, and must remain, a political decision.[7]

Notes

In these and later notes the following abbreviations are used:

JFE   *Journal of Farm Economics*
JAE   *Journal of Agricultural Economics*
AJAE   *American Journal of Agricultural Economics*

1 Samuelson, P. A., *Economics: An Introductory Analysis*, London, tenth edition, 1976, or earlier editions.

2 Galbraith, K. L., *The Modern Industrial State*, London, 1967. For an 'anti-Galbraith' viewpoint, see Allen, G. C., *Economic Fact and Fantasy* (Occasional Paper), Institute of Economic Affairs, 1969.

3 Mellor, John W., *The Economics of Agricultural Development*, New York, 1966, p. 250.

4 Kohler, H., *Scarcity Challenged*, New York, 1968, an excellent general review of economics which contains a summary of 'market socialism' in Chapter 20.

5 Abel, W., *Agrarpolitik*, Göttingen, 1958, p. 437.

6 Gide, C. and Rist, C., *A History of Economic Doctrines*, London, 1948, eighteenth- and nineteenth-century sections only—an older work, but one which makes the classical economists more intelligible than most subsequent books.

7 Walker, E. R., *From Economic Theory to Policy*, Chicago, 1943, which contains a penetrating discussion of the methodology of economics.

General Reading
This book should be read in conjunction with the appropriate sections in a general economics textbook—such as Samuelson, P. A., *Economics: An Introductory Analysis*—and a textbook on agricultural production economics. Two good American books (the first long and difficult, the second short and lucid) are:

Heady, Earl O., *Economics of Agricultural Production and Resource Use*, New York, 1952,
Bishop, C. E. and Toussaint, W. D., *Introduction to Agricultural Economic Analysis*, New York, 1958

A book specifically designed for those interested in tropical agriculture is:

Abbot, J. C. and Makehen, J. P., *Agricultural Marketing and Production in the Tropics*, London, 1979.

CHAPTER TWO

Problems of the Agricultural Industry

The two basic agricultural problems which give rise to state intervention are:

(1) low incomes;
(2) fluctuating incomes.

Studies for many countries and different periods often show incomes in agriculture as being below those in other occupations, whether the comparison is made with other self-employed persons, or with all wage and salary earners (Table 1). These comparisons of incomes in agriculture with those in other occupations must, however, be viewed with considerable caution. It is very difficult to measure agricultural income, or rather, one can often arrive at differing estimates of it. The valuation of non-financial advantages—such as food produced on the farm—and of capital assets, give rise to serious problems. Moreover, income from non-agricultural sources is often very important, and its exclusion can give a false picture of living standards; in the USA, it is calculated to be no less than one-third of total income of farm families. Finally, the income differences within agriculture are far greater than the differences between the average income in agriculture and in other occupations.

For these reasons, too much weight should not be given to any particular figure of average income in agriculture. But an impression of the financial position of agriculture can be obtained from various investigations, and these confirm that, without the current price support measures, agriculture in many countries would be in difficulties. In

TABLE 1

Estimated Average Incomes of Farmers as a Percentage
of Average Incomes in Other Occupations

	Early Industrial Era (Lipton)	1950–57	1961–65	1975
United States		58	54	81
Canada		130	106	
New Zealand		195	136	
United Kingdom	110 [1801]	108	92	72
West Germany	170 [1857]	66	78	72
France	110 [1830]			74
Denmark		94	75	66

Developing countries 1970 (Lipton's estimates)

Africa	60–3
Asia	45–4
Latin America	55–14

Developing countries 1969–71 (FAO estimates)

Level 1 (poorest)	19
Level 2	30
Level 3	30

Developed countries

Level 4	41
Level 5	67

Sources: Slattery, M., 'Relative incomes of farmers: some international comparisons', *Quarterly Review of Agricultural
Economics*, Vol. XIX, no. 3, 1966, p. 126; Lipton, M., *Why
Poor People Stay Poor*, London, 1977, p. 435; USDA; calculations from Eurostat; FAO, *State of Food and Agriculture*,
1975, p. 80.

this sense at least there is a problem of income disparity
between agriculture and other occupations.

In developed countries, the problem of income disparity
is paradoxically often increased by technical progress in

agricultural production. The application of scientific methods since the Second World War has led to sharp increases in output, which have sometimes outstripped the rise in demand and thus led to falls in the prices of agricultural products in relation to industrial prices, although not necessarily in relative farm income. A comparison made in West Germany between incomes in agriculture and in 'comparable occupations' in the annual 'Green Report' indicates that agricultural income has in recent years risen at the same rate as income in other sectors, but has been at roughly three-quarter its level. In the UK, the available national income statistics indicate that farmers' incomes rose relatively during the war, but have declined relatively since the early 1950s. The figures for the UK in Table 1, showing a fall from 108 in the early 1950s to 72 in 1975, probably give a reasonable indication of *relative* change, whatever the qualifications about the absolute level. Since 1975, there seems to have been a further fall, and in 1978–80 quite a sharp squeeze on farm incomes developed, arising from the same factors which squeezed the profits of manufacturing industry—a high inflation rate and high interest rates, combined with a strong sterling exchange rate based on the growth of North Sea oil revenues.[1]

These actual or potential problems of low incomes in agriculture are essentially the result of the industry not being able to adjust itself quickly enough to changed conditions. As incomes rise, the demand for food does not rise proportionately, whereas technical progress—at least in developed countries—causes a continuous rise in output. Fewer farmers are therefore needed to produce the food required but, because of various frictions, the reduction in the number of farmers does not take place at the required speed, leading to over-supplied markets, low prices, inadequate output per man, and low incomes. In developing countries, although to some extent for different reasons, relative income is even lower than in the developed countries, being usually 30 to 15 per cent and sometimes even less (see Chapter 14). This is not only much lower than in developed countries today but, as far as can be judged, much lower than it has ever been in the currently 'developed' countries since the beginning of industrialisation.

Fluctuating Incomes
The second basic agricultural problem is that of fluctuating incomes. This is largely a result of fluctuating prices, and can only be dealt with by means of price policy. But fluctuations in prices do not necessarily lead to fluctuations in incomes; the price change can be offset by a change in costs or in the quantity sold. For example, if income is to remain constant during a bumper crop or a short crop, prices will have to fall when the crop is heavy and rise when it is light. Constant prices would mean that total receipts varied in proportion to the crop; assuming that some harvesting costs varied with the crop, but that other costs did not, net income would fluctuate even more. Stabilisation of incomes does not therefore necessarily mean stabilisation of prices.

The prices of agricultural commodities on free markets are very 'flexible', whereas prices of manufactured goods tend to be 'sticky'. Prices of agricultural commodities are subject to large swings from day to day, week to week, and year to year. However, it is possible to distinguish five different types of fluctuation in these price movements (Fig. 1):

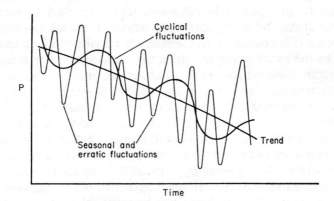

FIG. 1. Price fluctuations

(a) Long-term movements, stretching over many years and caused by basic changes in demand or supply conditions.

(b) Fluctuations resulting from the general trade cycle. Before 1939 the trade cycle was very marked, with a length of 6 to 9 years, but in the post-1945 period it has been less severe and shorter in length, causing 'recessions' rather than 'depressions'. However, the two booms-and-slumps of the 1970s have been of distinctly larger magnitude than previous fluctuations.

(c) Livestock and crop cycles of two years and upwards, in which shortages and high prices follow gluts and low prices.

(d) Seasonal variations within the course of a year.

(e) Erratic fluctuations, extending over days, weeks, months, or a few years.

The appropriate price policy varies according to the type of fluctuation. It is not desirable to shield agriculture permanently from the effects of long-term price movements. These reflect fundamental changes: either changes in demand; changes in production costs, mainly due to mechanisation; or changes in sources of supply, such as the opening up of new producing areas. Although it may well be justifiable to provide transitional price support in the face of rapid changes, there is no convincing case for doing so for ever; agriculture must be expected to adapt itself to changed circumstances. Similarly, seasonal variations of a regular type serve a useful purpose by reconciling demand with seasonally varying production costs. On the other hand, livestock and crop cycles are a form of fluctuation which have undesirable effects on income distribution and resource allocation, and which it is therefore desirable to moderate or eliminate; the cost and difficulty of doing so must, however, be balanced against the benefits obtained. Erratic price fluctuations, due to temporary gluts and shortages, although they serve a useful function in allocating available supplies, can have undesirable effects on income distribution and resource allocation, so that it may also be desirable to moderate this type of fluctuation. The fluctuations, caused by the general trade cycle are also harmful, but cannot be dealt with by policies confined to agriculture; they can only be tackled effectively by general economic policy.

Risk and Uncertainty in Agriculture
The arguments for governmental policies to reduce erratic price fluctuations rest partly on the undesirability of fluctuating incomes for producers, and fluctuating prices for consumers. A further argument, however, is that price stability reduces risk—or rather uncertainty—in agricultural production, and thus leads to cost reductions.

In ordinary language, the terms 'risk' and 'uncertainty' are virtually synonymous, but a distinction between them is often drawn in economic theory. In this specialised sense, 'risk' refers to occurrences, the probability of which is measurable. Thus the result of spinning a coin several times is subject to change, but it is known that heads are likely to come up on half the spins. Similarly, there are some occurrences in agriculture, such as egg breakages, or poultry deaths (in the absence of an epidemic) which tend to run at a constant level, and can therefore be allowed for. On the other hand, droughts, exceptionally cold winters, and livestock epidemics follow no obvious regular pattern. Price changes fall into the same category of 'uncertain' occurrences.

Uncertainty plays an important role in agricultural production since, for reasons discussed below, uncertainties regarding price and output are unusually large. But in addition to these uncertainties, agriculture faces difficulties in the supply of capital. Since share capital can in most cases be obtained only for unusually large farm companies (such as have developed in broiler production), a farmer has to rely on his own capital, or on loans of various types, including mortgages. Thus large capital investment often involves a heavy dependence on loans, interest on which has to be regularly repaid. To use a term from the business world, agriculture is 'highly geared', a condition which is dangerous if economic conditions deteriorate unexpectedly.

In addition to being largely restricted to repayable loan capital, the farmer is often limited in the amount he can obtain. Banks and other lending institutions often set a limit to the amount of credit they are willing to extend to any particular farmer, this limit being usually related to the security he can offer rather than the likely return on the capital. On the other hand, some farmers are themselves unwilling to take up a loan, since they regard being 'in debt' as reprehensible.

In so far as 'capital rationing' is imposed by the lender, it is partly an indirect outcome of the economic uncertainty facing the farmer himself; the lender is aware of this uncertainty and unwilling to risk losing his money. But there are often additional restraints of a structural type. Credit facilities available to farmers may be inadequate or the lending institutions may lack the 'know-how' to enable them to judge whether a farmer's plans are worth lending money on. In consequence, farmers in many countries have founded co-operative banks to provide credit for agriculture, and state institutions (such as the Agricultural Mortgage Corporation in Great Britain) have been set up for the same purpose. In many developing countries, however, provisions for the supply of agricultural credit are still very limited, and the interest rates charged by private money lenders are horrific. This can be the result of a general shortage of capital, or of a monopolistic position enjoyed by the lenders, or of genuinely high risks of default. Whatever the structural situation regarding the supply of credit, however, a reduction in the economic uncertainty facing the farmer is likely to put him in a better position for obtaining capital.

Problems in the supply of capital are not confined to agriculture. But agriculture suffers from the double difficulty of facing institutional problems in the supply of capital while at the same time needing relatively large amount of capital in relation to production. Agriculture's capital needs are illustrated in Table 2, which gives the rate of capital turnover in various industries in the UK in 1965. The figures are based on sample information, and subject to a wide range of error. They do, however, indicate the relatively slow rate of capital turnover in agriculture.

The capital intensity of modern agriculture does not

TABLE 2

Capital Turnover in Various Industries: UK 1965

Capital Turnover Annual Sales ÷ Fixed Assets	
Agriculture	0·25–0·4
Chemicals	2·0
Electrical Engineering	3·6
Retail Distribution	4·0

mean that incomes in agriculture need necessarily be lower than in other occupations, but it does mean that agriculture in developed countries is today very vulnerable to unexpected price falls. In the past, when less mechanised methods were employed, the capital turnover in agriculture was almost certainly higher, and the farmer's profit was higher in relation to receipts. Thus in bad times the farmer could carry on by tightening his belt; for this reason, the small farmer tended to weather depressions better than the large one. In modern capital-intensive agriculture, however, a reduction in the farmer's personal consumption would do very little to offset a substantial fall in prices.

The effect of economic uncertainty is to induce a farmer to adopt a more diversified, or a more flexible farming plan than he would otherwise do. Diversification means that a farmer carries on several enterprises, in order to avoid the dangers of having all his eggs in one basket. Flexibility means that he arranges his farming system so that, without too much cost, he can move out of one enterprise into another if economic conditions make this desirable. Diversification of flexibility thus provide a type of insurance against uncertainty. But there may well be a high price to be paid for this insurance, in that the farming system is less efficient, and less profitable, than a more specialised, inflexible system. Admittedly a certain degree of flexibility in farming systems (notably in farm buildings) is probably desirable in any case, since future developments are never wholly foreseeable. But erratic price fluctuations can encourage farmers to stay unduly diversified, or to hesitate to undertake the investment required for modern systems, and thus hold up the general level of costs per unit of output. Government action to damp down erratic price fluctuations can, by reducing farmers' uncertainty, be expected to encourage the adoption of more efficient farming systems.

However, having stated this case for price stabilising (as distinct from price-raising) policies, it must be added that some of the most rapid increases in efficiency have taken place in new branches of agricultural production, such as broilers, which have not generally been the subject of any official price policies, and have sometimes been subject to considerable instability. This type of production has been pioneered by progressive producers willing to adopt methods which have more in common with industrial production than with traditional agriculture. These new methods of production and marketing have brought considerable benefits to consumers; in recent years, retail poultry prices in Great Britain have fallen, in real terms, more than any other food prices (Table 4). Broiler and turkey production has probably benefitted from not being subject to official price policies and marketing boards, which might well have had the effect of holding up prices, and imposing restraints on more progressive producers for the sake of the less progressive. Thus although reasonable price stability probably encourages technical progress in agriculture, it does not in itself bring it about. Indeed, if price stability is combined with excessive price support and/or restrictions on the more enterprising producers, technical progress can be held back.

Peculiarities of Agricultural Supply and Demand
The twin problems of low farm income and price instability in income outlined above can be attributed to certain peculiarities of the supply of—and to a lesser extent the demand for—agricultural products. Admittedly, some of the traditional characteristics which distinguished agriculture from manufacturing industry—conservative techniques, primitive book-keeping, a non-pecuniary

approach—have largely been eliminated in modern agriculture. But it is a mistake to think that the modernisation of agriculture has eliminated the differences between agriculture and manufacturing industry; for example, agriculture still differs from most manufacturing industries in the number of firms in the industry. Thus the modernisation of agriculture has by no means removed its economic peculiarities. On the supply side, two peculiarities of agricultural production can be distinguished:

(1) The relatively small size of agricultural enterprises, which gives rise to:

  (a) the development of a separate system for collecting and processing agricultural products;
  (b) the immobility of factors of production and the inflexibility of output in relation to price changes.

(2) The biological nature of agricultural production, which leads to unplanned yearly fluctuations and a concentration of output into certain seasons. Added to this is the perishability of many agricultural products, making necessary storage or processing.

On the side of demand, the following characteristics can be noted:

(1) The generally low increase in consumption resulting from increases in consumers' real incomes (low income elasticity of demand).
(2) The often low increase in consumption resulting from falls in price (low price elasticity of demand).

We will examine these supply and demand characteristics in turn.

Size of Enterprise
In terms of labour, agricultural enterprises in the non-communist world are small or medium-sized. The family farm is the usual form in most countries of the 'free' world—including the USA, Canada, Australia and New Zealand—and the cases in which farms with more than two or three hired workers predominate are

exceptional. Farms with large numbers of non-family workers are found in the communist countries—although in the Soviet Union, contrary to all official doctrines, the workers' private plots supply a large proportion of total output—as well as in some South American countries, and in tropical countries where plantations have survived from colonial times. But even the largest agricultural enterprises are, in terms of numbers employed or market share, small in comparison with large industrial firms. Only in modern poultry production is there any likelihood of a situation developing which could become similar to that in manufacturing industry.

This small-scale structure of agricultural production is similar to that of industry in the nineteenth century and earlier. In developed countries nowadays this type of structure is, outside agriculture, to an increasing extent found only in such activities as garages or retail trade, which possess, however, a certain local monopoly. But the unusual organisation of agriculture is not a relic of the past; there are good grounds for it, in that the 'economies of scale' are soon exhausted as the number of workers rises, while the organisational problems increases sharply. These organisational problems arise because agricultural workers are usually spread out over a large area of land, and hence more difficult to supervise than in a factory. Moreover, the consequences of a lack of conscientiousness are often more serious than in manufacturing industry. Shoddy work in a car factory results merely in a dissatisfied car owner, but farm animals not tended with care are liable to die rather readily. These remarks do not apply to the same extent to 'factory farming', of the type which has been particularly developed for poultry, but even here the economies of scale, in terms of numbers employed, are soon exhausted. A further expansion in size merely involves a duplication of the plant, so that further economies must lie in the field of marketing or feed supply. The movement in costs as the size of enterprise increases can be represented as in Fig. 33(b). The various curves would represent farms with 1, 2, 3, 4 etc. workers cultivating the optimal amount of land in each case. The 'envelope curve' formed by the individual curves at first falls, but then flattens out. In practice, it is extremely difficult to say whether the lowest costs for a particular type of farm are reached with 2, 3, 4, or only 10 workers, but it is clear that the number is, by industrial standards, very small.

Since costs vary considerably according to the organising ability of the farmer—especially on farms with a large labour force—it is better to conceive of the cost curve as a fairly broad band rather than as a line. The upper edges of this band can be thought of as sloping slightly upwards as size increases beyond a certain point. As there is a fairly wide range of farm size over which the cost curve is a more or less horizontal band, it is difficult to speak of an *optimum* size of farm. But it is possible—at any particular time and for a given type of farming—to calculate a *minimum* economic size of full-time holding.

The Distributive System

The somewhat unusual organisation of agricultural production has the consequence that, in a modern economy, a distribution system is needed to collect, sort, process and pack farm products, and deliver them to retail traders. Many of these functions must also be carried out for manufactured products, but this often takes place inside the manufacturing firm itself. These functions were originally performed by the farmers themselves, who travelled into the nearby towns in order to sell their products. Even today this is still done in many developing countries, but in a developed economy it is too wasteful of labour, and tends to be confined to a few products such as eggs. A distributive system has therefore developed which is separate from agricultural production and often not in the producers' hands. In many cases, producers have joined together in order to found cooperative sales organisations, but these differ from the sales organisation of industrial firms, in so far as they have little influence on the level of production. In addition to voluntary groupings formed by farmers, organisations have been set up by law in various countries, with power to intervene in the marketing process. These organisations may represent merely producers—as in the case of the British Marketing

Boards and French 'groupements des producteurs' or they can represent producers, distributors and consumers —as in the case of the British Livestock Commission, or the Dutch 'Produktschappen' or they can be semi-governmental, as in the case of the American Commodity Credit Corporation. In the absence of co-operative or statutory groupings, a large number of competing farmers face a much smaller number of distributors, and may therefore be in a weak bargaining position.

Inflexibility of Supply

The second consequence of the small-scale organisation of agriculture is an inflexibility of supply in response to price changes, and particularly to price falls. The individual farmer produces such an infinitely small proportion of total production that he has no influence at all on the price. For the individual farmer, therefore, the price is given; he has merely to decide whether at this price it pays him to produce more, less, or the same amount. This is not always the case with industrial firms, who often have a sufficiently large share of the market to be able to influence the price.

The farmer changes the quantity produced in the light of a given price, but his reactions tend to be different according to whether the price change affects individual products or products as a whole. When the price of one product rises, and that of another falls, the farmer begins to produce more of the one and less of the other. The process takes time, and there are certain types of farm whose production possibilities are limited—such as hill farms which can only raise sheep or store cattle. But in general it is possible to alter farm outputs, and in fact enormous changes in the composition of agricultural production have taken place. The position is, however, different when the general price level of agricultural product falls, or lags behind the general price level. The question in this case is not that of altering the composition of production, but whether it pays to produce at all, and if so, how much. It is not only agricultural enterprises which have to ask themselves these questions, but these are in some ways in a peculiar position, in that their variable costs—namely those which vary with output—are unusually small. Whereas wages represent the largest cost item of most industrial firms, many agricultural enterprises employ no hired workers at all, and cannot therefore cut costs by laying off labour. The costs of agricultural machinery and buildings are also fixed in the short run, since used agricultural machinery fetches very little (especially in bad times) while buildings cannot be sold at all. Thus the 'salvage value' of agricultural assets is exceptionally low.[2] Variable costs are, in the short run, merely such items as purchased feeding stuffs, fertilisers and repairs; expenditure on these items can be cut when farm incomes fall, and it has, in fact, been usual in depressions for farmers to neglect repairs and run down the fertility of the land. But as long as receipts more than cover variable costs, and thus make some contribution to fixed costs, it is more profitable to continue in production than to go out of business; thus for many farmers the choice is between continuing a relatively unchanged level of production and giving up farming altogether. Since most farmers are traditionally attached to their farms, and would moreover find it difficult or impossible to obtain alternative work in the neighbourhood, they generally prefer to tighten their belts and continue production.

The consequence is that prices drop sharply when the demand for agricultural product falls or—as a result of technical progress—the supply increases more than the demand. This was particularly noticeable in the depression of the 1930s, when, as a result of an almost unchanged level of agricultural production, agricultural prices fell very much more than those of industrial products, the output of which was sharply reduced.[3]

Similar problems to those outlined above can also be observed in capital-intensive industries such as chemicals and steel, which are also burdened by high fixed costs. In these industries it is also more profitable for an individual firm to continue producing at low prices than to cease production altogether, so that at times when capacity greatly exceeds demand, competitive price-cutting easily sets in. In order to prevent price wars which would seriously reduce profits, firms in these industries have often entered into explicit or implicit agreements to maintain prices and restrict output (although experience suggests that when there is international competition and severe over-capacity, some degree of price-cutting always sets in, e.g., the world steel industry in the period 1965–67 and again in 1975–80). In agriculture, the number of enterprises is too large for similar policies to be followed, except through the exercise of statutory powers.

The Immobility of Factors of Production
The immobility of agricultural labour applies mainly to the farmer himself; it applies to a lesser extent to members of the family, and to a still lesser extent to hired workers, whose number throughout Europe has declined substantially in recent years. It is fairly easy to replace labour with machinery, when sufficient land is available to make full use of the machinery. A 150-acre farm, which in the nineteenth century may have employed ten workers, can be reorganised as a family farm with only one worker in addition to the farmer and his wife. But when it is a question of reorganising five 30-acre farms, the problem is extremely difficult. In the first place, farmers are very reluctant to give up their way of life, and when at last a farm does become vacant—usually through death—the neighbouring farm may not be in a position to take it over. In many countries—though not to any serious extent in the UK—the problem is complicated by an extreme fragmentation of farms.

At any one time, therefore, the structure of farms in a country or region diverges by a greater or lesser extent from that which would be optimal in the light of current techniques. These differences in the efficiency of the farm structure exert an important influence on national trade and price support policies. Countries with relatively efficient farm structures tend to have relatively low producer prices, and to favour freer international trade in agricultural products (e.g. New Zealand, Denmark, Canada). On the other hand, countries with relatively inefficient structures tend to have relatively high prices and generally wish to keep import restrictions in order to maintain these prices. Such national differences have been apparent in the negotiations over a common agricultural policy in the EEC and in the discussion over agricultural trade in the various 'rounds' of GATT negotiations. But even in this respect agriculture is not unique; coal mining is an example of an industry whose contraction, in the face of competition from other energy sources, has raised social and 'strategic' problems.

The Organisational Peculiarities of Agriculture
We can summarise the above discussion as follows. Since agriculture, unlike most industries, is organised primarily in family firms, the proportion of variable costs is generally lower than in manufacturing industry. Only in the long run therefore (at least under traditional agricultural systems), are market prices of agricultural products more or less closely related to the somewhat indefinable costs of production. In agriculture, the level of supply is not as directly linked to the cost-price relationship as in manufacturing industry; the prices of manufactured products are linked more closely with costs, those of agricultural products more closely with the current position of demand and supply.[4] The prices of agricultural products therefore fall particularly sharply when supply outruns demand.

The Influence of Natural Factors
The second peculiarity of agricultural production, in addition to its small-firm organisation, is its dependence on nature. In spite of technical progress, crop yields are still very much affected by the weather. Modern livestock husbandry is less dependent on the weather, but a hard winter or a dry summer can still have marked influence on production, and there is always the possibility of livestock epidemics. Fluctuations in production therefore take place which the farmer has not planned and cannot foresee. These fluctuations lead to an instability in supply and price which for some products, e.g. wheat, can to some extent be overcome by means of storage; for other products, such as potatoes, this is much more difficult.

Problems of this type are very rarely experienced in other industries.

A further consequence of the biological character of agricultural production is a seasonal grouping of production. Thus the cereal harvest takes place in Europe and North America in late summer or autumn. On the other hand, modern pig and poultry production is largely independent of the weather, although hens still persist in laying slightly more eggs in the spring. Cattle can be fattened indoors over the winter, and milk can also be produced in winter, but in both cases at higher costs. Thus the production of many foodstuffs is subject to seasonal fluctuations which are rarely matched by corresponding fluctuations in demand. Demand generally remains fairly constant throughout the year, apart from some fluctuations due to weather or tradition; a hot spell sends up milk sales, and the demand for turkeys is highest at Christmas.

There are three ways in which this discrepancy between supply and demand can be dealt with:

(1) The price at the time of peak supply can simply be allowed to fall, so that consumption at that time, and production in the off-season, is stimulated.

(2) Stocks can be built up at the time of peak supply, to be consumed later. However, the perishability of many agricultural products makes this in some cases an expensive operation.

(3) In the off-season, supplies can be imported from the southern hemisphere, or from more southerly lands (and vice versa for countries in the southern hemisphere).

In practice, each of the three methods is used for some commodities, and sometimes two or three together. A certain level of stocks is generally desirable in any case. For some products, such as cereals, the costs of storage are tolerable and quality losses are low, but for meat, dairy products and vegetables costs are higher and quality losses greater (although the quality problem is to an increasing extent being solved by modern techniques). Importing from countries with different seasons is not always practicable or profitable, but for fruit and some vegetables it plays a role, e.g. for North West Europe, new potatoes from the Mediterranean region or apples from Australia. In all cases, prices are lowest at times of peak supply; for some products this increases consumption, and in any case it makes storage more profitable. These seasonal fluctuations in production are peculiar to agriculture, and are found in hardly any other industry. They necessitate complicated storage arrangements, and produce a certain instability, since the extent of the fluctuations cannot always be forecast.

Peculiarities of Demand
On the demand side, foodstuffs—the largest class of agricultural products—also display certain peculiarities, the most noticeable of which is the trend of consumption as income increases. Adam Smith had already noted:

The rich man consumes no more food than his poor neighbour. In quality it may be very different, and to select and prepare it may require more labour and art: but in quantity it is very nearly the same. But compare the spacious palace and great wardrobe of the one with the hovel and few rags of the other, and you will be sensible that the difference between their clothing, lodging and household furniture is almost as great in quantity as it is in quality. The desire of food is limited in every man by the narrow capacity of the human stomach: but the desire of the conveniences and ornaments or building, dress, equipage, and household furniture, seems to have no limit or certain boundary.

It is still true, that—above a certain level—increasing income does not lead to an increase in the number of calories consumed. It is not, however, true that the pattern of consumption remains unchanged. With rising incomes there is a switch from cheap starchy foods such as cereals and potatoes to more expensive foods such as meat and fruit.

From week to week and month to month, on the other hand, the demand for foodstuffs remains very constant, and much less liable to seasonal fluctuations than commodities such as clothing, coal, sports goods or even motor-cars. In addition, the durability of certain manufactured goods, such as cars or television sets, can lead to long-term cycles in demand. Foodstuffs, however, have to be consumed every day, and this is an advantage for food marketing, since it enables stocks to be kept at a low level and labour and space to be fully utilised. As an American executive in the food industry put it: 'The wonderful thing about food from our point of view is that everyone uses it—and uses it only once.'[6]

Summary
The agricultural industry often suffers from low, and fluctuating, incomes. Low incomes are often a reflection of a condition of structural disequilibrium, in which a movement of labour out of the industry is proceeding. Fluctuating incomes are a consequence of the biological nature of production, which leads to unplanned fluctuations, combined with the characteristic structure of the industry, which approximates to 'perfect competition'. The 'family farm' is the most common type of production unit throughout the world, except under communist systems, and can be the most efficient. Such a production system, however, necessitates a separate processing and distribution system, as well as a publicly financed research programme. Some of the traditional differences between agriculture and industry are vanishing, but agriculture still retains several organisational peculiarities which give rise to special problems of policy.

Notes
1 'The squeeze on farm incomes', *Lloyd's Bank Economic Bulletin*, No. 18, June 1980.
2 Johnson, Glenn L., *Some Basic Problems for Economists and Statisticians arising from US Agricultural Policies*, Manchester Statistical Society, 1959.
3 Galbraith, K. K. and Black, J. D., 'The maintenance of agricultural production during the Depression. The explanations reviewed', *The Journal of Political Economy*, Vol. 46, No. 3, 1938, p. 305.
4 Hanau, A. 'The disparate stability of farm and non-farm prices', *Proceedings of the Tenth International Conference of Agricultural Economists*, London, 1960, p. 124.

5 Smith, Adam, *The Wealth of Nations*, Bk. 1, Ch. XI, Pt. 2. Everyman edition, 1964, pp. 149, 150.
6 Cassady, Ralph, *Competition and Price Making in Food Retailing*, New York, 1962, p. 3.

Further Reading

Bellerby, J. R., *Agriculture and Industry Relative Income*, London, 1956.
Cochrane, W. W., *Farm Prices: Myth and Reality*, Minnesota, 1958, Chs. 1–5.
Galbraith, J. K., *American Capitalism: The Concept of Countervailing Power*, Boston, 1952, Ch. 11, 'The Case of Agriculture'.
Giles, B. D., 'Agriculture and the price mechanism', in Wilson, T. and Andrews, P. W. S. (eds.), *Oxford Studies in the Price Mechanism*, Oxford, 1951.
Hathaway, D. E. and Perkins, B. B., 'Farm labor mobility, migration and income distribution', *AJAE*, May 1968.
Lipton, Michael, *Why Poor People Stay Poor*, London, 1977, Chs. 5, 6.
Milhau, J., *Traité d'Economie Rurale*, 2 vols., Paris, 1954.
Ojala, E. M., *Agriculture and Economic Progress*, Oxford, 1952.
Tweeten, L. G., 'Theories explaining the persistence of low resource returns in a growing farm economy', *AJAE*, November 1969.

CHAPTER THREE

Historical Movements in Agricultural Prices

Changes in the General Price Level

The problem of fluctuating—as distinct from low—farm income arises from the price fluctuations which characterise many primary products. In analysing these movements, however, it is first necessary to discount changes in the general price level. Movements in the general price level are connected with broad economic developments, especially with changes in total monetary demand compared with changes in the supply of goods and services. These movements of the general price level have in the past had a cyclical character; as can be seen in Fig. 2, the general price level since 1800 in the UK and Germany has displayed large and rather similar fluctuations. Large price rises often coincide with wars, e.g. the Napoleonic War, the Franco-Prussian War, the two World Wars, and the Korean War. The reason is that wars reduce the supply of civilian goods and services, whereas the government is rarely able to reduce monetary demand correspondingly by means of taxation, or to exclude price influences completely through price control. In the nineteenth century, the price level often fell after a war, but after the Second World War there was no relapse in prices at all. Price falls are often associated with periods of depression, since unemployment leads to a fall in monetary demand. When, on the other hand, the monetary demand increases much more rapidly than the supply of goods and services, this can lead to runaway inflation, such as Germany experienced in the years 1922–23.

The period from the 1840s to 1914 was an oasis of

stability in the history of prices. Before it, prices had
tended to move, very irregularly, upward, since the
fifteenth century. In the post-1945 period, prices in most
countries have shown a steady rise; falls in the retail price
index have been virtually unknown. The rate of increase,
however, has varied considerably. The lowest inflation rates
have been in West Germany and, until the 1970s, the USA.
The developing countries have had inflation rates ranging
from under 10 per cent to over 100 per cent in some South
American countries.

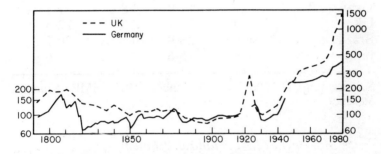

FIG. 2. Changes in the general wholesale price level in the
UK and Germany since 1800 (1910 = 100)

Sources: Layton, W. T. and Crowther, G., *An Introduction to the
Study of Prices*, London, 1938, p. 236; London and Cambridge
Economic Service, *The British Economy: Key Statistics
1900–1964*, London, 1964; *Statisches Jahresbuch für die
Bundesrepublik Deutschland*.

In the OECD countries, there was a tendency for
inflation rates to rise during the 1960s (see Table 3). After
the world-wide boom of 1973, the inflation rate peaked, at
levels ranging from over 20 per cent in the UK and Italy to
6 per cent in Germany. In the subsequent recession,
deepened by the sharp rise in oil prices, the rate of inflation
fell back, although rarely to the level of the 1960s. There
was an acceleration of inflation in 1979, although to very
different levels. In 1980 a new recession, also accentuated
by an oil price rise, again dampened down inflation rates.

TABLE 3

Annual Rise in Consumer Prices (Percentages)

	Average 1961–70	1974/5	1978	6 months to September 1979
OECD average	3·4	12·8	7·9	12·9
USA	2·8	11·1	7·7	14·1
Germany	2·7	5·8	2·6	4·4
France	4·0	13·9	9·1	12·9
Italy	3·9	23·3	12·1	16·8
Japan	5·8	13·9	3·8	7·4
UK	4·1	21·7	8·3	22·6
Brazil	n.a.	28·9	40·0	20·7
India	n.a.	5·6	2·5	17·6

Sources: OECD Outlook, December 1979; IMF, Financial Statistics.

Price Movement of Agricultural Products
Movements in the general price level reflect differing changes in the prices of individual products or groups of products. In considering the movement of agricultural prices over long periods of time, it is thus necessary to distinguish between *current prices* and *real prices*. Current prices are the actual prices at any particular time. Prices in real terms—real prices, or deflated prices—are nominal prices divided up by an appropriate index of the general price level: they therefore show how the current prices have moved in relation to the general price level. When producer prices of agricultural products are being expressed in real terms, the appropriate divisor will be an index of wholesale prices; when retail prices are being dealt with, the appropriate divisor will be an index of the cost of living. Fig. 3 shows, for example, in the upper graph the current wheat price and the index of wholesale prices index in the UK since 1800. By dividing the current wheat price by the index, one obtains the real price given in the lower graph. It can be seen that in the earlier part of the nineteenth century the real price was generally above, and in the last quarter of the century somewhat below, the 1910 level. In

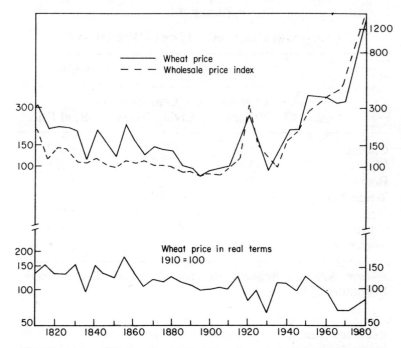

FIG. 3. Current and real prices for wheat, UK 1800–1965

Sources: Mitchell, B. R., *Abstract of British Historical Statistics*, Cambridge, 1962, p. 488; Layton, W. T. and Crowther, G., *An Introduction to the Study of Prices*, London, 1938, p. 236.

1930 it sank by two-thirds of this level. After the war it fell from 130 in 1950 to 74 in 1965, i.e. very nearly the 1930 level.

Retail food prices in real terms show the movement of retail prices movement in relation to the general retail price level. Table 4 shows the changes in real retail prices for some foodstuffs in the UK between 1956 and 1977 which are obtained by dividing the change in current prices by the rise in the general retail price index. The fall in the real price of poultry meat and eggs is striking.

The Influence of Rising Labour Productivity
The reasons for the divergence of the price movements for individual products from the general trend of prices

TABLE 4

Changes in Real Retail Prices UK 1956–77

1977 Prices (1956 = 100)

	Current Prices	Cost of Living Index	Real Prices
Cheese	333		83
Milk	303		75
Beef	305		76
White Bread	314	402	78
Eggs	242		60
Butter	298		74
Poultry	254		63

Source: Annual Reports of the National Food Survey Committee.

becomes particularly clear when some non-agricultural examples are taken. For example, in France the average hourly wage rose by 900 per cent between 1900 and 1937. During the same period, the price of a haircut rose by 1,050 per cent but that of a motor-car by only 150 per cent.[1] This means that, during this period, in relation to the cost of labour, the price of a haircut, rose from 100 to 117, whereas the price of a car fell from 100 to 17. The reason for this enormous divergence lies in the different changes in labour productivity. Haircutting is an activity which (up till now!) has been mechanised in only a small degree; a haircut in 1937 therefore occupied a hairdresser for roughly the same time as in 1900, so that its cost has to rise in roughly the same rate as the hairdresser's wages. On the other hand, the introduction of mass production in the motor-car industry led to a tremendous reduction in the number of man-hours needed to produce a car. In other words, the more labour productivity rises, as a result of technical progress, the more prices fall in comparison with hourly wages. Since hourly wages tend to rise, this means that goods and services requiring a good deal of hand work tend to become steadily dearer. Goods whose production can be mechanised tend to rise less in price, and sometimes fall in price.

This tendency is noticeable in comparisons between countries as well as in comparisons over time. Anyone who travels from a low-income to a high-income country (such as West Germay) notices that manufactured goods, and often basic foodstuffs are not much dearer. On the other hand, hotel rooms, repairs, handicraft objects, theatre seats and haircuts seem unduly dear. These are goods and services whose production cannot be mechanised sufficiently to offset the high wage levels; they are therefore either very dear or, if they can be transported, are imported instead of being produced at home. It is thus possible to think of a scale of goods and services—ranging from, say, cars to haircuts, according to their change in labour productivity over time. In this scale of price changes, agricultural products generally occupy a middle position.

There are, however, differences between agricultural products. In most countries there is a long-term tendency for the prices of those agricultural commodities whose production has not been mechanised to rise faster than the prices of those commodities whose production has been extensively mechanised. Among the products which up till now have been least mechanised are fruit and vegetables, beef, and milk. On the other hand, the commodity whose production has been more extensively mechanised— because of the combine harvester—is cereals. The marked fall in the real prices of cereals reflects this level of mechanisation.

Changes in labour productivity cannot, however, provide a complete explanation of the movement of agricultural prices. It is only one of the factors underlying changes in supply, which moreover, is not the sole determinant of price. Changes in demand are also important, especially in the short run.

An example of divergent movements in agricultural prices is given in Fig. 4, which shows the movement of real agricultural prices since 1900 in Canada, a country in which agricultural price formation has remained relatively free from state influence.[2] It can be seen that milk prices rose to

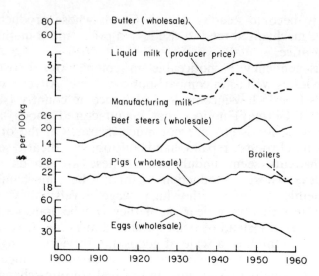

FIG. 4. Real prices of animal products. Canada (moving 5-year average, log. scale)

Source: Goeman, D., 'Die Preisrelationen zwischen landwirtschaftlichen Erzeugnissen', *Agrarwirtschaft*, Sonderheft 18, 1965, p. 125, Table 17.

a higher level during the 1939–45 war. Cattle prices show a rising tendency in spite of considerable fluctuations; on the other hand, pig prices have remained fairly constant in spite of a 3–5 year cycle. Egg prices have shown a fairly steady decline, while chicken prices have fallen very sharply since 1950.

Various factors underlie these price movements. In the production of eggs and poultry meat, an unusually large increase in labour productivity and in feed conversion has led to increased production and lower prices. The production of beef, on the other hand, is influenced by factors other than productivity. Beef is to some extent a joint product with milk; its production depends on the price of beef and milk, not on that of beef alone. Even when pure beef herds are kept, so that beef is not a joint product with milk, its production takes a considerable time, and reacts only slowly to price rises. There is also the influence of demand. With rising incomes, the demand for beef rises, whereas, after a certain consumption level has been reached, the demand for milk and milk products rises only slowly, or even falls. This greater rise in demand leads to a greater price rise for beef than milk.

There is therefore no contradiction between the theory that the differing development of labour productivity largely explains differing long-term price trends, and the well known thesis that price is determined by supply and demand. The supply of agricultural products is determined by many factors, among which the development of labour productivity is one of the most important. It is through its influence on supply—and only through this influence—that a rise in productivity affects prices.

Guaranteed Prices
When guaranteed producer prices for agricultural products are set by governments, as is nowadays the case in many countries, prices tend to be more stable than when there is no government intervention. Their general level may also be altered, usually in an upward direction. But it is a mistake to imagine that under these conditions price formation becomes a purely political decision. In the long run, the supply and demand influences discussed above have a tendency to assert themselves, even when prices are fixed by means of support buying, or import controls, or deficiency payments. If the price is fixed at a level which results in embarrassing surpluses, or excessive subsidy payments, there will be pressure to lower it. If it is fixed at a level which results in inadequate supplies, there will be pressure to increase it.

The larger the proportion of a country's food that it imports, the greater its ability to raise producer prices. If a country imports about half its food, as the UK did before the War, then it is both able to bear the burden of supporting relatively high prices for that part of food production which is grown at home, and also inclined to maintain the level of home production. When the degree of self-sufficiency rises—as it has done in the UK—the cost of price support rises, and the inclination to incur it also tends to fall. It can be seen from Table 5 that, as compared with

TABLE 5

Prices of Agricultural and Manufactured Products
UK 1938–76

	Producer Prices of Agricultural Products	Wholesale Prices of Manufactured Products
	1936–8 = 100	
1938	102	100
1945	196	169
1950	270	238
1955	328	288
1964	325	350
1976	1026	1142

Source: Annual Abstract of Statistics.

the wholesale prices of manufactured products, the producer prices of agricultural products have changed considerably since 1938. Agricultural prices were raised sharply during and after the War, in order to stimulate increased output. Thus between 1938 (admittedly a time of depressed prices) and 1955, they rose by more than three times, which was more than the rise in the prices of

TABLE 6

Average Producer Prices in Great Britain
(1955 = 100)

	1955	1965	1979
Wheat	100	83	328
Barley	100	96	346
Milk	100	112	305
Eggs	100	93	151
Lamb	100	101	414
Beef	100	125	583
Pigs	100	87	288

Source: Annual Price Review White Papers.

manufactured products. But after the mid-1950s, as shortages eased, world prices fell and home production increased, there was a tendency to reduce the level of support. Thus between 1955 and 1964 the index of agricultural prices remained virtually constant, whereas the index of manufactural products continued to rise. The 1970s saw something of a recovery in agricultural prices.

Within these broad price indices, there were changes in the relative prices of individual commodities (Table 6). These relative changes to a large extent reflect changes in the level, or method, of price support; although support prices are 'political' there is a tendency for productivity changes to work their way through.

Long Term Movements in the 'Terms of Trade'
The relation between the prices of agricultural products and industrial products is often a source of irate comment in discussions of agricultural policy. Farmers complain that all prices are rising except theirs—that in other words the 'terms of trade' between agriculture and industry are moving continually against agriculture. In the 1960s, this complaint was internationalised by Dr Prebisch and other United Nations economists. They argued that the terms of trade between manufactured and primary products (which were assumed to be broadly synonymous with those between 'developed' and 'developing' countries) had moved against primary products; that because of inherent flaws in market mechanisms this trend would continue indefinitely unless action was taken; that this trend was causing primary producers to become relatively poorer; and that existing trading arrangements should therefore be replaced by a new world trading system administered by United Nations organisations.[3] This was the original basis of the 'New International Economic Order' (see Chapter 16). One argument was that the prices of primary products move up and down, whereas (because of trade unions and 'full cost' pricing) the prices of manufactured goods rise continuously with inflation; this dichotomy gives rise to a 'ratchet effect' whereby, in the long run, the prices of primary products fall in relation to those of manufacturers.

This complex of arguments is worth examining because it

is still influential. It is open to several objections. Not all developing countries export primary products, and not all developed countries export manufactures; moreover, a fall in relative prices does not necessarily indicate a fall in relative income, since productivity growth has to be considered (see Chapter 6). Nor is it true that the prices of *all* manufactured goods rise steadily in money terms. The prices of some of them have shown dramatic declines: aluminium, nylon and transistor radios in the 1950s and 1960s; electronic calculators in the 1970s. Even if we take indices for the prices of the two categories of goods, it is far from clear that primary product prices have in fact fallen behind the prices of manufactures—or that the nature of price formation must bring this about. The greater volatility of primary product prices does not necessarily mean that they will rise less than the prices of manufactures. (A little thought by any mechanically minded reader should indicate the dubiousness of the 'ratchet' analogy.) Indeed, there have been periods when—on the basis of previous trends—a quite different prognosis has been made. The 'classical' economists of the early nineteenth century feared that because of diminishing returns in agriculture, food prices would *rise* in relation to prices of manufactured goods. This did not happen, because of the opening-up of the New World and because of technical improvements in agriculture. A similar view prevailed in Great Britain after 1945, when the shortage of food on the world market was expected to continue indefinitely. One courageous wartime forecast calculated that, compared with the period 1935–34, primary products would by 1960 have doubled in price in relation to manufactured goods.[4] In the event they hardly changed.

The terms of trade certainly moved against primary products during the 1950s and 1960s but, when their movement is studied over a long period, it is very difficult to establish that there has been a long term trend against primary products. For one thing, the experts disagree on the figures. In a much-quoted report of the League of Nations in 1945, it was stated that, in the sixty years from 1878 to 1938, the terms of trade had moved significantly against primary products.[5] A subsequent report of the

United Nations put the deterioration at 40 per cent.[6] But a still later report concluded that, although the terms of trade showed great changes, they revealed no clear trend, and that the evidence of the past offered no help in predicting future movements.[7]

One of the most thorough studies points out that the figures of UK prices used in most studies give an incorrect impression of the international terms of trade.[8] The prices of imported primary products include transport costs, while those of British manufactured goods do not. With the introduction of steamships, there was a large fall in transport costs in the nineteenth century, so that UK prices do not reflect the advantages which the primary producing countries obtained from cheaper transport for imports of manufactured goods. If figures for the USA instead of the UK are used, the movement of the terms of trade appears more favourable for primary products.

In spite of these qualifications, some figures of world prices prepared by Professor Arthur Lewis[9] (Fig. 5)

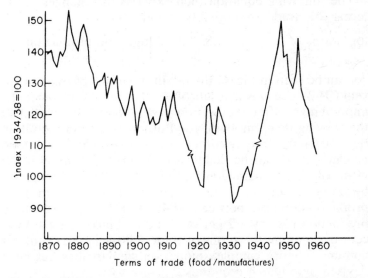

FIG. 5. Terms of trade (food/manufactures), 1870–1960

Source: Philpott, B. P., 'Trends in agriculture's terms of trade', *Proceedings of the New Zealand Institute of Agricultural Science*, 1962, p. 84, Diagram I.

probably give a reasonable idea of the trend of food prices. They suggest that the terms of trade moved slowly against foodstuffs in the last two decades of the nineteenth century. Since the First World War, the movements have been more erratic. The terms of trade moved sharply against agriculture in the depression of the 1930s, but in 1950 were again at the level of the 1880s, from which they have since fallen. Thus although there are large secular changes in the terms of trade between agricultural and industrial products it is difficult to generalise about their long-term trend.

Changes in the terms of trade are related to changes in the demand for, and the supply of, agricultural products, and various models have been constructed to explain the relationship. A simple but effective model relates the terms of trade to two variables:[10]

(1) world food production, representing supply;
(2) the national income, in real terms, of the main trading nations, representing demand.

The following equation then explains the changes in the terms of trade remarkably accurately:

log. terms of trade = 3·88 − 2·02 log. food production
+ 1·12 log. real income.

As can be seen in Fig. 6, the fall in the terms of trade in the years 1929–32 was a result of the fall in real income; the improvement after the Second World War was a result of the slowing down in world food production; and the fall in the 1950s was the result of the recovery in world food production. It can be deduced from the equation that the terms of trade remain constant when real income increases by 2 per cent for every 1 per cent increase in food production. Since, between 1949 and 1958, world food production rose by 3·2 per cent and real income by 4·4 per cent per annum, the terms of trade fell by 1·6 per cent per annum. A more complex model on similar lines has been devised by a Dutch economist.[11]

Thus, even in the 1960s, a study of the past gave little support to the view that commodity prices would fall continuously in relation to the prices of manufactures. Moreover, as soon as this view had become widely

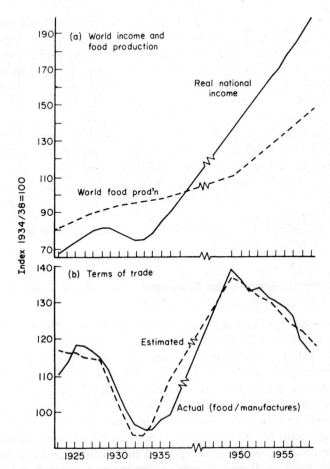

FIG. 6. World real national income and food production (5-year moving average). Terms of trade, actual and estimated (5-year moving average)

Source: Philpott, p. 84, Diagram II.

accepted, commodity prices shot up in the great boom of 1972/3.

Post-war Movements in Commodity Prices
Prices of individual commodities often show large fluctuations from month to month or year to year.

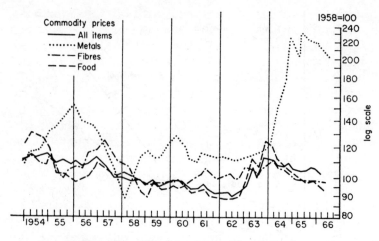

FIG. 7a. World commodity prices

Source: The Economist

However, indices of commodity prices—such as those produced by *The Economist* or, more recently UNCTAD and other organisations—smooth out fluctuations of commodities as a whole (Fig. 7). All such indices should be treated with caution, since different weightings can produce different results. However, all the main indices give broadly similar results over periods of 10 years or so. Long term comparison over decades or centuries become increasingly problematical as the time period increases. *The Economist* index for 'food' and 'fibres' indicates a general decline in the 1950s from the historically high levels—in relation to the prices of manufactures—attained in the 'Korean' boom. The early 1960s saw a recovery followed by a relapse. Then in 1973, there was an unprecedentedly sharp rise, taking commodity prices in real terms (i.e. in relation to those of manufactures) back to the level of the Korean boom. The sharpness of this boom was the result of many price-raising factors coming into operation at the same time. Commodity prices were depressed and due for a recovery anyway. There was then a sharp increase in the money supply in most countries, an upsurge of inflationary expectations, and poor harvests in the Soviet Union and some other countries, just when grain stocks in the USA had been run down to a very low level. The general economic boom was quickly followed by a recession, which depressed commodity prices. In 1975 (when the volume of world trade actually fell, by 4 per cent), commodity prices in real terms lost most of the gains they had made. This short recession was followed by a recovery, and several minor fluctuations in the late 1970s, in which commodity prices seemed to respond very sensitively to accelerations in the rate of growth of world economic activity. An index of 'real' commodity prices (i.e. in relation to the price of manufactures) is, in the opinion of some economists, a good guide to the level of 'over-heating' in the world economy. (For this type of comparison, there is a case for excluding petroleum from the commodity index, as the London Business School does, Fig. 7c). In any event, the relation of 'real' commodity prices and world industrial output suggests that the 'Philpott Model' discussed above is still relevant.

The price history of the post-War period leads therefore to the same broad conclusions as the history of the past two centuries. Week-to-week or month-to-month movements of individual commodity prices are often influenced by speculation and 'sentiment', rather than the basic demand and supply situation, but movements over a period of years do reflect the demand and supply situation. Commodity prices in general have tended to fluctuate around the movements of prices of manufactures, but show little sign of an upward or downward trend in relation to them. (This pattern is quite explicable in terms of the lagged adjustment to price changes discussed in Chapter 6.) As compared with the late 1950s and 1960s, the 1970s have tended to show somewhat more instability of commodity prices, in spite of all the international efforts to stabilise them. The decade ended with a boom in gold and silver which affected other commodities. Several explanations have been given for this instability: lower government-held stocks for some commodities; higher inflation rates and the consequent loss of faith in money; the erratic policies of many developing countries; the arrival of footloose 'petro-money'; even the greater speed and coverage of

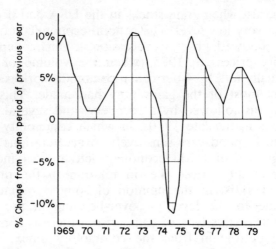

FIG. 7b. World industrial production 1969–79

Source: London Business School

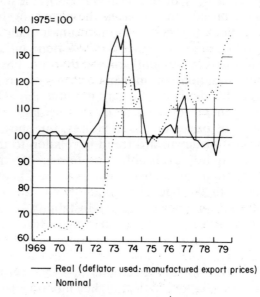

—— Real (deflator used: manufactured export prices)
····· Nominal

FIG. 7c. Non-oil commodity prices 1969–79

Source: London Business School

market data. An improvement in the 'perfection' of market information might, *ceteris paribus*, have been expected to produce greater stability but does not seem to have done so. In this, as in other fields, however, more and speedier information is not necessarily an advantage, unless it is interpreted by thoughtful, well-informed people who, for example, know something of the booms, slumps and panics of the past. In the absence of such interpretation, a flood of instantaneous data may lead to increased 'jumpiness' rather than better-informed decisions.

The Price of Farm Inputs

For the farmers of a particular country, the 'terms of trade' are the relationship between the prices received for agricultural commodities and the prices paid for farm inputs such as labour, machinery and fertilisers. This relationship has been used as a basis for setting agricultural prices in the USA. The 'parity' legislation was designed to maintain the relationship between the prices paid by farmers and the prices received by them in the years 1910–13, which was considered to be 'fair'. Since the 1939–45 War these 'terms of trade' have however, worsened in the USA, as they have done to a greater or lesser extent in most countries.

But any index figure for the price of farm inputs conceals important differences between various items, which in recent years have been very large. The most rapid rise has been in agricultural wages. Building costs have risen less than wages, machinery still less, while artificial fertilisers and pesticides have risen very little in money prices (in real terms they have therefore fallen). These different rates of change reflect mainly the varying progress of labour productivity, which has been highest in chemical products and lowest in building. Because of these changes in relative prices it becomes profitable for farmers to substitute machinery and chemicals for the increasingly expensive labour. It is not usually possible to do without buildings, but it becomes increasingly important that they should be as economical and flexible as possible.

Changes of this type in the relative prices of farm inputs, together with the discovery of new techniques, provide the pressure for the adoption of the new types of farming. These price changes cause difficulty and even hardship for some farmers, but there is always one group of farmers who adapt themselves to the new conditions and earn substantially higher profits than the average. Eventually the techniques of this group become common practice, but by this time the most enterprising farmers are using still newer techniques. It is in this way that the high rate of increase in agricultural productivity, observed in various periods, including the present, is maintained.

Summary
There has been a lively debate for over a century on the relative movements of prices of agricultural and industrial products. The 'classical economists' of the early nineteenth century—extrapolating recent trends into the future—feared that food prices would continue to rise in relation to the price of manufactures because of diminishing returns in food production. (A corollary was that farm rents would continue to rise in relation to income, so that agricultural landlords would 'make money, as it were, in their sleep'—J. S. Mill). This gloomy prognosis proved to be unfounded after about the middle of the nineteenth century. Similar predictions were made after 1945 but were disproved in the 1950s. In the 1960s some UN economists—extrapolating recent trends into the future—argued that there was a flow in the international trading system which caused the prices of agricultural products continually to *fall* in relation to the prices of manufactured goods. This was the original basis for the 'new international economic order'. The available studies—although not unanimous—suggest that the prices of agricultural products fluctuate around the movement of manufactured goods, but show no clear upward or downward trend. After periods during which production tends to outstrip demand, with consequently low prices, there tends to be a sharp recovery in price. The 1970s saw a commodity boom in 1973, but this was followed by a short, sharp recession; a subsequent recovery was followed by small-scale fluctuations. There may be problems of shortage for some commodities in the future (although of

minerals rather than of agricultural products and arising in the political as much as in the technical sphere). However, the historical record is a counter to excessively apocalyptic views.

Notes

1 Fourastie, Jean, *Le Grand Espoir du XXe Siècle*, Paris, 1952.
2 Goeman, D. 'Die Preisrelationen zwischen landwirtschaftlichen Erzeugnissen', *Agrarwirtschaft*, Sonderheft 18, 1965.
3 Prebisch, Paul, *Towards a New Trade Policy for Development*, United Nations, New York, 1964, especially Pt. 1, Ch. 2 and Pt. 2, Ch. 1.
4 Clark, Colin, *The Economics of 1960*, London, 1941.
5 League of Nations, *Industrialisation and Foreign Trade*, 1945.
6 United Nations, *Relative Prices of Exports and Imports of Under-Developed Countries*, New York, 1949.
7 United Nations, *Commodity Trade and Economic Development*, New York, 1953.
8 Morgan, T. 'Trends in terms of trade and their repercussions on primary producers', in Harrod, R. (ed.), *International Trade Theory in a Developing World* (Proceedings of a Conference of the International Economics Association), London, 1964.
9 Lewis, W. A. 'World production, prices and trade 1870–1960', *The Manchester School of Economic and Social Studies*, Vol. 20, 1952, p. 105.
10 Philpott, B. P., 'Trends in agriculture's terms of trade', *Proceedings of the New Zealand Institute of Agricutural Science*, Wellington, 1962, p. 83.
11 Attallah, M. K. *The Long Term Movements of the Terms of Trade between Agricultural and Industrial Products*, Netherlands Economics Institute, Rotterdam, 1958.

Further Reading

Clark, Colin, *The Value of Agricultural Land*, Oxford, 1973. (An analysis of the factors determining the rent and price of agricultural land, documented by statistics going back to Egypt, first century AD.)
'Prices, history of', in *Chambers Encyclopedia*.

CHAPTER FOUR

The Supply and Demand of Agricultural Products

The Role of Theory

The theory of supply and demand as applied to agriculture seeks to provide an explanation of the level and the fluctuations of the price of agricultural products. This explanation consists of an analysis of the factors which affect, on the one hand, the quantity demanded, and on the other hand, the amount supplied. Although one of the most basic and fruitful of economic theories, the theory of supply and demand is still only a theory or model, i.e. a logical structure designed to explain reality. Economic life is so complicated, and contains so many variables, that it would be impossible to understand without first simplifying it in some respects. An economic theory thus represents a simplified form of reality, which reveals the most important variables and explains their interconnection. A good theory should be based on practical observation and continually checked against actual events; when necessary, it should be amended or replaced by a better theory.

The analytical methods of economic theory are the same for agricultural and non-agricultural products. However, as there are sometimes organisational differences in the production and marketing of agricultural and industrial products, the theoretical assumptions sometimes have to differ in the two cases.

The Market

Prices are formed in markets, and the term 'market' is frequently employed in discussions of price movements.

Theoreticians speak of perfect or imperfect markets, market structures, and divided markets; economic correspondents speak of rising prices on the world wheat market, the market for American chickens, Brazil's share of the coffee market, an over-supplied sugar market, etc. The various meanings of the term 'market' become clearer when one examines its etymological development. The word originally denoted a meeting of buyers and sellers, at first in a street or square and later in a building, where goods were offered for sale. Markets of this type are still typical in the internal trade of developing countries, for some agricultural products they still exist in Europe and North America. At the retail level—and as in the case of weekly markets for flowers and fruit—they have no great commercial importance in developed countries, but at pre-retail levels—livestock auctions, wholesale fruit and vegetable markets, tobacco auctions in Zimbabwe or wool auctions in Australia—they still handle a large part of the trade.

But with the improvement of transport and communications, and the laying-down of objective quality grades for some commodities, it ceased to be necessary for the goods to be physically present at the place where buyers and sellers met. When both parties understood exactly what was meant by, for example, 'Manitoba No. 1' wheat, it was possible to arrange a sale in London even when the wheat was still in a Canadian elevator. Thus the commodity exchanges developed in commercial centres such as London, Chicago or Hamburg, where it became possible to buy wheat, cotton, sugar or vegetable oils lying thousands of miles away from the exchange itself. The men who buy and sell on these exchanges are dealers acting on behalf of firms with whom they are in touch by telephone or teleprinter. It may be convenient in such cases to conduct transactions at a particular place, but it is not essential to do so; if buyers and sellers are prepared to negotiate sales by telephone, they can by-pass the exchange or wholesale market.

There has, in fact, been such a tendency in the marketing of many agricultural products. Together with a concentration of the marketing channels, there has been a tendency to decentralisation, first noted in the American 'meat packing', i.e. slaughtering, industry but since apparent in many European countries as well. The number of distributors—creameries, slaughterhouses, egg packing stations—is falling, but at the same time the marketing channels are becoming more direct. There is an increasing tendency for cattle to be sold direct to a meat factory instead of going through an auction ring, for retail organisations to by-pass the wholesaler and buy meat direct from the meat factory or vegetables (under contract) direct from a farmer or group of farmers. It is more difficult in these cases to obtain price quotations and to follow the trend of prices, but there is no theoretical difference between a decentralised market of this type and one where the buyers and sellers actually meet. It can thus be seen that a market is formed by the meeting of supply and demand. The sellers who represent supply, with the buyers who represent demand can be scattered over a country or even the whole world, as long as they are in communication with each other, and are able to arrange purchases and sales.

Thus before the 1930s, Great Britain, Canada, the USA and Australia could be considered a single market for cereals, since trade between them was completely free. A similar position will exist in the EEC when a common market in agricultural products has been achieved. At the other extreme, physical or—nowadays more importantly—political barriers to trade can isolate one market completely from another, so that developments in one have no influence whatever on the other. Thus the fact that people in China are short of food, and would like more wheat, has no effect on the wheat market in Canada if imports into China are in the hands of the Chinese Government, and it decides not to use its foreign exchange for the purchase of wheat from abroad. If however, the shortage becomes so severe that it decides to do so, then the Chinese demand can have such an effect in Canada, as it did when the Chinese Government began buying Canadian wheat in 1962.

It is a well known conclusion in economic theory that, in a perfect market, only one price can exist at one time for a particular commodity. This is because, if all buyers and all sellers are fully informed about the state of the market, all sales will take place at the same price. This is, in fact, broadly speaking the case at commodity exchanges and wholesale markets, where the buyers and sellers are well-informed professionals (although the price can change very sharply from one time to another). At the retail and producer levels, however, market imperfections can give rise to differing prices at any one time. A farmer may, for example, be poorly informed about market prices, and so obtain less from a dealer than he could have obtained elsewhere. This is at least a theoretical possibility; whether it actually happens depends on the structure of the marketing system. Imperfections are likely to be greatest when ignorant and unorganised farmers sell to a small number of local dealers, which is not infrequently the case in developing countries. Imperfections will be least likely when farmers have the option of selling through a co-operative marketing organisation, when competition in marketing is strong, or when there are large, impersonal marketing organisations. This latter situation corresponds more or less to that in the more developed European countries such as Great Britain, the Netherlands, West Germany, and the Scandinavian countries; in spite of considerable criticism. It hardly seems likely that imperfections in agricultural marketing are today serious or extensive in these countries.

Regional Price Differences
The fact that there can be only one price in a perfect market at any one time does not exclude spatial price differences. Even when knowledge is perfect, there will be price differences between surplus and deficit areas equal to the transport and handling costs between them; if knowledge is imperfect, the price differences can be even greater. Thus the existence of transport costs leads to a spatial pattern of prices, which can exert an important influence on production. the model of 'von Thünen's circles' was an early attempt to explain these spatial price differences.[1]

Thus in the study of agricultural price movements, the

quotations used must either be average prices from various centres ('average auction prices, light steers, England and Wales'), or a price at a particular place ('Smithfield, English long sides'). When price formation is not free, but determined by some official body which regulates the market, or intervenes in it, the determination of regional price differences gives rise to considerable problems; e.g. in the price policies of the British Milk Marketing Board, or the 'regionalisation' of the cereal price in the EEC. We shall for the moment ignore regional differences and examine the determinants of supply and demand in a particular location.

The Determinants of Demand

Agricultural products are used mainly for food, although some—wool, cotton, rubber—are used for other purposes. We shall therefore mainly consider the determinants of demand for foodstuffs, and discuss later the peculiar problems of the non-food agricultural commodities. The total consumption of foodstuff depends, of course, on its *per capita* consumption and the size of the population; the main factors determining the *per capita* consumption are:

(1) Consumers' real income.
(2) The price of the foodstuff itself and of substitutes.
(3) Other factors such as living conditions, habits, advertising.

Population. Since the 1940s the growth of world population has accelerated in an unprecedented way, and the growth is concentrated in Asia, Africa and South America—where in many cases the difficulties of increasing food production are greatest (Table 7). In many European countries, on the other hand, the population is at present stable, or even falling. The rapid growth of population in the Third World presents grave problems—most economists believe—for food production, employment, and living conditions. However, there are signs that the growth is, very slightly, slowing down. (See Chapter 10).

Real Income. When real income *per capita* is very low, food is usually simple and often inadequate; with some

TABLE 7

The Growth of World Population

Region	Population (millions) 1960	Population (millions) 1977	Average Annual Increase 1970–77 (%)	Natural Increase latest year*	Density (Population per sq. km.)
Africa	273	424	2·7		14
North America	199	242	0·9		11
Latin America	216	342	2·8		17
China	654	866	1·7		88
Japan	94	114	1·2		90
South Asia	856	1,318	2·6		83
Europe†	425	478	0·6	10.0	97
USSR	214	260	1·0		12
USA	180	217	0·8	8·9	23
India	432	625	2·1	5·8	190
UK	52	56	0·1	19·3	229
France	45	53	0·6	0	97
West Germany	53	61	0·2	3·9	247
Italy	49	56	0·7	−2·0	187
Belgium	9	10	0·4	3·6	325
Netherlands	11	14	0·9	1·0	339
WORLD	2,986	4,124	1.9	4·6	30

*Birth rates *minus* death rates, per 1,000
†excluding USSR
Source: UN *Demographic Yearbook.*

exceptions—such as the Eskimos—it contains very little animal protein. With rising real income, there is a tendency to spend a large part of the increased income on food, and to consume more calories. But satisfaction in terms of calories is soon reached, and with further increases in real income the consumption of calorie-rich foods tends to fall. The consumer begins to attach more importance to quality, and the consumption of more expensive foods, such as meat, fruit and fine vegetables, rises at the expense of the cheap, starchy foods such as bread and potatoes. There is an increased demand for out of season fruits and vegetables, and for more prepared and processed foodstuffs.

The price of a foodstuff affects consumption, in so far as a rise in price causes a switch to cheaper foodstuffs, and vice versa. The 'price effect' therefore depends on the possibilities of substitution; this aspect is discussed more fully below.

Living conditions, habits, advertising. These influences are more difficult to measure than income and price, but are extremely important. They include religious or traditional customs, living and working conditions, climate, eating habits, fashions, fads, and advertising. For example, people in the tropics need less calories than those in colder climates; manual workers more than sedentary workers. For religious reasons the consumption of pigmeat in the Middle East is low as that of beef in India. Speculations about a connection between animal fat and heart disease have adversely affected the consumption of butter in the USA.

Many of the differences in eating habits have a historical or geographical background. Mutton is highly esteemed in Great Britain but not in Germany; on the other hand, rye is considered a normal bread grain in Germany but a speciality in Britain. Wine consumption is fifty times as high in France as in Britain, whereas milk consumption is one and a half times as high in Britain as in France.

Consumption is sometimes influenced by distribution methods. When milk is delivered to the door, as is usual in Great Britain, this probably leads to higher consumption than when no milk has to be carried home from the shop. Advertising is another of the rather intangible determinants of consumption. It is debatable how far advertising can influence the consumption of a particular foodstuff. It can certainly—provided that the quality of the product lives up to the advertising claims—benefit the sales of a particular brand of products from a particular country, e.g. Danish bacon or Dutch tomatoes as against English, but whether it can significantly increase the total consumption of bacon or tomatoes is not so certain. A certain level of advertising can probably influence consumption; mouth-watering pictures of salads or grilled bacon may well act as an appetiser. But one suspects (it is difficult to get evidence) that diminishing returns soon set in, and that, as in all advertising, it is easy to exceed the limits both of profitability and of good taste.

We can therefore say that the consumption (C) of a certain foodstuff (x) is a function of the following variables:

population (P);
per capita income (Y);
the price of the foodstuff (Px);
the price of substitute foodstuffs (Ps);
a residual factor (Z) representing the influence of advertising, habits, living conditions etc.

The relationship between the variables can be represented by the equation:

$$Cx = f(\overset{+}{P}, \overset{\pm}{Y}, \overset{-}{Px}, \overset{+}{Ps}, \overset{\pm}{Z})$$

The plus or minus signs show whether the relationship is positive or negative. For example, a rise in the price of a product always leads, *ceteris paribus*, to a fall in consumption (with the unimportant theoretical exception, discussed below, of the 'Giffen case'), and a rise in population to an increase. On the other hand, a rise in real income leads to an increase in the consumption of some products and a decrease in that of of others. Similarly, the changes that take place with time in habits and living conditions can either increase or decrease consumption.

In order to explain changes in consumption, it is necessary to isolate the various determinants and study them separately. The influence of population is easy to isolate, since adequate population statistics are available for most countries. It is more difficult to establish the influence of price and income on *per capita* consumption. As price, income and other factors are constantly changing, it is difficult, in spite of statistical techniques, to assess their individual influence on consumption. However, they can at least be separated theoretically, which is useful for a logical analysis of the situation.

Price Determination by Demand and Supply

The essence of the theory of supply and demand is represented in the well-known diagram of the demand and the supply curves (Fig. 8). In this, it is assumed that income, living conditions, tastes—in short, everything except price—remain constant. The demand—i.e. the hypothetical consumption, depends on the price, and therefore reacts negatively to price changes. Similarly, on the supply side everything except price remains constant—production methods, costs of agricultural inputs, crop yields and livestock performances. Under these conditions the supply, i.e. the production, will react

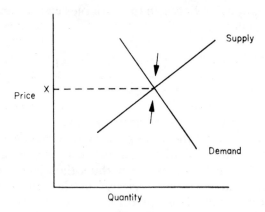

FIG. 8

positively to price changes. The intersection of the two curves indicates the equilibrium price and quantity, towards which actual price and quantity will always tend to move. When the price lies above the equilibrium level, supply will exceed demand, unsold goods will begin to pile up with the wholesalers or retailers, and prices will have to be cut. When the price lies under the equilibrium level, the demand will exceed the supply, stocks will be exhausted, and prices will rise.

Substitution Effect and Income Effect
The fact that the demand curve falls from left to right—i.e. that with rising prices, consumption falls—is mainly the result of substitution. When beef prices rise, housewives begin, perhaps after a time lag, to switch to pork. When all meat prices rise, they may—although to a lesser extent—begin to replace meat with fish, eggs or cheese. There is, however, another consequence of a price movement. An increase in the price of an important product or group of products, in the absence of a corresponding change in money income, makes consumers poorer; a decrease makes them richer. A price rise thus resembles a fall in income, and forces consumers to restrict their consumption—although not necessarily their consumption of the goods concerned. This 'income effect' is insignificant in the case of products accounting for only a small proportion of total expenditure. On the other hand, price changes for important foodstuffs can have a signficant income effect, especially when the income level is low. In England and Wales in 1978, consumers spent on average 24·1 per cent of their total expenditure on food, and the proportion rose to 35 per cent among low-income pensioners.[2]

The effect of a rise in the price of basic foodstuffs is not necessarily to cut down on their consumption: savings may well be made on other, less essential goods. The income effect can thus work in a different direction to the substitution effect. It could, theoretically, even outweigh it. Alfred Marshall quotes the 'Giffen paradox' that an increase in bread price leads to an increase in the bread consumption among poorer people.[3] Expenditure on bread is such a large proportion of their total expenditure that when its price rises they are forced to cut down their already low consumption of meat and other expensive foodstuffs, and replace it with more bread. However, such cases have never been satisfactorily documented; they could in any case arise only in a very poor society.

The possibilities for substitution differ from foodstuff to foodstuff. Pork and chicken meat are fairly close substitutes, so that there is a fairly rapid switch when chicken meat becomes relatively cheaper. On the other hand, there are relatively few substitutes for liquid milk, so that its consumption does not react so much to price changes.

Coefficients of Elasticity
We have till now spoken merely of demand being 'more elastic' or 'less elastic'. There is, however, a precise measure of elasticity, the coefficient of elasticity, which in broad terms can be defined as:

$$\frac{\% \text{ change in the quantity bought}}{\% \text{ change in price}}$$

When, therefore, a price change of 1 per cent leads to a 2 per cent change in the quantity bought, elasticity is $\frac{2}{1} = 2$. If, on the other hand, this price change leads to a change of only $\frac{1}{2}$ per cent in the quantity bought, the elasticity will be only 0·5. If the change in the quantity bought is 1 per cent, the elasticity will be 1. It is common to speak of demand being 'elastic' when the coefficient is more than one, and as 'inelastic' when it is less than one. The coefficients are sometimes written with minus signs because a price increase leads to a fall in consumption and vice versa. It is usual, however, to omit the minus signs.

Coefficients of elasticity can be measured in two ways:

(a) at a point on the curve (point elasticity);
(b) between two points on the curve (arc elasticity).

In Fig. 9 the slope of the tangent to the demand curve at point p indicates the elasticity at that point, which

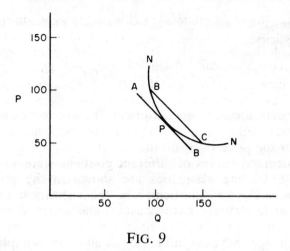

FIG. 9

corresponds to the formula

$$\frac{dQ}{dP} \cdot \frac{P}{Q}$$

In practice, however, one is mainly dealing with finite changes, e.g. the price rises from 50 to 100, and sales fall from 150 to 100. In Fig. 9, the straight line *BC* joins these two points, and the elasticity calculated from it represents an average of the point elasticities along the curve. But with this method there are several ways of calculating the 'percentage change' in price and quantity. For example, a price rise from 50 to 100 represents a rise of 100 per cent, if one takes the initial price of 50 as the divisor, whereas a fall from 100 to 50 represents a fall of 50 per cent, taking 100 as the divisor. To avoid these problems it is usual to use the 'Allen' formula, which is:

$$\frac{\Delta Q}{\Delta P} \cdot \frac{P_1 + P_2}{Q_1 + Q_2},$$

where ΔQ = change in quantity
         ΔP = change in price
         P_1 = first price
         P_2 = second price
         Q_1 = first quantity
         Q_2 = second quantity

In the case quoted above, this formula gives the following elasticity:

$$\frac{50}{50} \cdot \frac{50 + 100}{150 + 100} = 0{\cdot}6$$

The 'Allen' formula uses, in effect, the average of the two quantities and prices, and thus gives the same elasticity whether the price rises or falls.

Six demand curves of different elasticities are shown in Fig. 10. Income elasticities are shown in the left-hand column, and price elasticities in the right-hand column. The first five curves have constant elasticities along their length, and represent elasticities ranging from zero, when price changes have no influences at all on consumption, to infinity, when any price change would lead to consumption either rising to infinity or falling to nothing—an admittedly unrealistic case. (The price elasticities have a negative sign, $-0{\cdot}5$, -1 etc.) The sixth curve has an elasticity which alters along its length. The price elasticity changes from $0{\cdot}45$ to $1{\cdot}19$, so that at high prices the demand is elastic, at low prices, inelastic. This is a realistic case. It can be easily imagined that with rising prices a point is eventually reached where consumers stop buying; on the other hand, consumption will not expand beyond a certain point, even if the price falls to zero.

The monetary value of expenditure at any point on the demand curve consists of price × quantity. It is thus possible, on the basis of the demand curve, to construct a receipts curve, showing receipts in relation to either quantity (or price). When the price elasticity is 1, the expenditure remains constant; the change in the price exactly offsets the change in the quantity sold. When the elasticity is less than unity receipts fall as the quantity rises; when the elasticity is above 1 receipts rise as the quantity rises.

Price Flexibility
In the calculation of price elasticity, it is tacitly assumed that the price is the independent, and the quantity the dependent variable. The price elasticity shows the change

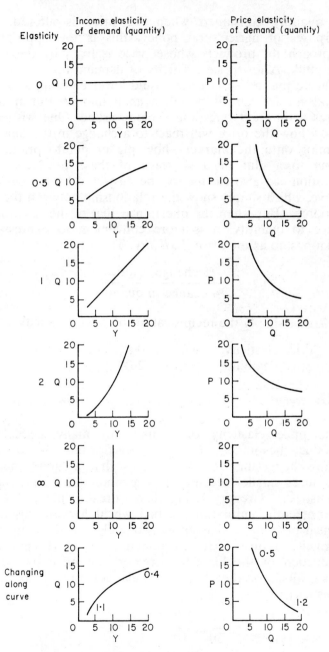

FIG. 10. Price and income elasticities of demand

in quantity consumed when the price is altered. For purposes of agricultural policy, this is the appropriate approach for products whose price is fixed by the state, e.g. milk. A low price elasticity of demand for milk would indicate that a rise in price would lower consumption, and a fall in price raise it by only a small amount. But in many cases a different question is being asked. One wishes to know how the price will react to a change in the quantity coming onto the market—how pig or potato prices will react to a glut or a shortage of these products. This question can also (in theory) be answered by the demand curve, which simply show the relationship between the two variables. But when the question is that of the reaction of price to quantity, it is more convenient to express the relationship as the *price flexibility*. This is:

$$\frac{\% \text{ change in price}}{\% \text{ change in quantity}}$$

It is thus simply the reciprocal of the price elasticity.

Price elasticity	0	0·5	1	2·0	∞
Price flexibility	∞	2·0	1	0·5	0

The Relationship between Quantity, Production and Receipts

The price elasticity of demand of many agricultural products lies under 1 (i.e. the price flexibility lies over 1). Thus the strange situation arises that a 'good' harvest produces smaller receipts than a 'poor' one. The English statistician Gregory King had already noted in the seventeenth century that a bad wheat harvest raised the wheat price more than proportionately and thus improved farmers' returns. He calculated that a 10 per cent reduction of the harvest increased the price by 30 per cent, which, on the 'Allen' formula, corresponds to a price elasticity of:

$$-\frac{10}{30} \cdot \frac{100 + 130}{100 + 90} = -0.45.[4]$$

Nowadays, however, it is in practice no longer true that

a poor harvest brings better returns to wheat growers than a good one. King wrote at a time when international trade was very undeveloped. Nowadays, harvest fluctuations are largely offset by changes in stocks, or in imports and exports. But when international trade or stock-holding is limited by high costs—as is often the case with fruit, vegetables and potatoes—it still happens that a 'good' harvest can bring lower returns than a 'bad' one. This is particularly true of the returns to the farmer, for, because of the behaviour of distributive margins discussed below, the price elasticity of demand at the farm-gate level is lower than at the retail level.

From the point of view of agricultural policy, the price elasticity of demand of agricultural products is extremely important, in that the acceptability of the market mechanism is greater, the higher the elasticity of demand. If the elasticity is fairly high, even if not over one, then the price changes resulting from fluctuating production will remain within tolerable limits. When, however, the elasticity is low, the price fluctuations can be so large, and the effect on farm incomes and resource allocations so considerable, that official intervention in the market becomes necessary.

The Supply Curve

Just as the demand curve indicates the reaction of consumption to price, so the supply curve indicates the reaction of supply. And the elasticity of supply is measured in a similar way.

$$\text{Price elasticity of supply} = \frac{\text{\% change in quantity supplied}}{\text{\% change in price}}$$

The two extremes, between which supply elasticities can theoretically lie, are nil, when the curve is vertical and supply does not react at all to price changes, and infinity, when the curve is horizontal, which means that any desired quantity can be supplied at the given price.

There is, however, an important theoretical difference between demand and supply, in that the period being considered is far more important in the case of supply.

Inside a certain period of time—days, weeks or months—it is virtually impossible to alter the level of planned agricultural production. Once the seed is sown, the farmer can only wait for the harvest. With livestock he has a little more flexibility. Milk production can to some extent be altered by altering the level of concentrate feeding. The slaughtering of breeding or young stock can rapidly raise the level of meat production, but only at the cost of a sharp falling-off later, so that farmers do not do it willingly. On the other hand, the farmer can hold back his fatstock from the market and fatten the animals further, although only with incurring higher costs and quality losses; in any case the delay cannot be more than a matter of weeks for pigs and months for cattle. We can thus say that within a certain period—up to perhaps six months or a year according to the product—the supply is very inelastic.

Over a longer period—one, two or three years—the possibilities for altering the level of production are much greater, since crop acreages or livestock numbers can be increased or reduced. In the case of crops, the planted acreage can be changed at the next seed-time, and production thus altered within about eighteen months. The production of eggs or pigmeat can be altered in about the same time. In the case of cattle, where the breeding period is nine months and the time to maturity about two years, the length of the production process is considerably longer. Even in this medium-term period of several years, there are limits to the extent to which production can be altered, since fixed equipment such as buildings cannot be quickly expanded or abandoned. The longer the period, the greater are the possibilities for altering the whole mechanism of production and the greater therefore the elasticity of supply. The supply curve is therefore not a single curve but a whole series of curves, according to the length of time being considered (Fig. 11). Moreover, each curve can be thought of as having a band on either side, the central curve representing supply under normal weather, with good or bad weather increasing or reducing the supply.

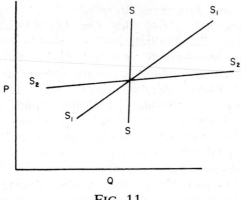

FIG. 11

Another characteristic of the supply curve is that it is not always 'reversible'. A rise in price leads after a certain time-lag to increased investment and thus higher production, but if the price then falls to its original level, the production does not fall correspondingly. The investment in reclaimed land, fences, water supply, drainage, buildings, etc. will not at once be abandoned when the price falls; it may well be perfectly economic in the short run to make use of this investment and maintain production at almost the same level as before. The supply curve can thus take the form shown in Fig. 12.

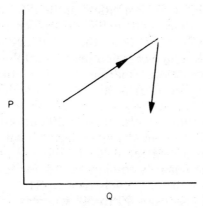

FIG. 12

Distributive and Processing Margins
It was explained above that the equilibrium price is established by the interaction of the supply and demand curves. The conventional diagram (Fig. 8) tacitly assumes, however, that the producer sells direct to the consumer, so that the retail price paid by the consumer and the price received by the producer are the same. For most agricultural products, however, this is not the case, Between the retail price and the price received by the farmer there lie various distributive and processing margins which exercise an important influence in price formation.

One question which therefore arises is whether the price formation takes place at the retail or the producer level, in other words, whether the retail price depends on the producer price or vice versa. In one sense, prices at all levels can only be considered as part of an inter-related complex. Professor Schmitt, however, argues convincingly that price formation takes place primarily at the wholesale level.[5] At wholesale markets such as Six Elms or Smithfield the conditions of a perfect market and perfect competition are largely realised, in that there are large numbers of well-informed buyers and sellers. Both producer and retail prices are thus largely derived from the prices established in the wholesale markets, by adding or deducting the normal margins.

Because of the margin between the retail price and the producer price, price elasticities can be different at the two levels. This is illustrated in Fig. 13, which shows demand and supply curves for both the retail and the producer levels. The difference between the two levels represents the trading and processing margin, which in this case is the same absolute size (20) at all prices. The intersections of the *D* and *S* curves give the equilibrium prices at the producer and retail levels, namely 20 and 40. It is easy to see that in this case the demand elasticity will be less at the producer than at the retail level (and the price flexibility greater). If the quantity coming on the market falls from 40 to 30, the price at both levels rises by 10. But at the retail level this is a rise from 40 to 50, whereas at the producer level it is from 20 to 30, and thus proportionately greater. If the elasticities are calculated on the basis of the

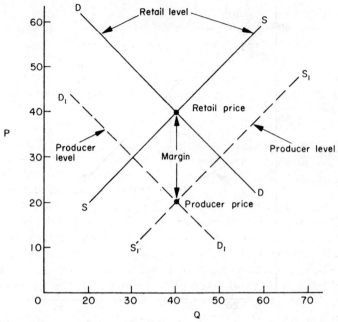

FIG. 13. Demand curves at producer and retail level
(fixed margin)

arithmetical mean (the 'Allen' formula) the following
results are obtained:

Elasticity at the retail level $\quad \dfrac{10}{35} \div \dfrac{10}{45} = 1\cdot29$

Elasticity of the producer level $\quad \dfrac{10}{35} \div \dfrac{10}{25} = 0\cdot71$

The fact that the price flexibility at the producer level is
higher than at the retail level means that a given change in
quantity leads to a proportionally greater price change at
the producer level. In the case above, a one per cent
change in quantity would lead to the following price
changes:

Retail level $\quad \dfrac{1}{1\cdot29} = 0\cdot78$

Producer level $\quad \dfrac{1}{0\cdot71} = 1\cdot41$

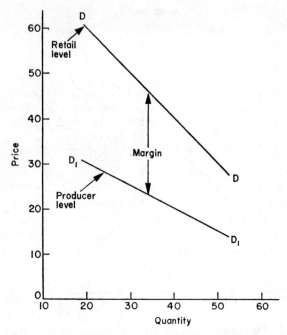

FIG. 14. Demand curves at producer and
retail level (percentage margin)

Thus when the margin is fixed in absolute terms the price flexibility at the producer level will be greater than at the retail level. When, on the other hand, the margin remains a constant proportion of the price, the price flexibility will be the same at both levels. In Fig. 14, a margin of 50 per cent of the retail price is illustrated. If under these conditions the quantity falls from 40 to 30, the following results can be calculated:

Price elasticity at the retail level $\dfrac{10}{35} \div \dfrac{10}{45} = 1\cdot29$

Price elasticity at the producer level $\dfrac{10}{35} \div \dfrac{5}{22\cdot5} = 1\cdot29$

The price elasticity (and flexibility) is thus the same at both levels, so that a change in the quantity coming on the market will produce the same proportionate price changes at both retail and producer levels. The question of distributive margins is examined further in Chapter 9.

Summary
Prices are formed in 'markets', which were originally physical locations but can today consist of a national or international nexus of buyers and sellers linked by continuous and virtually instantaneous means of communication. The quantity demanded of an agricultural commodity can be expressed as a function of price, income, and (less quantifiably) 'tastes'. It is analytically useful to isolate the effect of price and income, on the assumption that all other factors remain constant. The relation of quantity demanded with price or income can be expressed by an 'elasticity' which is a relationship between proportionate changes. A similar relation can be applied to supply, but the supply curve is more complex as it varies according to the time-period being considered. It is necessary to distinguish between elasticities at the retail and farm-gate level, as they are not necessarily the same.

Notes
1 Thünen, J. H. von, *The Isolated State*, London, 1966. For a summary of the agricultural and urban applications see Hallett, G., *Urban Land Economics: Principles and Policy*, London, 1979, p. 47ff.
2 *Family Expenditure Survey, 1978*, HMSO, London, 1978.
3 Marshall, Alfred, *Principles of Economics*, eighth edition, London, 1920, p. 132. But no one ever found such a case in the writings of Sir Robert Giffen, and it is doubtful whether it actually existed. The 'Giffen case' is *not* merely than of an 'inferior good', and ought to be forgotten.
4 Stackelburg, H. von, *The Theory of the Market Economy*, trans. A. T. Peacock, London, 1952, p. 146.
5 Schmitt, G., 'Die Handels- und Verarbeitungsspannen bei Nahrungsmitteln', *Berichte über Landwirtschaft*, Sonderheft 171, 1959, pp. 115–19.

CHAPTER FIVE

Market Forms in Agricultural Production and Distribution

Perfect Competition
Agricultural production is one of the very few industries in which there are thousands of firms in direct competition with each other. It corresponds closely, therefore, to the theoretical model of perfect competition, which lies at one extreme of the scale of market forms ranging from perfect competition at one end to monopoly at the other (Table 8). *Perfect Competition* assumes the existence of a homogenous product and so many producers that the individual producer has no influence on the price. Most agricultural products are in fact homogenous when they leave the farm, in the sense that wheat or pigmeat from one farm—within certain quality grades—is identical with wheat or pigmeat from another farm. The individual farmers cannot therefore influence the price of the product by altering his level of output, or by advertising. Only in the case of direct sales (e.g. eggs) can an individual producer achieve a premium price for a certain level of sales as a result of consumers' preference for real or imagined quality differences. Normally, however, the price is completely outside the control of the individual producer; the demand curve for his production is infinitely elastic (Fig. 15). He is a 'price taker'.

An industry characterised by perfect competition displays marked weaknesses when, through an increase in production or a decline in consumption, prices fall below the level which ensures normal profitability to the majority of producers. The restoration of equilibrium should, in theory, take place through the least profitable producers moving out of the industry, but as a result of immobility this movement is often very long delayed. The whole industry therefore suffers a loss in income and cuts down on investment and repairs; sometimes the whole industry becomes rather derelict, in other cases some producers eventually succeed in developing cheaper methods of production. This process is particularly noticeable in the case of agriculture, but it can also be seen in other industries with a similar atomistic structure, such as the British cotton industry in the long period of decline after the First World War.

Monopoly
Because of these weaknesses in the adjustment process, the state often intervenes in industries characterised by perfect competition, either to accelerate structural change or to maintain prices, or both. Examples of policies designed to accelerate structural change are the various schemes since the 1920s for encouraging concentration and re-equipment in the British cotton industry, or policies for reforming the size and layout of farm holdings. Examples of price support policies are the control of cotton cloth imports by means of quotas, or levies on imports of agricultural products, or import control by an official importing organisation. These policies of price support are often based on the principle of *Monopoly*, which is thus important for the explanation of agricultural price formation, even though the structure of agricultural production is the very opposite of monopolistic. The Milk Marketing Boards, possess in Great Britain, for example, a monopoly in the purchase and sale of milk. Official agencies in many countries exercise monopolistic control over imports, either directly or by means of import quotas; e.g. butter and bacon in Great Britain, or cereals in West Germany and France before the introduction of the Common Market regulations. Exports are sometimes controlled by an official monopoly, either on a national basis, e.g. the Canadian Wheat Board or the American Commodity Credit Corporation, or on an international basis through international commodity agreements, e.g. the International Coffee Agreement.

TABLE 8

Market Forms

Perfect Competition Polyopoly	Imperfect Competition, Oligopoly, Oligopsony	Monopoly, Monopsony
Homogeneous product (wheat, wool)	Heterogeneous goods; product differentiation, real or induced by advertising	Single seller, single buyer of product.
Many small buyers or sellers	A few large buyers or sellers, or agreements about prices	No competition (although possibility of new entrants may influence policy).
Free entry	Entry sometimes difficult	
No preferences between firms	Objective or subjective preferences between firms	

Price-taker; production or purchases adjusted to given price	Some control over price. Price must be set in light of competition and demand conditions	Sales depend on price set, according to D curve for the product. The monopolist can set any price (subject to D curve). The price can be above normal costs and yield above-normal profits.
Demand curve of individual firm horizontal		
Uniform market price	No uniform market price. The attitude, not the number, of buyers or sellers determines policy on price and output	

Examples

Commodity exchanges, wholesale markets for many foodstuffs, larger auction markets for livestock	Commerce, retail trade and manufacturing industry	Public monopolies (e.g. railways). Natural monopolies through control of sources of supply (rare). Collective monopolies with official sanction (e.g. milk, although not full monopoly in absence of supply control).

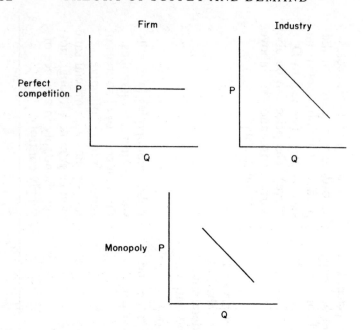

FIG. 15. Demand curves under perfect competition and monopoly

When there is only one seller of a product, the demand curve facing this seller is the demand curve for the product, so that the monopolist has it in his power to raise prices by restricting supply. The extent to which prices can be raised in this way depends, however, on the elasticity of the demand curve. It will only pay to restrict output when demand is price inelastic, because only then will receipts (price × quantity sold) rise as the price rises; the more inelastic the curve, the more profitable will be a policy of output restriction. The demand for most agricultural products is in fact price inelastic, so that a restriction of output does raise receipts.

A statutory monopoly can only make use of its monopoly power if it is in a position to control the quantity of the product coming on to the market. If it is bound to sell all the produce delivered to it by producers over whose output it has no control, the price it can obtain will be the same as would have prevailed under perfect competition. The supply of the product can, however, be controlled, and the price raised, in two ways:

(a) Quota restriction of the output (or, less directly, of the planted acreage) of individual producers. A restriction of this type can, however, be enforced by a statutory authority even when it possesses no monopoly of buying and selling. The British Potato Marketing Board, the American acreage control programmes, and the acreage quotas for sugar beet employed in many countries, are all examples of output restriction without a selling monopoly.

(b) Price discrimination. When a product is sold in two separate markets, which have differing price elasticities, a monopoly can obtain higher returns by charging different prices in the different markets. This can, however, only be done if it is possible to keep the two markets separate; otherwise buyers in the higher-priced markets will switch to the lower-priced market, until the price difference is eliminated.

Price Discrimination
The conditions for maximising total revenue are that marginal revenue (MR) is the same in the two markets and is falling and that, at the price corresponding to this level of MR, the quantities sold in the two markets add up to total production. Thus if P_1 and P_2, Q_1 and Q_2, MR_1 and MR_2, represent prices, quantities sold, and marginal revenues in the two markets respectively, and Q_T the total production, the conditions for the most profitable division of supplies between the two markets are:

$$Q_1 + Q_2 = Q_T \dots (1)$$
$$MR_1 = MR_2 \dots (2)$$

Marginal revenue is the derivative of total revenue ($R = P \times Q$) with respect to quantity (dR/dQ). Given the function of the D curve, which expresses P in terms of Q, these two equations can, theoretically, be solved to find the optimal price and quantity in the two markets.

Price discrimination is usually illustrated by a diagram showing two arithmetic-linear D curves with differing

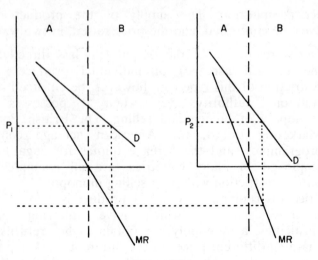

FIG. 16

slopes, both of above unitary elasticity (the sections marked A in Fig. 16). The profit-maximising prices in the two markets then correspond to the quantities at which MR is equal. It is usually stated that a monopolist would never produce at a price at which elasticity of demand was below unity, and MR thus negative, since at this level of production, total revenue could be increased by producing less. But a monopolist selling on farmers' behalf, e.g. a marketing board, might well continue to sell under these conditions; it could admittedly increase its receipts by destroying part of the supply, but might well decide against this course of action because of the likely public outcry. If, therefore, we consider the sections of the D curves for which the corresponding MR is negative and downward-sloping (section B), the principle still applies that the most profitable prices are those at which MR is equal in the two markets, e.g. P_1 and P_2.

Among agricultural products, the conditions necessary for price discrimination are met particularly well in the case of milk, since the demand for fluid milk is less price elastic than that for milk products such as butter and cheese. Thus in many countries the markets for fluid and manufactured milk have been separated, either by the setting up of an explicit monopoly, as in Great Britain, or by means of administrative controls and transfer payments from one market to the other, as in West Germany. This separation of the markets enables higher prices to be charged in the liquid than in the manufacturing market and results (at least in the short run) in a higher average price to the producer.

At current prices, demand is generally inelastic in the liquid milk market and elastic in the manufacturing milk market. This means that marginal revenue is negative in the liquid and positive in the manufacturing market. It would therefore be in the interest of the monopolistic seller to raise the price in the liquid market (thereby selling less) and continue raising it until demand in the liquid market becomes elastic, as it is bound to do at a sufficiently high price. In other words, the existing situation means that the monopolist has not fully exploited the monopoly power he would possess if he had full control over price.

In most countries, however, the price in the liquid market is generally set by some public body. The selling agency is thus faced with a fixed price in the more profitable market, and naturally seeks to sell as much as possible in this market.

Except where it is deliberately maintained by the state, a pure monopoly is seldom found in developed economies, and cases where private monopoly power is clearly exploited to produce above-normal profits are even more seldom. In spite of the process of concentration in modern industry, there are usually two or more firms producing competitive products for a given market and if it appears that there are profits to be made, firms in other sectors are quick to enter the field. In the British fertiliser market, for example, the 'monopoly' position of ICI has been challenged first by Fisons and then by Shell. Thus the threat of potential competition imposes limits on the extent to which a monopoly can make use of its power.

The undeniable existence of monopolistic elements in the rest of the economy may, however, aggravate the problems of an industry such as agriculture which—in the absence of intervention by statutory authorities or even co-operatives—has many of the characteristics of perfect competition. Farmers' complaints of excessive prices for fertilisers, machinery etc. may well be unfounded as such. Nevertheless the existence of powerful trade unions, exercising their monopoly power to raise wages, and of 'imperfect competition' among firms may, in a general way, put agriculture at a disadvantage. Industries in which trade unions are weak tend to get left behind in the wage race—unless labour in them is very scarce—and this has been recognised in the United Kingdom in the settling of Wages Boards for determining minimum wages in both catering and agriculture. The same may apply—in the absence of price support policies—to farmers' incomes. It is true that the problem of farmers' incomes arises basically from the fact that, because of technical progress, there tend at any one time to be more farmers in the industry than are needed. But his situation is confined to agriculture. Several reports on the British newspaper industry have reported about 30 per cent overstaffing, but by means of restrictive working agreements and limitation on entry the printing unions have nevertheless been able to maintain wages at a relatively high level. (It is quite possible, however, that the printing unions will eventually kill the industry.) Thus the pressure on industries facing the same problems as agriculture are sometimes reduced in a way not possible for agriculture. There is, of course, a strong case for pushing ahead with structural reforms both in printing and in agriculture; two blacks do not make a white. But although the existence of inefficiencies and monopolistic practices in other industries is no reason for condoning an inefficient agriculture, it may nevertheless be a further reason why so many governments have felt it necessary to take measures to support agricultural prices and incomes.

We have used the word 'monopoly' in the strict economic, and etymological, sense of a 'single seller', without any implication that this form of organisation is good or bad. In ordinary usage the word does, however, have pejorative undertones, and the question therefore arises of whether monopoly really is good or bad. The traditional argument against monopoly is that it enables the monopolistic to enjoy excessive profits. It is implicitly assumed that a monopolistic is an already wealthy man or group of men whose further enrichment through monopoly profits is unjustified. But there are cases, such as those of statutory monopolies for agricultural products, where the beneficiaries of monopoly are groups of producers with below-average incomes. In such cases a raising of incomes may be regarded as socially desirable, and the employment of monopolistic practices can be defended as means to this end.

Whether in fact farmers' incomes should be supported, and at what level, is of course a matter on which opinions will vary; furthermore, argument is possible as to whether monopolistic market organisations are a better way of raising incomes than direct payments or structural reform. It is nevertheless stressed in modern 'welfare economics' that the effect on income distribution cannot be ignored in discussion of economic policy.[1] (This conclusion is just about the only one that modern welfare economics has in fact reached.) This means that the setting up of a monopolistic marketing board for agricultural products cannot be rejected merely on the ground that it is monopolistic, or even on the ground that it would not benefit the nations as a whole. The effect on the income of particular groups must be assessed; a decision reached as to whether such a change is desirable or undesirable; and the question considered, whether the desired change in income distribution could be better achieved in other ways.

Imperfect Competition

The form of competition typical for the manufacturing industry—and also for the production and sale of processed agricultural products—is neither perfect competition nor monopoly, but something between the two. The typical situation is that the number of sellers of the product is small, while several of them have a substantial share of the market. This type of competition has been variously called 'imperfect competition' or 'monopolistic competition', or 'oligopoly'. The various terms have different shades of meaning, but there cannot be said to be clear-cut and universally accepted definitions of the terms, mainly because economists disagree, or have in the past disagreed, as to how this type of competition actually functions. Professor Wiles—who has provided one of the most convincing post-1945 expositions of the subject[2]—simply refers to the 'full cost sector' within which he makes further sub-divisions. We will use the term 'oligopoly' and 'oligopolistic competition', although aware that many economists would use these terms in a more restricted sense. However, 'oligopoly' does not mean 'a few' sellers and at least fits neatly into the tripartite division: polyopoly, oligopoly, monopoly.

It is a characteristic of oligopolistic competition that the firm has, at least in the short run, some influence on the price of its product. Unlike the farmer producing under conditions of perfect competition, the firm must decide, not only how much to produce but at what price to offer its product—bearing in mind that the price will affect sales, and that limits are imposed by the actions of competitors.

Oligopolistic competition is frequently characterised by *product differentiation*. Motor cars, or tractors, or men's clothes from one firm, possess real or imagined differences from those of other firms; the goods are not homogenous and can therefore command different prices. Someone who wishes to buy a car has a choice between a variety of models, all of which have advantages and disadvantages and whose prices are not identical. Each model is unique in that it offers differences in design or styling or workmanship; in the sense that each product is unique, every manufacturer can be said to possess a monopoly in its manufacturing. On the other hand, the various models are sufficiently similar in their general performance that the manufacturers are in fact engaged in fierce competition with each other. Competition therefore exists, and is not necessarily a diluted form of 'perfect competition' as the name 'imperfect competition' suggests; it is, however, different from the type of anonymous competition found in agricultural production.

Oligopolistic competition is found even in the marketing of agricultural products, when they have reached the stage of being processed and packaged. The dividing line between perfect and oligopolistic competition is indicated by whether the product of a single producer or distributor is advertised or branded. Farmers who sell milk wholesale do not engage in advertising, because they can sell as much as they wish at the existing price. (A farmer who retails his milk, on the other hand, may find it profitable to advertise.) When the milk has reached the form of tins of condensed milk, however, it is normally branded and advertised. In fact, the possession of an established brand gives a manufacturer an advantage which may enable him to charge higher prices than his competitors. When a firm sells agricultural products of a variable character, it may be able to raise the average price it receives by sorting out those of higher quality and selling them under a brand name. This has increasingly been done in recent years even with what might be considered unpromising material. For example, the United Fruit Company—which controls the banana output of several South American countries—has sought to counter a fall in the price of bananas by selling especially well developed fruit under a brand name at a higher price per pound.

All foodstuffs which are sold under brand names are *ipso facto* being marketed under conditions of oligopolistic competition. The processing and marketing firms concerned—whether private or co-operative—are engaged in a form of competition in which advertising, reputation, and sales contacts play an important role. Even when the product is not branded, as in the case of bread (from small bakeries) and meat or meat products (from butchers) many of the characteristics of oligopolistic competition are present. The consumer knows that so and so's bread or so and so's sausage tastes particularly good and is therefore sometimes prepared to pay a slightly above-average price.

Oligopoly on the International Level
The theory of oligopoly can be applied, however, not only to firms but also to nations, in as far as governments or statutory organisations control external trade. This is today relatively frequent in the case of agricultural products. The USA and Canada, for example, have in

recent years dominated the world market for wheat, supplying roughly two-thirds of total world exports. In both cases the supply of wheat onto the world markets is controlled by statutory agencies which, in the short run, can regulate supplies by increasing or decreasing their stocks. Both the Canadian Wheat Board and the Commodity Credit Corporation can therefore, in the short run, influence the supplies coming on to the world market, and thus influence the world price. The demand curve facing them is neither the infinitely elastic curve of the perfect competitor (such as that facing small suppliers like Iraq, whose exports are too small to affect the price) nor is it a monopolist's demand curve; the curve depends on the reaction of the competitors and is therefore indeterminate. At this point one enters a field which has more in common with a poker game than with intersecting demand and supply curves; the outcome is largely a matter of psychology. In the 1950s and 1960s, the American and Canadian authorities followed each other's actions closely and maintained a stable world wheat price. The 1973 price explosion followed the abandonment of this policy by the USA and the running down of stocks.

The counterpart on the buying side is *oligopsony* (a few buyers). Just as a small number of selling nations account for a large share of world agricultural exports, so a small number of buying nations account for a large share of imports. Great Britain, the EEC countries and Japan, take the greater part of world exports of temperate agricultural products—at least of commercial sales as distinct from food aid. Actions by one of these buyers can thus have a significant effect on the sales of the exporting countries, and measures to hamper imports can give rise to retaliation by the exporters. The 'chicken war' of 1964–65, in which the United States retaliated to a rise in EEC import duties on chickens by raising import duties on various industrial products coming mainly from EEC countries, is a typical example.[3]

In a similar way, the threat of potential competition, which limits the power of manufacturing industries to exploit a quasi-monopolistic position, applies at the international level; it imposes limits on the extent to which international commodity agreements (for rubber, sugar, etc.) are able to raise world prices by restricting supplies. When a group of countries seeks to raise prices by restricting output, there is always the danger that production will be stimulated in countries which remain outside the agreement. Thus the efforts in the 1920s of certain rubber-exporting countries to raise prices were frustrated by the increased production in the Dutch East Indies, which remained outside the scheme.[4] Today, potential competition takes another form, namely the competition between agricultural materials and synthetic substitutes. If, for example, the price of natural rubber rises above a certain level it becomes profitable to expand the production of synthetic rubber.

Assessment of Oligopolistic Competition
Although economists hold different views on the virtues and vices of competition, certain general trends in the attitude to competition can be observed in the history of economic thought. These changing attitudes have to some extent been caused by changes in the nature of competition, for although economic theorists are inclined to present their conclusions as eternal truths based on pure reason, it can be seen in retrospect that these theorists were in fact deeply influenced by contemporary conditions.

The liberal economists of the nineteenth century assumed in most cases that competition brought about the most efficient distribution of resources. They did not define competition very closely, but presupposed the existence of a large number of directly competing firms, at that time a not unrealistic assumption. In the 1920s and 1930s, it became apparent to economists that changes had taken place in industrial organisation and that, in an age of giant organisations, obviously possessing considerable market power, many of the old ideas about competition needed to be revised. Theories of 'imperfect' or 'monopolistic' competition were developed by Chamberlin in the United States,[5] Joan Robinson[6] in England and Stackelberg in Germany virtually contemporaneously. The very name 'imperfect' competition suggests that this form of competition is defective and, in spite of some subsequent qualifications, there is little doubt that this was what the early theorists believed. As regards the marketing of agricultural products, both at the pre-retail and at the retail level, some economists used the theory to postulate the existence of serious inefficiencies and monopolistic profits.[7] These criticisms were mainly deductive, i.e. they were based on abstract principles rather than on empirical investigations. Nevertheless the intellectual climate in which they were made was dominated by the depression which began in 1929. Not a few economists came to the conclusion that the capitalistic system had collapsed, and sought a solution in Marxism or Fascism. A theory showing that competition did not work fell therefore on fruitful ground. Indeed, the depression showed up many weaknesses in the marketing system but—as can now be seen more clearly than then—the depression itself had quite other causes.

With the recovery from the depression, and with dynamic new developments in economic organisation, economists began to find theories about the 'wastes of imperfect competition' less and less convincing. For example, the concentration of food retailing into chains, voluntary chains and co-operatives has not led to a weakening of competition or a decline in efficiency—quite the reverse. These inconsistencies were sharply pointed out by Schumpeter,[8] who stressed the dynamic element in economic organisaion. The fear that a firm would use its 'monopoly' position in order to restrict production and exploit the public assumes a static situation; in practice, he argued, such a firm would soon be forced out of business. Other writers pointed out that the theorists of imperfect competition had attributed unrealistically short-sighted attitudes to firms and tried to develop a theory of 'workable' competition which explains the facts of modern industrial behaviour. A typically incisive contribution was made by Galbraith with the concept of 'countervailing power'.[9] According to this theory, the monopoly power of any economic group is neutralised by the concentration of power among opposing groups. Trade unions offset the power of employers; chain stores offset the power of food processors; farms offset the power of their market partners, partly by forming trading co-operatives, partly by means of political action.

At the present time, the concensus of opinion among economists is that the gloomier conclusions of the earlier theorists of imperfect competition were unjustified, and that the usefulness of the theory is in many ways limited. Stackelberg in his later years was able to see 'imperfect competition' in better perspective than some of his English-speaking counterparts, and in his last book he incorporated the most important elements of his early work in a synthesis in which the 'neo-classical' principles were partially re-instated.[10] The distinction between a homogeneous product and a differentiated product, between 'price takers' and 'price makers' is today accepted by economists, but it is also realised that it is the *behaviour* rather than the *number* of competitors which is decisive for the character of competition. For the explanation of firms' behaviour there is, however, no simple theory comparable to the theories of perfect competition or monopoly. It is possible to describe various business motives (e.g. the desire to expand, to develop new products) and the influence of different market arrangements (e.g. greater or lesser freedom of entry to the industry, the extent of international competition). But the sector lying between the poles of perfect competition and monopoly cannot be explained in terms of a diagram.

In one respect, which is important for the price formation of primary products, the emerging concensus on 'oligopoly' re-introduces a simple 'demand and supply' analysis. The price of primary products—apart from short-term speculative wobbles—depends on demand and supply, and market forms can exert a permanent influence on price *only in so far as they affect demand and supply*. This applies both to the ability of sellers to raise prices, and to the ability of buyers to hold them down. Oligopolistic sellers, acting either informally or in a formal cartel, can raise prices (above the level which would otherwise have prevailed) only if they agree, explicitly or implicitly, on a reduction in supply. At the time of writing (Christmas 1979) the Organisation of Petroleum Exports Countries is being unjustifiably criticised for raising the price of oil. In fact, the price is rising because of the market situation, with demand tending to outstrip supply. OPEC has not imposed national quotas, and so acted as a price-raising cartel—although some individual member countries are unwilling or unable to increase production. In the same way, groupings of countries exporting cocoa, coffee, etc. can raise prices, in the long run, only if they can impose coordinated national sales quotas.

The same principle applies to oligopsonistic buyers. For example, the price of tea has been somewhat depressed in the 1970s. One explanation—put forward by businessmen and taken up by some anti-market economists—has been the increased concentration of the tea-blending industry. However, this could be expected to depress the price permanently only if the tea buyers throughout the world reached and maintained an agreement to reduce their purchases, which has certainly not happened. An alternative explanation is that the demand for tea has been growing slowly (*per capita* consumption in tea-drinking Britain has fallen). At the same time, production has been increased by the development of production in new areas, notably East Africa (partly through the efforts of international agencies to provide new employment in these countries). The result has been a 'buyers' market'. But a drastic reduction in supplies would establish a 'sellers' market', irrespective of the fairly high degree of concentration in the blending industry; the sharp rises in the price of coffee (in 1976), in oil, etc., illustrate the point.

Summary
Market forms can be divided into a spectrum ranging from 'perfect competition' to 'monopoly'. These two cases can be represented by diagrams; what lies between them—the competition between a small number of large firms characteristic of manufacturing and wholesaling—cannot. The theories of 'imperfect competition', which attempted to give an explanation in terms of 'curves', and suggested gross inefficiencies in anything other than 'perfect' competition, have been rejected by subsequent economists. From a dynamic point of view, 'perfect competition' can

have disadvantages, and oligopoly can have advantages. Agriculture has examples of all three market forms: perfect competition in production; monopoly in state control of supply; oligopoly in marketing. Perfect competition and oligopoly give rise to different short-term price movements, perfect competition leading to greater price volatility, but in both cases the general level of prices is dominated by supply and demand.

Notes

1 Little, I. M. D., *A Critique of Welfare Economics*, second edition, Oxford, 1957.

2 Wiles, P., *Price, Cost and Output*, second edition, Oxford, 1961.

3 This little episode illustrates the way in which a round of retaliatory tariff rises between two countries, or economic groupings, can harm them both. Scitovsky has shown theoretically that two countries, trading with each other and each raising tariffs in a way which is in their own interest, can get into a position which is in the interest of neither ('A reconsideration of the theory of tariffs' in *Readings in the Theory of International Trade*, American Economic Association, 1949.)

However, whereas in this model the imposition of a tariff benefits a country by improving the terms of trade, the motivation in practice is more often to assist a local industry, or to 'hit back' at another country. The higher unemployment rates of the late 1970s have led to a 'creeping protectionism', in spite of the efforts of GATT to maintain progress towards freer trade, and the agricultural protectionism of the EEC has contributed to this trend. Many economists feel that protectionist policies can harm all parties, although the 'New Cambridge School' strongly supports import controls, as did some economists in the 1930s.

4 Rowe, J. W. F., *Primary Commodities in International Trade*, Cambridge, 1965, p. 120.

5 Chamberlin, E. H., *Theory of Monopolistic Competition*, Cambridge, Mass., 1933.

6 Robinson, J., *Economics of Imperfect Competition*, London, 1933.

7 Nicholls, W. H., *Imperfect Competition within Agricultural Industries*, Iowa, 1941.

8 Schumpeter, J. A., *Capitalism, Socialism and Democracy*, New York, 1942, Chs. 7–8.

9 Galbraith, J. K., *American Capitalism: The Concept of Countervailing Power*, Boston, 1952.
10 Stackelberg, H. von, *The Theory of the Market Economy*, trans. A. T. Peacock, London, 1952.

Further Reading

The 'mainstream' consensus on market forms and welfare economics is summarised in general textbooks such as Samuelson, P. A., *Economics: An Introductory Analysis*, or more fully in a book such as Mansfield, E., *Microeconomics: Theory and Applications*, New York, 1970. Graduate students can be referred to Wiles (see n. 2 above), a sometimes obscure but important book, and Schumpeter (see n. 8 above), which is thought-provoking. Neither, however, is specifically agricultural. Rowe (see n. 4 above) gives a good account of internationally traded commodities, and Kohls, R. L. and Downey, D., *Marketing of Agricultural Products*, fourth edition, New York, 1970, contains a clear discussion of economic organisation as related to agricultural marketing.

CHAPTER SIX

Shifts in the Demand and Supply Curves

The demand and supply curves are based on the assumption that all factors other than the price of the commodity remain constant. But in the real world these factors are continually changing, and the extent and speed of these changes are of the greatest importance for the prices of agricultural products. Such changes are represented graphically by new D or S curves lying either to right or left of the original ones. In Fig. 17(a) the curve D_2 represents a shift to the right compared with curve D_1, i.e. at each price a larger quantity will be demanded. Such a shift could be brought about by a rise in population or, in the case of a foodstuff such as meat, by a rise in real income per head. The curve D_3, on the other hand, represents a shift to the left of the D curve, i.e. a fall in demand.

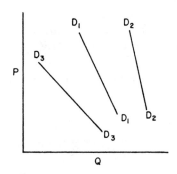 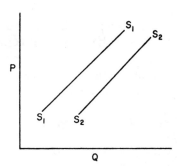

FIG. 17

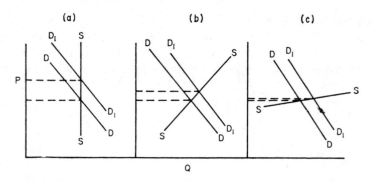

FIG. 18

Shifts of the curves produce new equilibrium positions. Since, however, there are short, medium and long-term supply curves (or rather a whole range of curves), there are correspondingly short, medium and long-term equilibrium positions. Take the case of a sharp increase in demand. The short-term S curve will be completely inelastic—except in so far as imports can be increased or stocks run down—and the price will therefore rise without any change in quantity (Fig. 18(a)). Over a medium-term period, farmers are able to increase production to some extent: the supply increases and the price rises slightly from its previous high level (Fig. 18(b)). Over a long period, the supply is much more elastic, so that in the long-term equilibrium, the supply has increased considerably, whereas the price is hardly higher than at the beginning (Fig. 18(c)). Price movements do not, however, always proceed smoothly from a short-term, over a medium-term, to a long-term equilibrium. During the adjustment period, demand or long-term supply can again alter, so that the movement is towards a long-term equilibrium which is itself moving. Or the supply can overshoot the long-term equilibrium and give rise to the formation of cycles.

The Cobweb Theorem
For a number of agricultural products, regular fluctuations in price and output have been observed over long periods of time. These cyclical fluctuations are most marked in the case of pigs, which in many countries show a regular cycle

of large supplies and low prices, followed by low supplies and high prices. The length of the pig cycle was in the past 3–4 years, but more recently—no doubt as a result of shorter fattening periods—the length of the cycle has been reduced to 2–3 years. Vegetables often show regular fluctuations from one harvest to another, i.e. a two-year cycle. A cattle cycle of 10–15 years has been noted in the USA, and coffee shows cycles of varying length.

An explanation for the persistence of these cycles is given by the cobweb theorem, which was first put forward in theoretical terms, and has subsequently proved particularly useful in explaining the pig cycle.[*1] The assumptions of the theorem are:

(1) There is perfect competition, and the total supply is solely determined by the reaction of individual producers to the price. In particular, it is assumed that each producer plans his production on the assumption that the future price will be the same as the present one, and that his own production will not significantly affect the market.

(2) There is a production period of a certain length, so that supply does not react to price directly, but only after a time-lag.

(3) The price is determined by the quantity coming on to the market and reacts immediately to it.

To explain the cobweb theorem, let us assume that supply is originally in a position of equilibrium, but that it is in some way moved away from this position. In Fig. 19, Case I, the equilibrium point is when the price is 10, and the quantity 10; some disturbance (e.g. a high death rate among piglets during a hard winter) now causes the quantity supplied to fall to 9. Thus in Period 1, the quantity has fallen to 9 and the price has consequently risen to 11. The rise in price leads producers to plan a larger production, which, as can be seen from the supply curve, amounts, at the price of 11, to 11 units. In Period 2, after the appropriate time-lag, this production comes on to the market and causes the price to sink to 9. This low price now causes producers to plan a reduced production, but this again takes time. In Period 3, the supply has again sunk

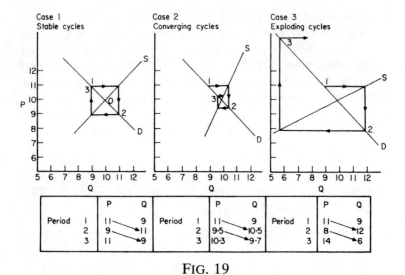

FIG. 19

to 9, the price risen to 11, and the cycle starts all over again.

In this case, the S and D curves have been drawn so that their slopes are the same. If the curves are drawn so that the S curve is steeper than the D curve, the cycle takes a different form (Case 2). In period 2, the supply has risen to only 10·5 and the price has therefore fallen to only 9·5. In Period 3, price and quantity are 10·3 and 9·7 respectively. The cycles clearly become smaller and smaller and converge on the equilibrium position. If, on the other hand, the slope of the demand curve is steeper than that of the S curve, the cycles become larger and larger; the cycle 'explodes', until the price falls to zero.

But although it is geometrically the *slope* of the curves that determines the form of the cycle, it is more useful for practical purposes to think in terms of their *elasticities*. The more price and quantity diverge from the equilibrium, the greater the divergence between the ratio of slopes and elasticities. This difficulty can be overcome by using a diagram with a double log. scale, so that a constant slope indicates a constant elasticity. Case 1 will then represent a situation in which the elasticity of demand (η) equals the elasticity of supply (ε). Case 2 a situation in which η is less than ε, and Case 3 a situation in which η is less than ε. Thus we can say the cycles are stable when the numerical value of the elasticity of demand equals that of the elasticity of supply; converge when it is greater; and explode when it is less. The case in which the cycles keep on exploding is, of course, an unrealistic one; it will not happen if at high or low prices η increases or ε decreases sufficiently, and this many well happen at high prices. Given these changes in the elasticities, the cycle will cease to explode, and will become a stable cycle of the first type.

These three cases are theoretical models which never correspond exactly to reality. Nevertheless, the cobweb theorem gives a valuable explanation of how cycles can arise and persist. The reasons why cycles of this type are more common in the case of (some) agricultural products than of industrial products are two-fold. Firstly, the assumption of perfect competition does not hold good to the same extent in manufacturing industry. The number of producers is smaller, and they take some account of the influence on the market of their own policies. Secondly, manufacturers tend to take a longer view. When the market is flooded they may know from their market research department that in a few years consumption will again have risen, and that panic measures to contract production would therefore be unwise. And when there is a shortage they know that excessive expansion by all producers could easily lead to a surplus. Farmers, on the other hand, tend to react in a less well-informed way. They are too optimistic when prices are high and too pessimistic when they are low; thus by their reactions they perpetuate the cycle. It is noteworthy that the very large-scale 'factory' producers of poultry, eggs and pigs maintain a far more constant level of production than the smaller producers. Perhaps the concentration of a greater part of production in enterprises of this type, which is going on in all advanced countries, will lead to a dimunition of 'cobweb' cycles.

The reason why pig production shows particularly marked cyclical fluctuations is that pig production reacts so quickly and so sharply to price changes, i.e. the elasticity of supply over a short period is relatively high. In the case of cereals and other crops, where supply elasticities seem to be lower, fluctuations are—as in Case 2—soon damped, and in the case of cattle, which have a very long production period, cycles are not so clearly defined because demand may well change in the course of a cycle.

Agriculture during a Depression

It was mentioned in Chapter 3 that agricultural prices tend to fall more than industrial prices in a depression; this can be explained by means of D and S curves. In Fig. 20 the effect is shown of a fall in demand, i.e. a shift to the left of the D curve, in the case of an inelastic 'agricultural' and an elastic 'industrial' supply curve. In the case of 'agriculture' the shift of the D curve causes a slight fall in the quantity supplied and a big drop in the price; and in the case of 'industry' it causes a big drop in quantity and a slight fall in price.

In this diagram, the S curve has been shown as very inelastic. There is, however, an alternative explanation for the maintenance of agricultural production in depression. Instead of being so inelastic, it may be that the S curve is moved to the right in a depression.[2] This could be the result of a change in the supply of agricultural labour (mainly the supply of farmers). The movement of labour out of agriculture proceeds fastest when other occupations are booming and jobs are easy to get. In a general depression,

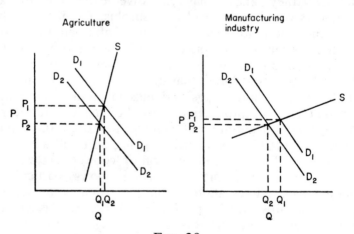

FIG. 20

when there is unemployment in industry, the movement out of agriculture slows down, or even reverses, becoming a movement back into agriculture, as was the case in the USA in the 1930s. On the farm there was at least enough to eat, and thus many families who had left farming returned to it. This development is represented in Fig. 21, where a simultaneous shift is shown of the *D* curve to the left and of the *S* curve to the right. The actual movement of price and quantity (shown by the dotted line A_1) is the same as the very inelastic *S* curve as shown in Fig. 20, but is not in fact a true supply curve.

What actually happens in a slump probably lies between the two cases represented in Figs. 20 and 21. This example shows, however, how difficult it is to calculate the true elasticity of supply from actual changes in prices and production. It suggests that agriculture will react more readily to price changes in a time of general prosperity than in a time of depression. In the light of post-war experience, we can say that *ceteris paribus* this is probably so, but in fact things do not remain equal. In a period of prosperity the application of science to agriculture seems to proceed more rapidly than in times of depression, so that the effect

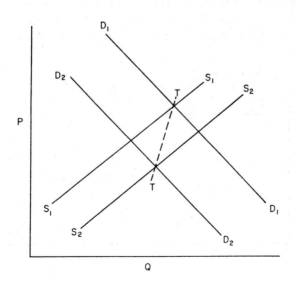

FIG. 21

of the increased migration out of agriculture—which would move the S curve to the left—is more than made up for by increased technical progress, which moves the S curve to the right. Thus both prosperity and depression bring difficulties for agriculture. There is, fortunately, no doubt that the problems of prosperity are easier to solve than those of depression.

Agriculture in Conditions of General Economic Prosperity
When the economy in general is prosperous, the demand for agricultural products rises—until a very high level of real income is reached—but the supply also tends to increase, unless natural conditions are very unfavourable. There is thus a kind of 'race' between supply and demand, which determines the level of agricultural prices. If supply and demand rise by the same amount—i.e. if the horizontal shift of the S and D curves is the same—then prices remain unaltered (Fig. 22(a)). If supply rises more than demand, the price falls (Fig. 22(b)). If the supply rises less than the demand, the price rises (Fig. 22(c)). This assumes that the

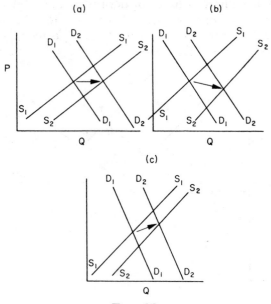

FIG. 22

general price level remains unaltered. When dealing with actual situations, when the general price level rises or falls, the agricultural prices would have to be expressed in 'real' terms.

Historical examples of a rise in the real agricultural price level are seen in Great Britain and Germany in the middle of the nineteenth century; in both cases an increase in demand brought about by rising population and real incomes impinged upon an agricultural industry which was able to raise production only slowly. On the other hand, in the USA since 1945 there has also been an increase in demand, arising mainly from population increase, but the increase in production brought about by technical progress has been even greater; this has led to a fall in real agricultural prices.

The Influence of Price Elasticities on Price Changes
When price rises or falls occur as a result of shifts in the S and D curves, the elasticity of the curves determines the size of the price change. Fig. 23 represents the effect of a shift in the S curve with differing elasticities of demand and supply. It can be seen that in (a) the price fall when the curve D_b is very inelastic (from P_0 to P_2) is greater than when the curve D_a is very elastic (from P_0 to P_1). Fig. 23(b) shows that the shift of the inelastic supply curve,

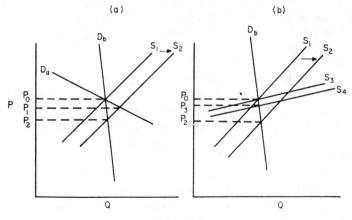

FIG. 23

$S_1 - S_2$, causes a greater price fall $(P_0 - P_2)$ than the shift of the elastic curve $S_3 - S_4$ $(P_0 - P_3)$.

Thus the lower the elasticities of demand and supply, the greater will be the price change for any given shift in supply (or in demand).

Productivity and Income
When supply increases more than demand, the (real) prices of agricultural products will fall. It does not, however, necessarily follow that farmers' (real) incomes will fall, because these are affected by two further factors:

(a) the price of farm inputs,
(b) changes in agricultural productivity.

The relationship between the price of agricultural inputs and those of agricultural products constitutes the 'terms of trade' between agriculture and industry, in the same way that the relationship between a country's import prices and export prices constitutes the country's international terms of trade. There has been a tendency in many countries since the war for agriculture's terms of trade to worsen, but the position varies from country to country, depending largely on the agricultural price policies followed. The point needs to be made, however, that it is the terms of trade rather than merely the product price that is decisive.

The productivity concept relates to the relationship between the quantity of input and the quantity of output. The question of its definition can become extremely complicated,[3] but the two most commonly used versions—gross and net (labour) productivity—are basically fairly simple. Both relate to the gross or net output per worker in agriculture, or per man-hour.

The number of workers, or of man hours, is in practice difficult to measure, because of part-time farming, and the contribution of wives and other members of the family. Thus figures from different countries are by no means completely comparable. Total gross output relates to the total quantity of cereals, meat, etc. sold off the 'national farm', and, in order to compare differing years, when the combination of products will be different, it is necessary to reduce the various products to a common unit. This is generally the value at constant prices, although other methods can be adopted—such as the German method of expressing output in 'cereal units'.

The figures of Gross Output published by the Food and Agriculture Organisation of the United Nations are obtained by valuing the various products at the prices ruling in a given base year, and these figures are used in Table 9 to show the growth of production in various countries between 1950 and 1960. The reduction in the agricultural labour force is shown in column *b*, and the division of *a* by *b* gives the change in Gross Output per head (gross productivity). It can be seen that the Gross Output of British agriculture in this period rose by 30 per cent, while the labour force fell to 84 per cent of the original figure; thus the Gross Productivity rose by 55 per

TABLE 9

Gross Output, Labour Input and Gross Productivity
1950–60

| | Level in 1960 1950 = 100 | | | Average Annual Increase 1950–60 | |
	Gross Output *a*	Labour Input *b*	Gross Productivity $c = a \div b$	*a*	*c*
				%	%
Italy	132	66	200	2·8	7·2
West Germany	130	70	186	2·7	6·4
Belgium	128	70	183	2·4	6·3
France	118	83	142	2·8	6·0
Netherlands	131	81	162	2·7	4·9
USA	120	76	157	1·8	4·6
UK	130	84	155	2·7	4·5
Sweden	109	71	153	0·9	4·3

Source: FAO, *Monthly Bulletin of Agricultural Economics and Statistics*, quoted in Peters, G. H., 'Agriculture's contribution to economic growth', *Westminster Bank Review*, October 1963.

cent. In Italy, where Gross Output rose by virtually the same amount, the labour force fell even more—to 66 per cent of the original figure—so that the Gross Productivity doubled during the period. (The higher figure for Italy represents the *change* in Gross Output per head; the actual figure was, even in 1960, considerably higher in the UK.)

These increases in Gross Output were achieved, however, by means of increased inputs of industrial products such as machinery, fertilisers, etc. If these payments to other industries are deducted, a figure of Net Output is arrived at which corresponds to the incomes of those engaged in agriculture. Changes in Net Output per head (based on constant prices) indicates the increase in the efficiency of agricultural production, and the rate at which agricultural income per head would rise if all prices remained constant. Figures of the yearly growth in Net Output—on this definition—are given in Table 10, and are sometimes larger and sometimes smaller than the figures of Gross Output given in Table 9, according to whether the input of industrial products rose more or less than Gross Output.

It can be seen from Table 10 that, for all the countries listed, the rise in net productivity from 1950 to 1960 was higher in agriculture than in industry. If, therefore, the

TABLE 10

Rates of Growth in Net Productivity 1950–60

	Agriculture %	Manufacturing Industry %
West Germany	6·7	3·7
Italy	6·3	4·6
Netherlands	5·5	3·3
Belgium	5·3	2·1
France	4·8	4·1
UK	4·1	1·8
USA	3·5	2·2

Source: Peters, 'Agriculture's contribution to economic growth'.

terms of trade between agriculture and industry had remained constant, incomes in agriculture would have risen faster than in industry. But in only a few countries during this period did the terms of trade in fact remain constant. In many they worsened, and so agricultural incomes did not rise as fast as they otherwise would have done.

Table 11 shows the changes in the terms of trade, and in the real agricultural income over the period. In West Germany, France and Italy, the terms of trade remained fairly constant—thanks largely to price support measures—but in Belgium and the Netherlands they worsened considerably. (Statistics for the UK were not available.) Thus, real income did not in all countries rise at the same rate as net productivity. Farmers did not, that is to say, enjoy the benefit of the whole of their increase in productivity, but, in the listed countries, real income fell only in the USA, and there only by one per cent.

More recent data suggest that these general trends have continued. One study estimates that the average rate of productivity growth in UK agriculture *with regard to all inputs* between 1963 and 1972 was $3 \cdot 06$ per cent, which was higher than in most other sectors.[4] The German figures of gross productivity per employee for 1967–77 show an average growth of $6 \cdot 2$ per cent in agriculture as against $3 \cdot 7$ per cent in other sectors.[5] The comparable figure for EEC agriculture was $6 \cdot 3$ per cent.[6] Agriculture in the USA has shown a similar trend.[7]

To sum up the relationship between the various factors which determine income per head in agriculture, it can be said that income per head in agriculture (I) is a function of the terms of trade (T) and net productivity (PR).

$$I = f(T, PR)$$

Or if Q_o is the quantity of agricultural production, and P_o its price, Q_i the quantity of non-agricultural inputs, and P their price, and L the agricultural labour force, then

$$I = \frac{(Q_o \times P_o) - (Q_i \times P_i)}{L}$$

The level of agricultural prices depends on the supply of agricultural products in relation to the demand for them.

TABLE 11

Changes in Prices and Incomes in Agriculture 1950–60

| | 1950–51 = 100 | | | |
	Price of Agricultural Products *a*	Price of Inputs *b*	Terms of Trade $c = a \div b$	Real Income Per Head* *d*
West Germany	127	128	100	188
Netherlands	103	157	66	163
Belgium	103	137	75	134
France	163	159	102	126
Italy	106	104	101	121
UK	106	—	—	107
USA	93	117	79	99

*Gross domestic product of agriculture, forestry and fishing per worker, divided by the change in the cost of living index.
Source: OECD, *General Statistics,* July and October 1962.

On the other hand, the price of agricultural inputs is primarily dependent on the level of wages and the course of productivity in the industrial sector. The terms of trade can be influenced by official policies to support the prices of agricultural products and subsidise prices of non-agricultural inputs, such as fertilisers, but there are often economic limits to policies of this type.

To summarise this somewhat involved discussion of productivity and agriculture's terms of trade, it may be helpful to represent the interaction of the factors affecting real income per head in agriculture as follows:

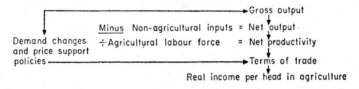

Factors in Agricultural Price Formation

To summarise Part I of this book, we can illustrate the interaction of the various price determining factors in Fig. 24. On the supply side, the general level of home production will be influenced by costs and technical progress, in relation to price. Imports also contribute to total supply, and can be influenced both by the same considerations as affect home production and also by import policy. In the short run, the supply can be affected by weather or epidemics.

On the demand side, the determining factors—in addition to price—are population, disposable real income per head and, in the case of an individual product, the price of alternatives. Whereas supply impinges on the producer price, demand impinges in the first instance on the retail price. But the distributive margin links the two prices, and is determined by costs, competition and productivity in distribution, together with the amount of processing required.

Some factors influence both supply and demand and the distributive margin simultaneously. For example, a rise in real wages raises production costs, distributive costs and—for some products—the demand. In addition,

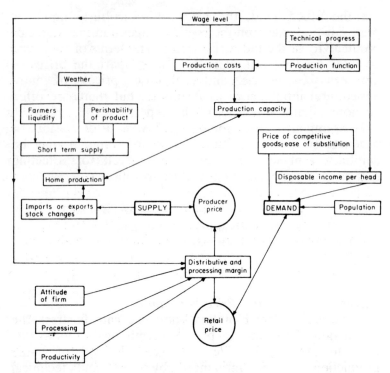

FIG. 24. Factors in the price formation of agricultural commodities

improvements in productivity in production and distribution often go together. Although the connection is not invariable, a country with an inefficient agriculture often has an inefficient distributive system as well.

The relationships shown in Fig. 24 are valid even when price support policies are being operated. When the state intervenes to support market prices, it does so by restricting the supply—either by means of a restriction of home production (acreage quotas), an increase in stocks (support buying), a restriction of import (levies, quotas) or an increase in exports (export subsidies). If, on the other hand, producer prices are supported by means of subsidies, the producer price, including subsidy, becomes separated from the market price.

Summary
The demand and supply curves for agricultural products are subject to shifts. Some are steady shifts resulting from secular economic change but—especially in the case of supply—some are violent and erratic. These shifts can give rise to price fluctuations, which sometimes take a cyclical form (the 'cobweb theorem'). The supply curve is shifted to the right by technical progress. If, as is often the case in 'developed' economies, this shift tends to out-run the shift in the demand curve, there can be a tendency for agricultural prices to fall in real terms. This in itself tends to cause a fall in farm income in relation to income in other sectors, but productivity growth can offset this tendency. The growth of agricultural productivity—although its measurement is problematical—has been very high in most developed economies in the post-War era. It is closely related to the movement of population out of agriculture.

Notes
1 Ezekiel, M., 'The cobwen theorem', *Quarterly Journal of Economics*, Vol. 52, 1938, p. 255. The work by agricultural economists on the cobweb theorem, and other subjects, appears to be largely unknown among general economists in Britain, even those who use illustrations drawn from agriculture. An introduction to mathematical economics (Archibald, G. C. and Lipsey, R. G., *An Introduction to a Mathematical Treatment of Economics*, London, 1967, p. 298 n.), which contains a useful mathematical exposition of the cobweb theorem, cites Professor Kaldor, in 1941, as one of the first writers to realise that it was more than a theoretical curiosity. This seems a little hard on the German and American agricultural economists who used the concept in the 1930s for the detailed analysis of livestock cycles.
2 Johnson, D. G., 'The nature of the supply function for agricultural products', *The American Economic Review*, Vol. XL, no. 4, 1950.
3 Peters, G. H., 'Agriculture's contribution to economic growth', *Westminster Bank Review*, October 1963.
4 Doyle, C. J., 'A comparative study of agricultural productivity in the UK and Europe', *JAE*, Vol. XXX, no. 3, 1979, p. 275.
5 *Agrarbericht der Bundesregierung 1979: Materialband*, Bonn, 1979, p. 35.

6 —'Measured in constant prices, final agricultural production increased at an annual rate of 1·8 in EUR 8 (excluding the UK) between 1968 and 1976. During the same period, agricultural employment and the utilised agricultural area for EUR 9 declined at an average annual rate of 4·2% and 0·6% respectively. Productivity per hectare increased at an annual rate of 2·4% during the period' (*The Agricultural Situation in the Community, 1978 Report*, Brussels, 1979, p. 56).

7 Gross output per worker-hour in US agriculture grew by an annual average of 7·9 per cent between 1963 and 1975. The 'parity ratio' fell from around 80 in the 1950s and 1960s to around 70 in the 1970s. But the ratio of *per capita* income of farm people to that of non-farm people rose from 50–60 per cent in the 1960s to around 70 per cent in the 1960s, and around 80 per cent in the late 1970s. It briefly rose above 100 per cent during the commodity boom of 1973/4. (USDA figures).

Further Reading

Allen, G. R., *Agricultural Marketing Policies*, Oxford, 1959, Ch. 3.

Cochrane, W. W., *Farm Prices: Myth and Reality*, Minnesota, 1959, Chs. 4, 5.

OEEC, *Agriculture and Economic Growth*, Paris, 1965.

PART II

The Quantification of Supply and Demand

CHAPTER SEVEN

Price and Income Elasticities of Demand

The Demand Function
As we have seen, the demand function for a foodstuff can be expressed as follows:

$$Qi = f(Pi, Pj \ldots Pn, Y)$$

where Pi represents the price of the foodstuff in question and $Pj \ldots Pn$ the prices of competitive foodstuffs, while Y represents income. Given empirical data on prices, income and consumption, it is possible to derive mathematical functions indicating the relationship between consumption, prices and income. Since a straight-line demand curve often corresponds closely to empirical data, it is often convenient to represent the price function as arithmetic-linear. On the other hand, the consumption of many foodstuffs tends to 'level off' as income increases, and this can best be represented by a log-linear function. Thus (using different subscripts) the demand for beef could be represented by the following—hypothetical but not wildly unreasonable—function:

$$Qb = -37 - 27Pb + 13Pp + 31 \log Y$$

where Qb is average *per capita* consumption of beef in lb. per annum.

Pb is the price of beef in £ per lb.
Pp is the price of pork in £ per lb.
Y is average *per capita* income in £ per annum.

If the price of beef and pork is taken as £1·50 and £1 per lb. respectively, and Y as £3000 p.a., the equation becomes

$$Qb = -37 - 27 \times 1 \cdot 5 + 13 \times 1 + 30 \log_{10} 3000$$
$$\simeq 40.$$

Thus the consumption of beef will be 40 lb. per head per annum.

It can be seen from the equation that if the price of beef rises (other things remaining unchanged) consumption will fall, whereas if the price of pork or the level of income rises, consumption will rise. The relationship between a change in price and in consumption can be represented as $\Delta Q / \Delta P$ or, for those familiar with calculus, as the partial derivative $\partial Q / \partial P$. In the equation, the relationship between the price of beef and the consumption of beef is 27; a rise of £0·1 in the beef price would cause beef consumption to fall by 2·7 lb. But it is often more convenient to think in terms of *proportionate* rather than *absolute* changes; when changes are expressed in this way, the expression is known as an 'elasticity'.

The Concept of Elasticity
The concept of elasticity was first formulated in theoretical terms by the English economist Alfred Marshall. It has subsequently proved possible to calculate empirical elasticities in a number of cases. In the most general terms, an elasticity is the relationship between the relative change in one economic variable and the relative change in another variable with which it is linked. Various types of elasticity are listed below, and the following symbols used. The Greek letters ε and η indicate supply elasticity and demand elasticity while P, Q, and E represent price, quantity and expenditure of a product a and a competitive product b. The elasticities can be expressed either as 'point' or 'arc' elasticities. In the case of arc elasticities there is the problem discussed in Chapter 4 of choosing an appropriate denominator for price and quantity, most conveniently resolved by the 'Allen' formula.

For convenience and accuracy the derivative notation will be used below. But the 'Allen' formula could equally well be employed, and the reader who has no idea what a derivative is will lose very little if he continues to think in terms of the elementary definition, elasticity =

$$\frac{\%\ \text{change in quantity}}{\%\ \text{change in price (or income)}}$$

This definition is adequate for a general appreciation of the relationships involved, even if it begs certain questions as far as prices are concerned. For the purpose of agricultural price analysis, the most useful types of elasticity are as follows:

SUPPLY ELASTICITY
Price elasticity of supply. The relationship between the supply of an agricultural product and

(a) its own price $\varepsilon_i = \dfrac{\partial Qi}{\partial Pi} \cdot \dfrac{Pi}{Qi}$

Arc elasticity would be $\dfrac{\Delta Q1}{\Delta P1} \cdot \dfrac{P1 + P2}{Q1 + Q2}$

(b) the price of another product $\varepsilon_j = \dfrac{\partial Qi}{\partial Pj} \cdot \dfrac{Pj}{Qi}$
       (cross elasticity)

DEMAND ELASTICITIES
Price elasticity of the quantity purchased. The relationship between the quantity purchased of a foodstuff and:

(a) its own price $\varepsilon_i = \dfrac{\partial Qi}{\partial Pi} \cdot \dfrac{Pi}{Qi}$

(b) the price of another foodstuff $\varepsilon_j = \dfrac{\partial Qi}{\partial Pj} \cdot \dfrac{Pj}{Qi}$
       (cross elasticity)

Income elasticity of the quantity purchased. The relationship between the quantity purchased of a foodstuff and the income of the purchasers.

$$\eta_q = \frac{\partial Qi}{\partial Y} \cdot \frac{Y}{Q}$$

Income elasticity of expenditure. The relationship between the expenditure on a foodstuff and the income of the purchasers.

$$\eta_e = \frac{\partial Ei}{\partial Y} \cdot \frac{Y}{E}$$

All these elasticities rest on the assumption that other variables remain unaltered, i.e. one excludes the influence of other variables in order to establish the relationship between the two variables being considered.

Elasticities can be either negative or positive. The 'own price' elasticity of demand is always negative, indicating, for example, that a rise in the price of beef will, other things being equal, lead to a fall in its consumption. The cross elasticity of demand is positive for competitive foodstuffs, indicating, for example, that a rise in the price of pork will increase the consumption of beef. The income elasticity of demand can be either positive or negative, according to whether the foodstuff is a 'superior' or an 'inferior' good. The 'own price' supply elasticity is normally considered to be positive, although the possibility that it could be negative (i.e. that a price increase could lead to a fall in supply) will be discussed below. The cross elasticity of supply is negative for competitive products such as wheat and barley, but positive for joint products such as—to some extent—milk and beef.

Income and Price Elasticities

There are both income and price demand elasticities. The income elasticities show the relationship between income and the quantity or the value purchased, on the assumption that the price remains constant. The price elasticity shows the relationship between the price and the quantity purchased, on the assumption that income remains constant. The price elasticity thus refers to movements along the D curve, whereas the income elasticity refers to shifts in the D curve.

In Fig. 25(a), two D curves are shown, corresponding to incomes of x_1 and x_2. If the income rises from x_1 to x_2 while the price remains unaltered, at d, the quantity bought will rise from ab to ac. Fig. 25(b) gives a curve

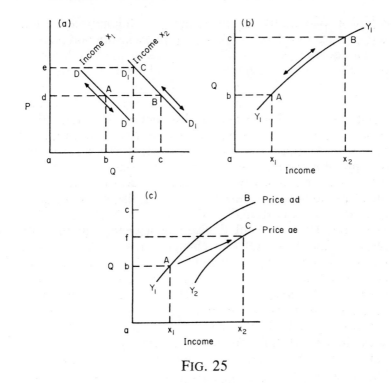

FIG. 25

showing the relationship between income and the quantity bought, on the assumption that the price remains constant at *d*. In practice, however, both price and income may change simultaneously. For example, if the price rises (in 25a) from *ad* to *ae*, while at the same time income rises from x_1 to x_2 then the movement will—in Fig. 25(a)—be from point *A* to point *C*. Fig. 25(c) shows the same change using income curves, where the movement is from point *A* on the income curve corresponding to the first price to point *C* on an income curve corresponding to a higher price. This means that the increase in purchases which would have followed from the rise in income has been damped by the rise in price.

The practical usefulness of the relationships so far discussed in this chapter lies in the way in which they enable the effect on demand of changes in prices and incomes to be calculated. This opens up a large and complex field, but an introductory explanation should suffice for an understanding of the relationships involved.

If a demand function is known, such as the simple linear type given at the beginning of the chapter, the effect on consumption of a change in prices or income can be calculated by substituting the new values for price and income. But this tends to lead into deep econometrical waters. A simpler alternative approach (at least for analytical purposes) is to select a set of elasticities from the published information and work out the effect of proportionate changes in price and income, assuming that the elasticities remain unchanged over the range of price and income in question.

On this basis, the relationship of a change in quantity purchased of foodstuff i to changes in its own price, the price of foodstuff j, and income, can be expressed by the equation:

$$\frac{\Delta Qi}{Qi} = \varepsilon_i \frac{\Delta Pi}{Pi} + \varepsilon_j \frac{\Delta Pi}{Pj} + \eta_q \frac{\Delta Y}{Y}$$

This indicates that proportionate change in quantity consumed will be determined by three factors:

(1) the proportionate change in the price of foodstuff i, multiplied by the 'own price' elasticity of demand
(2) the proportionate change in the price of one or more competitive foodstuffs, multiplied by the cross elasticity of demand
(3) the proportionate change in real income, multiplied by the income elasticity of demand.

For example, let us assume the following demand elasticities for beef, which are derived from the demand function given above:

$$
\begin{aligned}
\text{Own price elasticity} &= -1\cdot0 \\
\text{Cross price elasticity} &= +0\cdot3 \\
\text{Income elasticity} &= +0\cdot3
\end{aligned}
$$

If the prices of pork and beef, and income, all rise by 5 per cent, the percentage change in the consumption of beef will be:

$$-1 \times 5 + 0\cdot3 \times 5 + 0\cdot3 \times 5 = -2\%$$

The assumption that the change in consumption equals the price elasticity of demand multiplied by the percentage change in price applies, strictly speaking, only to *small* price changes. As price changes become larger, the result given by this simple formula diverges from the correct one. This can be illustrated by a simple example. Since $P \times Q$ is constant when the price elasticity of demand is unity, a rise in P from 4 to 5 will lead to a fall in Q from 5 to 4. But a rise from 4 to 5 is an increase of 25 per cent, whereas a fall from 5 to 4 is a fall of 20 per cent.

This difficulty can be overcome by a calculation based on the equation for a curve of constant elasticity. There is, however, a rule of thumb which is accurate enough for many purposes.[1] The percentage price rise is multiplied by the elasticity (without the minus sign), e.g. if the price rise is 20 per cent and the elasticity is 0·5, this gives 10 per cent. The ratio of the new to the old quantity (Q_2/Q_1) is then 100/100 + 10. Thus the fall in consumption is 10/110 or 9·1 per cent.

Although changes in taste etc. are very important in the long run, changes in income and price account for most shifts of demand in the short run. In consequence, since adequate price and income statistics became available a number of empirical studies of the demand for foodstuffs have been undertaken. Most demand studies have, in fact, been of foodstuffs, because the nature of the product changes less rapidly than in the case of manufactured goods. The pioneering work was done in the 1920s and 1930s in the USA by Schultz and Ezekiel,[2] among others, and today studies for various European countries are available. We will examine income elasticities before going on to price elasticity.

The researcher who wishes to study the effect of income or price changes cannot employ the experimental method; he cannot change the income or the price level in order to measure the results. There are thus only two ways in which the effect of income changes on food consumption can be measured. One is to compare consumption at a particular time in households (or countries) with differing incomes. The other is to examine changes in consumption over a period in which real income has changed—and to seek to exclude the influence of price changes. There is thus:

(1) cross-section analysis, using
   (a) household comparisons,
   (b) international comparisons;
(2) time-series analysis.

Cross-section Analysis: Engel's Law
Studies of expenditure in households in different income groups show differences in the absolute and proportionate expenditure on food. In the nineteenth century the German statistician Ernst Engel examined these differences in the expenditure of households in Saxony and Belgium, and sought to explain them by what has become known as 'Engel's Law'[3] He stated that the poorer a family was, the higher the proportion of its total expenditure spent on food. In other words as income rises the amount spent on food also rises, but not the same degree; thus food expenditure falls as a percentage of total expenditure. This relationship has since been observed in many countries and at many different times. See Fig. 26.

When one compares countries with differing real incomes, a similar picture emerges (Table 12), In the poorer countries expenditure on food accounted for half or more of total consumption expenditure. In the richer countries it had fallen to one quarter or less.. These international comparisons must naturally be regarded with the greatest caution. National eating habits enter into the picture, and international comparisons of real income are always rather problematical. But the general tendency is unmistakable.

The results of cross-section analysis using family budget data can be shown on a scatter diagram (Fig. 27). Income is measured on the horizontal and expenditure on the vertical axis, and the points represent the income and food expenditure of the individual families. A curve can be drawn through these points by means of regression analysis, and this curve is known as an 'Engel curve'. The slope of the curve then shows how food expenditure reacts to a change in income. For example, a rise of income from £600 to £800 is accompanied by a rise in food expenditure from

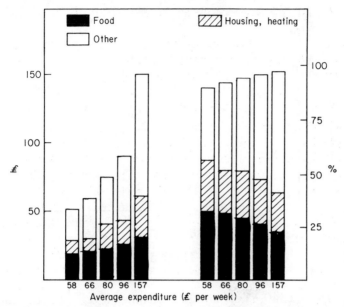

FIG. 26. Expenditure according to expenditure groups (one man, one woman, two children households, UK, 1978)

Source: Family Expenditure Survey, HMSO, London, 1978.

TABLE 12

Food Expenditure as a Percentage of Total Consumption Expenditure

	1960–62	around 1970
Ghana	49	53
Korea (Republic of)	51	41–47
Japan†	38	33
Philippines	54	n.a.
Sweden	26	26
UK	30	24*
USA	22	n.a.

*1977   †includes beverages
Source: FAO, *The State of Food and Agriculture*, 1965 and 1974.

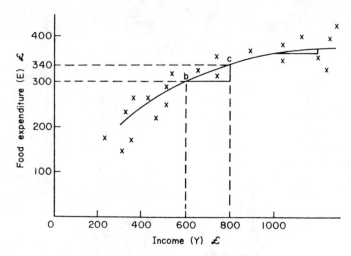

FIG. 27. The Engel Curve

£300 to £340, i.e. at this income level out of each additional pound of income an extra 40/200 = £0·2 is spent on food. This figure of 0·2 is the *marginal propensity to consume*.

A more useful measure is, however, the *income elasticity* which represents the relative changes of the two variables, and will in this case be:

$$\frac{\text{\% change in food expenditure}}{\text{\% change in income}}$$

The elasticity can be measured either by the 'point' formula:

$$\frac{\partial E}{\partial Y} \cdot \frac{Y}{E}$$

or, by the 'Allen' formula:

$$\frac{\Delta E}{\Delta Y} \cdot \frac{Y_1 + Y_2}{E_1 + E_2}$$

According to this formula, the income elasticity between

points *b* and *c* is:

$$\frac{40}{200} \times \frac{600 + 800}{300 + 340} = +0 \cdot 44$$

This means that a rise of 1 per cent in income leads to a rise of 0·44 per cent in expenditure on food. In empirical work, Engel curves, and demand curves, are often drawn with a double logarithmic rather than an arithmetical scale. This scale has the useful characteristic that the slope of the curve shows the elasticity. A curve of 1:1, i.e. 45°, indicates an elasticity of 1; a slope of 1:0·5 indicates an elasticity of 0·5, etc. A straight line indicates a constant elasticity and a curved, a changing one.

The income elasticity of total food expenditure tends to fall as income rises. This is particularly noticeable when comparisons are made between countries with different levels (Fig. 28). The curve *TU* shows that the elasticity falls

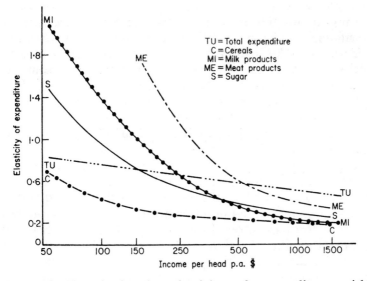

FIG. 28. Trends in the elasticity of expenditure with changing incomes

Source: Goreux, L., *Income and Elasticity and the Demand for Food: Household Survey Analysis*, FAO, Rome, 1959.

from about 0·8 in the developing countries to about 0·4 in the more developed countries. But for individual products the elasticities at low income levels are very high—from 1·0 to 2·0—but they fall sharply with rising incomes. For cereals, the figure is about 0·7 in India, whereas in some wealthy countries it is negative; in this case, cereals are an 'inferior good', in that consumption falls as income increases.

Income Elasticities of Expenditure and of Quantity Purchased
We have up till now dealt only with expenditure on food, i.e. the monetary value. But a rise in expenditure can indicate one or any of the following: a rise in the quantity of food consumed, the replacement of cheap foodstuffs with dearer ones, the purchase of better qualities or of more processed products, a rise in the number of meals eaten in restaurants. The income elasticity of expenditure does not indicate which of these possibilities has occurred, or what their relative importance is. In order to find this out, the consumption must be measured in quantitative terms—in weight or calories. Expenditure on restaurant meals can also be excluded from expenditure and measured separately. The arithmetic for calculating the income elasticity of the quantity purchased is exactly the same as that for the income elasticity of expenditure. Instead of expenditure, one measures consumption—in weight or calories—on the vertical axis in Fig. 27.

At high incomes, the elasticity of quantity purchased is generally lower than that of expenditure; this results from the consumption of better qualities and more expensive foodstuffs as income rises. An example is given in Table 13. It can be seen that the three elasticities of quantity purchased—measured in terms of calories, fat content, and animal protein—are lower than the elasticity of expenditure although they are all positive. The elasticity for fat and animal protein are, however, notably higher than that for calories.

Table 14 gives elasticities calculated for England and Wales in 1977 on the basis of family budget surveys. The negative figures indicate that better-off households consumed *less* sugar, bread, etc. Compared with the

TABLE 13

Income Elasticities in European Countries

Elasticity of expenditure on food	+0·68
Elasticity of quantity consumed	
(a) in terms of calories	+0·11
(b) ,, ,, ,, fat	+0·30
(c) ,, ,, ,, animal protein	+0·35

Source: FAO/ECE, *European Agriculture in 1965*.

TABLE 14

Income Elasticities of Expenditure and Quantity Purchased:
England and Wales 1977

	Expenditure	Quantity purchased
Frozen peas	0·72	0·73
Cream	0·35	0·33
Leafy salads	0·64	0·41
Poultry	0·24	0·19
Oranges	0·45	0·43
Pork	0·43	0·46
Mutton and lamb	0·40	0·34
Milk	0·08	0·06
Butter	0·13	0·13
Cheese	0·35	0·33
Eggs	0·03	0·01
Beef and veal	0·39	0·42
Potatoes	−0·20	−0·19
Sugar	−0·17	−0·20
Bread	−0·05	−0·08
Canned peas	−0·51	−0·52
Canned meat	−0·09	−0·03
Magarine	−0·16	−0·21

Source: Household Food Consumption and Expenditure 1977,
National Food Survey, HMSO, London, 1977.

corresponding figures for the early 1960s, the 1977 elasticities were generally lower, sometimes very much so. This is in keeping with the growing uniformity of eating habits. The figure for frozen peas halved between 1962 and 1977—indicating that their use is now more widespread partly because of the more widespread ownership of refrigerators. The figure for canned peas changed from -0.16 to -0.52, indicating that only a few lower-income households buy them any more. On the other hand, some figures rose. The figure for margarine rose from -0.27 to -0.21. Can one detect here a tendency for the professional family, which knows about cholesterol and poly-unsaturated fats, to switch from butter to margarine?

An income elasticity of demand derived from household budgets merely indicates that, at a particular time, there is a certain relationship between income and consumption. If such figures are used to forecast future consumption, an implicit assumption is made that the present low-income groups will emulate the consumption pattern of the present higher-income groups as their income rises. This has often happened. The luxuries of one generation (chicken or turkey) can become the everyday fare of the next, although the reverse can also happen (some fish and shell-fish). Experience indicates that elasticities based on household budgets can be used with reasonable success for forecasts of up to 5 years or so.[4] One expert argues that they are more reliable than elasticities based on time series.[5] But neither type of calculation provides an infallible guide to the future, since there can always be unforeseen changes, not only in incomes and prices, but also in the more intangible area of tastes and life-style.

International Comparisons
International comparisons can also be used to make rough calculations of the income elasticity of the quantity consumed, although differences in climate have to be taken into account. In addition, foods have to be grouped into broad classes in order to make comparisons possible. The diagrams in Fig. 29 are based on data for 1950 but in most cases the general conclusions are still valid.[6]

It can be seen from Fig. 29(a) that there is a fairly close connection between income and the consumption of meat

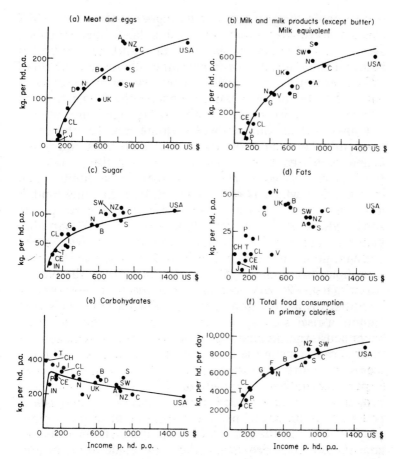

FIG. 29. Income and consumption (adjusted for price differences) in various countries, 1950

Source: Müller, p. 105 (see n. 6).

Key to countries: A = Australia; C = Canada; Ce = Ceylon (now Sri Lanka); CL = Chile; CH = China; D = Denmark; F = France; G = Germany (West); I = Italy; IN = India; J = Japan; N = Netherlands; NZ = New Zealand; P = Portugal; S = Switzerland; SW = Sweden; T = Turkey; UK = United Kingdom; USA = United States; V = Venezuela.

and eggs, and that elasticity at European income levels is about one; the elasticity falls off sharply, however, when a consumption of around 100 kg per head is reached, as is the case in Australia, New Zealand, Canada and the USA. Milk and milk products show a similar picture, although it is noticeable that, in spite of its higher income, the USA consumes less than Sweden or Switzerland. Sugar shows a good fit, with consumption flattening-off noticeably at higher income levels. For fats, on the other hand, no curve can be drawn. There appear to be two distinct groups of countries. On the one hand, there are the European and North American countries, with a fairly high consumption, not linked at all directly with income, and on the other hand there are the tropical countries such as India and China, which have lower incomes but are also situated in the tropics. It seems clear that there is a limit to fat consumption which is soon reached, and that this limit is lower in warm countries than in those in the temperate zone, where it is around 20 kg. (45–50 lb.). Another factor is that fat consumption is often linked with bread consumption, and that when this declines, the fat consumption also declines. The consumption of carbohydrate foods (Fig. 29(e))—cereals, potatoes etc.—shows a clear but distinctive trend. At very low income levels consumption rises sharply, as income rises, but after a certain point consumption beings to fall.

The total consumption of food is shown in Fig. 29(f) in terms of 'primary calories'. This represents the number of calories contained in vegetable goodstuffs and in the vegetable matter needed to produce meat or dairy products. It therefore provides a better measure of total crop production than if food consumption is measured in consumption calories, since the conversion of vegetable into animal food involves considerable calory losses. It can be seen that there is a fairly steady relationship between income and primary calories, with the curve flattening off at higher income levels in the familiar way.

Time-series Analysis
A different method of calculating income elasticities is by the analysis of time-series. This involves comparing the changes in consumption over a certain period with the corresponding changes in income. The difficulty in this method is that over the period not only income but also factors such as price, tastes etc. may well have changed. In order to calculate the effect of income changes alone, one

must seek by means of multiple correlation analysis to eliminate the effects of these other factors. The basic principle is fairly straightforward. If, for example, the prices in two years of a ten year period are the same, it can reasonably be assumed that any change in consumption between the two years is mainly the result of income changes. The details of multiple correlation analysis are complicated, but the result is that an equation is obtained which best explains the observed changes in consumption, income and price. A time series analysis thus yields both an income and a price elasticity.

Neither multiple correlation analysis nor any other statistical technique is able, however, to separate out the influence of income from that of other variables when changes in price or in economic conditions are too great. An analysis, for example, using data for Britain for the period 1900 to 1966, would not yield any meaningful elasticities. It is therefore necessary to choose periods which are long enough to contain significant changes in real income, but short enough to avoid profound changes in economic conditions—not an easy task. An analysis of a period of this type is, however, represented in Fig. 30, which relates to fruit consumption in West Germany

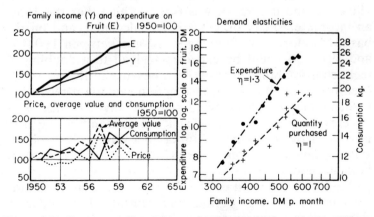

FIG. 30. Income elasticity of demand for fruit, West Germany, 1950–60

Source: Institute for Agricultural Marketing, Göttingen.

between 1950 and 1960. The expenditure on fruit rose faster than disposable income (top left), so that the Engel curve (right) shows an income elasticity of more than one, namely 1·3. The curve for the quantity consumed has a lower elasticity, however, namely 1·0. This indicates that, after allowing for changes in real prices, the quantity of fruit consumed rose in the same proportion as income.

Long Term Trends in Consumption

The country and time period used in the above example—namely West Germany in the 1950s—shows a very rapid rise in real income which is very pleasing for the purpose of calculating income elasticities. When one examines long term trends in consumption, however, one realises that the usefulness of such elasticities for long-term forecasting is often limited. Another example from Germany illustrates the point.

Table 15 compares the change in meat consumption per head, real income per head, and the retail price (in real terms) over the last century. It can be seen that in 1951–54 meat consumption was lower than before the Second or even before the First World War, and that it was only in 1955–58 that it exceeded the level of 1904–13. But real income in 1955–58 was 64 per cent higher than in 1904–13, and in 1958 it was twice as high. For the 1950s an income elasticity of 1 has been calculated, and on this basis, therefore, the doubling of income between 1904–13 and 1913–50 could be expected to lead to a doubling of meat consumption, or rather less, because of the price rise. Clearly the small rise in consumption cannot be reconciled with an income elasticity of one, or anything like it. It appears that there was a shift of demand away from meat—partly in favour of other foodstuffs, but probably also in favour of other goods such as television, cars, holidays, etc.

What has happened can be thought of as a movement of consumption along periodically shifting Engel curves. Before 1914 consumption rose along one curve. After the Second World War the curve had shifted to the right. Consumption began at a very low level and rose until it eventually reached, although it did not greatly exceed, the pre-1914 level.

TABLE 15

Long Term Trends in Meat Consumption in Germany

	1851–1860	1904–1913	1926–1929	1931–1934	1935–1938	1951–1954	1955–1958	1958
Income (1904–13 = 100)	50	100	102	90	109	125	164	180
Consumption per head (kg.)	25	51	50	51	53	42	51	54
Prices (1904–13 = 100)	50	100	95	77	82	112	114	121

Source: E. Wöhlken, 'Langfristige Tendenzen auf dem deutschen Schlachtvieh- und Fleischmarkt', *Berichte über Landwirtschaft*, Bd. 38, 1960.

The Use of Income Elasticities

Income elasticities calculated from cross-section or time-series analysis provide useful help in the forecasting of food demands. They do not, however, provide a crystal ball in which one can foresee the future. Not only is it very difficult to forecast future income and prices, but there are also shifts in demand as well as new products or processing methods which can considerably affect consumption. Thus one should not lay too much weight on the exact size of any measurement of elasticity.

The various types of elasticity are useful for different purposes. From the point of view of agriculture, the elasticity of expenditure is of no great interest, since it does not distinguish between the producer price and the distributive margin. Increased expenditure which goes to the distributor does not benefit the farmer, except in so far as farmers' co-operatives participate in processing and distribution. As far as agricultural production is concerned, however, the elasticity of quantity purchased is what matters, and, as can be seen from Table 16 they are, in the wealthier countries low or even negative for many products.

Price Elasticities

Price elasticities can be calculated only from a correlation analysis of time series of price, quantity, and income. The following estimates shown in Table 17 are for England and Wales over the period 1972–77. It can be seen that, as might be expected, product groups have a numerically lower figure than the individual foods within them; the figure for carcase meat is -0.23 as against -1.31 for beef and veal. The range of elasticities is considerable, but for many foodstuffs the figures are well below one. It must also be remembered that these figures are for the retail level; those for the farm-gate level would normally be lower (Chapter 9). These low elasticities mean that fluctuations in supply tend to lead to large price fluctuations.

Just as income elasticities decline with rising income, so do price elasticities decline as real incomes rise and/or prices fall. In these circumstances consumers tend to take less account of the price and buy simply what they fancy.

TABLE 16

Income Elasticities of Demand (Quantity)*

	Cereals	Potatoes	Sugar etc.	Vegetables	Meat	Eggs	Milk	Cheese	Fats	Coffee	Tea
USA 1965/66	−0·06	−0·03	−0·09	0·02	0·09	−0·05	0·19	0·23	−0·04	0·02	−0·07
France 1969	−0·16	−0·16	−0·11	−0·08	0·07	−0·03	−0·12	0·13	0·02	−0·04	
UK 1972	−0·20	−0·26	−0·29	0·04	0·08	0·03	0·11	0·10	−0·10	0·38	−0·36
Morocco 1970–71	0·33	0·36	0·37	0·48	0·71		0·68	2·40	0·47	0·48	0·33
Zaïre 1971	0·54	0·23†	0·42	0·24	0·36		1·82		0·25		
Trinidad & Tobago 1970	0·00	−0·07	0·02	0·05	0·29			0·23	0·06		
Brazil (Rio) 1973	0·11	0·06†	0·10	0·37	0·41	0·56	0·21	1·58	0·15	0·29	
Iran (urban) 1969	0·10	0·15	0·39	0·52	0·49	0·77	0·77	0·54	0·66		0·20
India (Mahendergarh) 1974	0·18		1·27	0·31			0·40		1·36		
Pakistan 1968/69	0·02	0·32	0·69		2·21‡	2·42	0·98	0·40			1·10

*log-inverse function †starchy roots ‡mutton

Source: Income elasticities of demand for agricultural products', FAO Internal Document.

This can be seen particularly well in the case of eggs, whose real price has fallen sharply in developed countries in recent years. Thus the price elasticity in West Germany fell from 0·94 in 1952 to 0·30 in 1962. During this period consumption rose from 134 to 218 eggs per head per annum, while at the same time real incomes doubled and real prices fell by one third. The same fall in the price elasticity when consumption rises over almost 200 eggs per year has been noted in the UK.

TABLE 17

Estimated Price Elasticities of Demand, England and Wales, 1972–77: Retail Level

Liquid milk	−0·18
Cheese	−0·23
All carcase meat	−0·23
Beef and veal	−1·31
Pork	−1·49
Broiler chickens	−0·89
Eggs	−0·11
Butter	−0·30
Sugar	−0·47
Potatoes	−0·17
Peas, fresh	−3·60
Peas, frozen	−1·04
Apples	−0·64
Bread	−0·03

Source: Household Food Consumption and Expenditure 1977.

Changes in UK Food Consumption
It has already been indicated that there is no unchanging relation between consumption, price, and income, so that elasticities of demand cannot be relied on to yield precise forecasts of consumption. The point is an important one,

TABLE 18

Consumption and Price Changes, U.K., 1956–77

	Consumption (lb. per head p.a.)			Price Changes (1956 = 100)	
	1956	1966	1977	Nominal	In Relation to Retail Prices
Beef	47·4	45·8	52·0	305	76
Bacon	24·7	25·8	19·8	327	81
Pork	18·7	25·8	22·7	292	73
Lamb	24·5	23·1	18·3	333	83
Poultry	6·4	16·7	25·1	254	63
TOTAL MEAT	117·7	129·1	125·6	306	76
Cheese	9·3	10·4	12·2	333	83
Eggs	29·4	34·2	31·8	242	60
Milk (pints)	255·0	250·0	242·0	303	75
Potatoes	224·0	224·0	213·0	350	87
Butter	15·5	20·0	17·1	298	74
Margarine	17·1	12·1	14·3	298	74
Fruit	131·4	145·5	116·7	286	72
Grain products	192·9	169·1	163·0	306	76
				ALL FOOD 332	83
Energy k.cal.	3,170	3,140	2,920		
Protein total	83·5	86·4	84·7		
animal	48·2	51·3	50·8		
vegetable	35·3	35·1	31·9		

Source: Domestic Food Consumption and Expenditure, HMSO., published annually.

and can be illustrated by reference to British food consumption since the 1950s. Over this period, *per capita* real income has risen on average by around 2 per cent *per annum* and it rose in all years except 1973–75 when there was a slight 'dip'. There were significant changes in food consumption patterns over this period. Although food consumption changes little from year to year, considerable change can occur over a decade or more. Total meat consumption began to rise after the end of rationing in 1954. In 1956 it reached the pre-War level, and it continued rising until the late 1960s; thereafter it fell to only slightly above the 1956 level in 1977. The composition of total meat consumption changed far more. Between 1956 and 1977 the consumption of poultry meat quadrupled, and that of pork rose by one-fifth; on the other hand the consumption of lamb and bacon fell, and the consumption of beef fluctuated around the 1955 level.

The growth of poultry meat consumption can largely be explained by price changes, resulting from the 'industrialisation' of this branch of production. But the decline in other kinds of meat consumption cannot wholly be explained by price changes. Over the period since 1956, all meat prices and other food prices have fallen in relation to the retail price index. Cheese prices rose in relation to meat prices, and yet cheese consumption went up. Egg prices since 1956 (and 1966) fell markedly more than the average of food prices. Yet consumption rose between 1956 and 1966 and fell between 1966 and 1977. It seems clear that (as with the long-term changes in German meat consumption) there have been shifts in the demand curves and Engel curves—a creeping vegetarianism, perhaps, or the change from father carving the baron of beef to food on a tray in front of the television? There is little firm evidence on these points. It should merely be stressed that, for all the apparent precision of econometric studies, the influence of readily measurable factors such as price and income can often be outweighed by more intangible changes in eating and buying habits. The tools of demand analysis are useful as far as they go, but they need to be used with an appreciation of the wider context.

The general fall in price elasticities means that supply fluctuations have a greater effect on prices. This means that it is more necessary to ensure that production matches demand, since an excessive level of production will result in seriously low prices. Careful market research therefore comes into its own, together possibly with arrangements for taking excessive supplies off the market and either storing them or using them for some less profitable purpose, e.g. breaking out eggs for manufacturing purposes.

The decline in price elasticities also applies to tropical agricultural products imported from developing countries, such as tea, coffee, sugar and cocoa. The UK does not tax these products, but the USA and many Continental European countries do so, and it has often been argued by developing countries that their exports would be increased if these taxes were reduced or removed. However, studies have shown that the retail price elasticities for these products are now quite low and falling continually. A price elasticity of 0·24 for coffee has for example, been calculated for West Germany. Thus unless taxes on these products are a very large proportion of the retail price, a removal on the tax would not cause any very great increase in consumption.

Summary
By means of correlation analysis, it is possible to calculate empirical elasticities of demand. Time-series yield both income and price elasticities; household budget data yield only income elasticities. Considerable caution has to be used in interpreting such elasticities, and in using them to make forecasts of future consumption. The movements along demand and Engel curves resulting from changes in (real) prices and income are often less important than shifts of the curves resulting from changes in tastes, eating habits, and life-styles. This is particularly true in fairly 'affluent societies', when both income and price elasticities tend to be low.

Notes

1 The equation of a D curve of -0.5 elasticity is:

$$Q = kP^{-\frac{1}{2}} = \frac{k}{\sqrt{P}}$$

$$\therefore Q_1 = \frac{k}{\sqrt{P}} : Q_2 = \frac{k}{\sqrt{1.2P}}$$

$$\frac{Q_2}{Q_1} = \frac{\sqrt{P}}{\sqrt{1.2P}} = \frac{1}{\sqrt{1.2}} = 0.9133 \text{ (the correct figure)}$$

$$\simeq \frac{1}{1.0 + \dfrac{0.2}{2}} = \frac{1}{1.1} \text{ or } \frac{100}{100 + 10} = 0.9091$$

2 Schultz, H., *The Theory and Measurement of Demand*, second imp., Illinois, 1957, and Ezekiel, M. and Fox, K., *Methods of Correlation and Regression Analysis*, third edition, New York, 1959.
3 Burk, M. C., 'Ramifications of the relationships between income and food', *JFE*, Vol. 44, 1962, p. 115.
4 Brown, J. A. C., *The Use of Income Statistics in Predicting Food Consumption*, Department of Applied Economics, Cambridge, 1959.
5 Jones, G. T., 'Some elements in a forecast of demand: are your time series really necessary? *JAE*, Vol. XXIX, no. 3, 1978, p. 291.
6 Müller, R., 'Langfristige Entwicklungstendenzen der Nachfrage nach Nahrungsmitteln', *Agrarwirtschaft*, 1955, p. 105.

Further Reading

Angel, L. J. and Hurdle, G. E., 'The nation's food—40 years of change', *Economic Trends*, HMSO, April 1979.
Daly, R. F., 'Demand for farm products at retail and the farm level', *Journal of the American Statistical Association*, Vol. 53, no. 283, 1958, p. 656.
Houthakker, H. S., 'An international comparison of household expenditure, commemorating the centenary of Engel's Law', *Econometrica*, Vol. 25, no. 4, 1957.
Shepherd, G. S., *Agricultural Price Analysis*, fifth edition, Iowa, 1963.
Waugh, F. V., *Demand Analysis: Some Examples from Agriculture*, USDA Technical Bulletin no. 1316, Washington DC, 1964.

Working, E. J., 'How much progress has been made in the study of the demand for farm products?' *JFE*, Vol. 37, 1955, p. 968.

Working, E. J., 'What do statistical demand curves show?' *Quarterly Journal of Economics*, 1927. Reprinted in Boulding, K. E. and Stigler, G. J., *Readings in Price Theory* (Blakiston series of republished articles on economics, American Economic Association), London, 1951.

CHAPTER EIGHT

The Analysis of Agricultural Supply

In the neo-classical theory of supply and demand, the supply curve is in most respects the counterpart of the demand curve. Just as the demand curve shows the relationship between price and the amount demanded, so the supply curve shows the relationship between price and the amount supplied. The numerical relationship is in both cases expressed in the form of an elasticity. But in the practical application of the theory to agricultural products there is a noticeable difference. On the demand side, the concepts of price and income elasticity have been applied statistically so as to explain the relationship between income, price and consumption, and to make forecasts which, in the short run at least, are accurate enough to be useful. On the supply side, however, the picture is very different. Statistical studies of supply elasticity are few in number, and obviously less reliable. One of the most elaborate studies of supply elasticity includes the revealing statement 'Estimates of the elasticity of cotton acreage . . . range between 0·7 and 4·5. The reason for such a large range . . . is that two different estimation techniques have been employed. . . . The reasons such a large difference occurs between the estimation derived by the two procedures are not definitely known.[1]

Estimates of supply elasticity have so far proved of little practical value. For example, there has been considerable controversy in the European Economic Community on the question whether rises in guaranteed prices for various commodities would stimulate production and lead to the emergence of burdensome surpluses, or whether, as some farmers' leaders argued, they would damp down production. This is, in fact, simply a question of the size of the elasticity of supply, but the available statistical studies of supply elasticity have not been found to be of much assistance in answering the question.

The first attempts to measure supply elasticity were made in the USA in the 1920s, and many agricultural economists have subsequently concerned themselves with the subject. Yet for most products it still remains an open question whether it is possible to calculate supply elasticities of any value for forecasting purposes. This lack of success is a result not so much of statistical difficulties as of the characteristics of agricultural supply. In the short term, the supply curve is very inelastic but subject to violent shifts. The longer the time period involved, the more elastic is the supply curve; there is not a single curve but a fan-like spread of curves. Even this 'fan' is being continually shifted by technical and economic changes. Technical progress shifts the curves to the right, the movement of labour out of agriculture and the rise in agricultural wages shifts them to the left. The actual movement is thus the outcome of opposing forces, and in recent years these forces tending to increase production have been stronger than those tending to reduce it.

It is true that the demand curve is also subject to shifts, but there is a difference between supply and demand which is fundamental for empirical work. Changes in income, which account for the greater part of demand shifts in the medium term, are statistically measurable and to some extent foreseeable. On the other hand, the many influences which cause shifts in the supply curve are not represented by any statistically measurable variable, and are very different to forecast. It is thus much more difficult than in the case of demand to distinguish between movements along the curve and shifts of the curve, i.e. to determine what part is played by price changes and what by other changes. The supply curve is thus a useful abstract concept, but whether it can serve as a basis for econometrical studies is rather questionable.

In order to examine how far the concept of the supply curve can be used in agricultural price analysis, we will first discuss the difference between production and supply. Then the relationship between costs and supply in general economic theory will be outlined, and the question raised, how far this theory helps to explain the facts.

Production and Supply
The supply of an agricultural product on the market consists of the following elements:

   domestic production;
   minus consumption on the farm;
   plus or *minus* changes in stocks;
   minus exports;
   plus imports.

In developed countries, consumption on the farms by the farm family is generally of no importance compared with the total supply, although it can sometimes affect the market supply. For example, in many countries a substantial proportion of the total fruit and vegetable production is produced by small growers as a sideline for personal consumption or sale to acquaintances, and only occasionally does it spill over onto the commercial market. Sometimes, however, the use of crops for livestock feeding affects the market supply; in some central European countries, notably Germany, potatoes are used for feeding pigs, so that the supply of potatoes depends to some extent on the number of pigs being fattened and the price of alternative feed, especially cereals. But in the developing countries on the other hand, consumption on farms accounts for a large part of production. The greater part of the world's rice production, for example, is consumed on the farms where it is grown.[2] When a high proportion of production is consumed on the farm, this has consequences for the supply response which are discussed below.

   Changes in stocks can, in the short run, exercise a considerable influence on supply. As far as stocks in private hands are concerned, the traditional theory is that speculators will buy up goods when they are plentiful and cheap, store them, and sell them when they are scarce and dear. This type of speculation has a price stabilising effect, since the increased demand at the time of purchase raises prices when they are low, while the increased supply at the time of sale lowers prices when they are high. This type of speculation is therefore to be welcomed, and the only thing that could be said against it is that a public—or farmer controlled—body might do it better, and appropriate the speculators' profits for the public or the farmers. (This argument was used in Western Canada in the 1920s as a justification for the wheat growers' co-operatives, the 'Pools', playing the part of the speculator and holding large wheat stocks. It was partly hard luck, but also rather significant, that the Pools were holding large stocks when prices slumped catastrophically in the Depression; they were forced into bankruptcy and their debts taken over by the Canadian Government.[3]

But there is another type of speculation, which can be destabilising. When prices rise, speculators expect them to rise still further and hold on to stocks, forcing up the price still more; when prices fall, speculators expect them to fall still further and sell their stocks. It has been alleged that Indian grain traders behave in this way. There is also the 'stock (or inventory) accelerator'. This means that if processing or manufacturing firms—rubber or cocoa manufacturers, sugar refiners—maintain large stocks, in a certain relation to their output, fluctuations in their output can be passed on in an amplified form to the producers. When output is rising, stocks are also having to be built up, so that an amount over that needed for production is required. When output flattens off, the building up of stocks stops abruptly. If output falls, stocks can be run down, so that purchases are less than the level needed for current output.

For these reasons, the changes of stocks in private hands do not always act in a stabilising manner. Stocks held in importing countries have not prevented fantastic price fluctuations for sugar and cocoa in recent years, and seem in some ways to have even made them greater. But for many temperate agricultural products, the largest stocks are held by public authorities such as the Commodity Credit Corporation in the USA and the Canadian Wheat Board which do not speculate in the ordinary sense, but exercise an important stabilising influence. For example, the

Canadian and American stocks helped to tide over the period between the period of good crops and rather low foreign demand in the 1950s and the period of strong foreign demand in the 1960s brought about by shortages in Russia, China and India. However, by the early 1970s the USA had become tired of maintaining expensive stocks, and had allowed them to fall to a very low level. Then, in 1972, came the 'great grain robbery'. The Russians, after a bad harvest, surreptitiously bought up 18 million tons of grain; this, together with a general upsurge in world demand, caused US stocks to fall to virtually zero and the price to shoot up.

Changes in stocks can only influence supply in the relatively short run (unless the stocks are destroyed or diverted into other markets) so that their influence on supply is limited. Supply thus depends mainly on production, and the chief question in supply analysis is to explain the effect of price on production. But total production is made up of the production of individual enterprises, and its reaction can only be explained in terms of the reaction of the individual enterprise.

The Relationship between Costs and Supply
In general economic theory, it is postulated that the supply function (or curve) of the product depends on the supply functions of individual firms which either produce the product, or could do so. The supply function of the individual firm further depends on its cost function, since it is assumed that the *entrepreneur* will determine his production in the light of costs and prices.

The cost functions of the individual firm, and the input-output relationships underlying them, can only be mentioned briefly. A basic concept is the famous 'Law of diminishing returns', which in general terms can be expressed as follows. 'When one input factor is increased, while others remain constant, increased inputs bring continually smaller increases in output.' The most profitable level of input is when the consequent increase in output (the marginal product) is equal to the cost of the input. Thus *so long as technical conditions remain unaltered* the prices of inputs and products will determine the most profitable level of production. This 'Law' is often illustrated with an agricultural example, although it is one which will seem rather odd to agriculturalists, namely the relationship between wheat yield and increased labour input. The relationship between yield and fertiliser application would be a more realistic example.

In terms of costs per unit of output, the law of diminishing returns means that if one factor is held constant—which in the case of agriculture is generally land—marginal costs will rise after a certain point. Most farms, however, produce several products (although specialisation is increasing), and in this case the most profitable combination of products is when the marginal cost of each product is equal to its price. Thus a rise in the price of any product will, *ceteris paribus*, lead to an increase in its production.

Joint Supply

The case of joint supply represents something of an exception to the above rule. Joint supply means that a certain production process inevitably results in the production of two or more products. There are several well known agricultural examples: mutton and wool; milk and beef; sugar and sugar-beet pulp; cotton, cotton wool and cotton seed. If the relationship between the products cannot be altered at all, they have to be considered as a single product for purposes of production planning. If a sheep rearer keeps to one breed of sheep, he cannot alter the relative production of meat and wool, and it therefore makes no sense to talk about separate costs of production. The receipts from wool and meat have to be added together and compared with the costs of producing the entire sheep (although, as is mentioned below, the calculation should be based on 'opportunity' rather than 'enterprise' costs). In many cases, however, it is possible to alter relative production by using different livestock breeds or crop strains. The replacement of meat breeds of sheep by Merinos, for example, will increase the output of wool at the expense of meat. It will be profitable to adjust the production of meat and wool to the point at which the *marginal* cost of each is equal to its price, since the marginal cost of a joint product can be calculated even though its average cost cannot. The marginal cost of wool, for example, is the difference between the total cost of producing x cwt. of meat plus y cwt. of wool and the total cost of producing x cwt. of meat plus y plus 1 cwt. of wool.[4]

Thus a change in the relative price of meat and wool will affect their *relative* production in the normal way. However a fall in the price of one product can, under some cost conditions, be accompanied by an *absolute* rise in output. For example, a rise in the mutton price accompanied by a fall in the wool price could lead to a rise in sheep numbers and an increase in the output of wool, even though, as a result of the substitution of meat breeds, the relative increase in wool output was less than that of mutton output. This rather special case of joint products, when a price fall can be accompanied by an increase in output, needs to be distinguished from the case of a truly 'perverse' reaction of supply to price, which is discussed below.

The Costs of the Individual Firm

It is assumed in neo-classical theory that the *entrepreneur*—whether he is a factory director or a farmer—so organises his production that his profit, namely the difference between costs and receipts, is as large as possible. But it could equally well be assumed that the *entrepreneur* maximises some other variable, and an appropriate variable for a farmer might be 'net satisfaction', derived both from money profits and the type of life he leads. Thus farmers in traditional cattle-raising areas could often increase their profits by going over to milk production. They prefer not to do so because rearing enables them to lead a more pleasant life, free from the daily grind of milking. (And there is nothing economically wrong in such a decision provided that the farmer does not then demand a subsidy to give him a 'normal income.) This sort of consideration should be borne in mind as an important qualification to the following analysis, which will assume the 'profit maximisation' approach.

Costs can be expressed in various ways, and Fig. 31 shows for a single product, marginal costs (MC), and average total costs (ATC), which are made up of average fixed costs (AFC) and average variable costs (AVC).

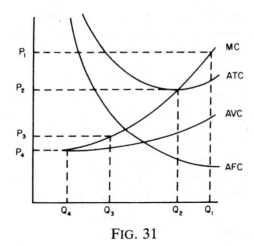

FIG. 31

Since the most profitable level of production is that at which marginal cost equals price, the supply curve of the enterprise will—over a certain range—be the same as its marginal cost curve. If the price is P_2, the production Q_2 will represent the most profitable level of production. This is also the point at which the average total costs are at their lowest. If the price rises to P_1, it pays to increase production to the level Q_1. If the price falls to P_3, it pays to reduce production to the level Q_3. This price lies under average total costs, so that the producer is not receiving enough to cover his fixed costs, including a normal profit. The price is, however, above average variable costs, so that the producer is covering his outgoings and obtaining something towards his fixed costs; in this situation it is more profitable to keep producing rather than to shut down, provided there is a prospect that prices will later rise again. If, however, the price falls to P_4 or below, i.e. under the average variable costs, it will be more profitable to shut down than to go on producing. Thus to the right of Q_4 the supply curve of the firm corresponds to the MC curve; to the left of Q_4, it runs horizontally.

The curves in Fig. 31 are drawn so that the fixed costs are high in relation to the variable costs, as is often the case in agriculture. When the curves are of this shape, it is worthwhile continuing production even when prices sink below average total costs. When, however, vaiable costs are high in relation to fixed costs, as is the case in pig or poultry production, production will cease at a relatively higher level.

The Aggregate Cost Function

On the basis of the cost functions of individual firms, a cost function for the product can, in theory, be constructed. This function shows the relationship between total production and costs, on the assumption that prices remain constant. It is at the same time a supply function for the product because, as we have seen, production is related to costs. The cost function can be of three types:

(1) rising costs (diminishing returns);
(2) constant costs (constant returns);
(3) falling costs (increasing returns).

Of these three possibilities, rising costs are often regarded as typical for agricultural production, since the limited area of good agricultural land leads to diminishing returns. The second case, constant costs, is regarded as typical of manufacturing industry, since it is not subject to such limitations, and can expand all factors of production at will. The third case, decreasing costs, has caused economists a good deal of worry, because it is incompatible with a long-term equilibrium, so long as there is more than one firm in the industry. This incompatibility led to the development of the theory of imperfect competition, which postulates a 'world of competing monopolies'. As far as agricultural production is concerned, it is clear that the first case is the most usual, although examples occur of the other two types. First, however, an examination of the first type of cost function.

Rising Costs (Diminishing Returns)

All firms do not have the same costs. When the price rises, new firms begin production; when the price falls, they cease. Thus total output changes because:

(a) firms increase or reduce their production;
(b) firms come into or go out of production.

In Fig. 32 a simple case of two firms with differing costs is

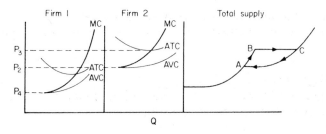

FIG. 32

shown. At first, only Firm 1 is in production, and its *MC* curve is also the supply curve for the product. If, however, the price rises above P_3, Firm 2 will begin production, and thereafter the total supply curve will consist of the sum of the two individual supply curves.

This theory has a consequence which is not sufficiently stressed in most presentations, and is particularly important for agricultural production. *When the commencement of production by new firms involves capital investment, the supply curve will not be the same for a price rise as for a price fall.* If Firm 2 is not yet in production, it will not undertake the investment necessary for production until the price rises to at least P_3, when average total costs are covered. Thus the total supply curve up to this point will be the supply curve of Firm 1, i.e. *AB*. When the second firm begins production, the supply will jump from *B* to *C*. If later the price falls, however, Firm 2 will for the time being continue in production, as long as its variable costs are being covered. Its supply curve will be the same as its marginal cost curve, so that the total supply curve between P_3 and P_2 will be the sum of the two firms *MC* curves, represented by the line *CA*. Thus the supply curve is, in the short run, irreversible, and this irreversibility is particularly important in agriculture, where a reduction in production is very difficult to bring about. Land is brought into cultivation when prices rise but does not go out of cultivation when prices fall.

Constant Costs
When marginal firms to not have higher costs than those already in production, the aggregate supply surve is

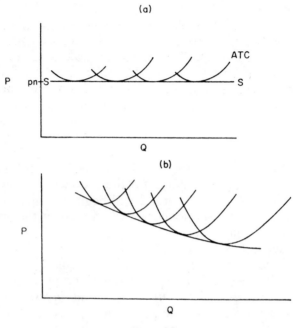

FIG. 33

horizontal (Fig. 33(a)). In this case, the long-term elasticity of supply is infinite, and increases or decreases in production take place without any changes in price or costs. Short-term changes in demand can, however, cause the price to be above or below the normal cost-covering level (*pn*), and cyclical fluctuations around this price—e.g. the pig cycle—are possible.

In agricultural production, the nearest equivalent to constant costs is the 'factory' production of pigs and poultry. As long as ample supplies of cereals are available at the ruling price, and all producers are equally efficient, the production of these commodities can be increased without any change in costs. In practice, there is at any one time a shortage of top-level producers, so that supply in the short run is not completely elastic. On the other hand, very large production units are now possible, so that the more efficient producers may well be able to expand production without incurring significantly increased costs.

Falling Costs
Falling costs (Fig. 33(b)) are found in agriculture in the case of small farms whose costs would be lower if they had more land or livestock. This means that the industry is not in long-term equilibrium. As the farm size is below the optimum, there is a tendency to amalgamation, but for social and practical reasons this can only take place at a certain place. In the meantime, the purchase of concentrated feeding stuffs enables the farmer to expand his production and so reach a medium-term equilibrium.

The Applicability of the Theory
In examining how far the model outlined above can be used to explain changes in the level of agricultural production, it is first necessary to distinguish between the influence of price on total agricultural production, which is often limited, and on individual commodities, which can be very great. These two cases will be discussed in turn. Total agricultural production nearly always shows an upward trend, although the rate of increase varies from period to period and from country to country. Except as a result of war, political disturbances or climatic changes, falls in total agricultural production are extremely rare. The rate of growth of total production is closely linked with technological progress and its application in agriculture, which does not directly depend on the price level.

Changes in total production can, as discussed above, be due to changes in the level of production of established firms or to the arrival or departure of marginal firms. In agricultural production this means:

(a) more or less intensive cultivation of the existing cultivated area;
(b) extension or contraction of the cultivated area.

There is, in other words, in *intensive margin* and an *extensive margin*. The intensive margin depends on the state of agricultural technique and the price level. The extensive margin i.e. the point at which cultivation in general or the cultivation of one particular crop ceases, depends on one of many factors; these can be physical, or

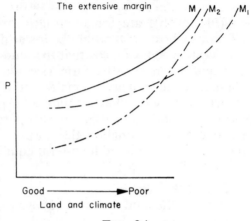

FIG. 34

economic, or historical, such as the time when the area was first settled.

The relationship between price and the extensive margin is represented in Fig. 34. The horizontal axis represents consecutive units of successively poorer land, and the curve indicates the relationship between the prevailing price and the extensive margin, the curves M, M_1 and M_2 representing three different relationships. Since the horizontal axis represents land rather than output, the M curve is not the same as the aggregate supply curve, although related to it, according to the yields on the successive units of land. Like the supply curve, however, the M curve assumes unchanged agricultural techniques; technical progress can move it downwards and to the right. But technical progress does not necessarily affect all types of land in the same degree, so there is no certainty that the curve will be moved bodily, remaining the same shape. A technical improvement that raised the productivity of poorer land more than that of better land, e.g. irrigation and dry-farming techniques, or better grasses for hill pastures, would cause a shift from M to a curve like M_1; an improvement that raised productivity more on the better land, such as the development of cultivating machinery that works best on level, stone-free land, would cause a shift to a curve like M_2. Although a given M curve indicates the extensive margin at a given price, a shift in the curve may cause the price to alter; if improvements on the better land cause output to rise further than demand, the price will fall, leading to a contraction of the extensive margin. Thus technical progress can cause either a contraction or an expansion of the extensive margin.

But in practice the extensive margin does not react sensitively to price changes. A favourable price situation is generally the background to an expansion or a contraction of the cultivated area, but technical change has often precipitated the change, especially in the case of an extension. The building of railways opened up the Great Plains of North America and the Pampas of Argentina; the breeding of new, quick-ripening wheat varieties made wheat cultivation in the Canadian prairies possible, and artificial fertilisers have enabled cereals to be grown on the British Downs. Sometimes the cultivation of new land takes place more under the influence of an expansionist philosophy than of cool economic calculation; this was especially true on the North American 'frontier'.

The Intensive Margin
The increase in production which results from higher yields is governed by very different influences. The nineteenth and twentieth centuries have seen a steady increase in crop and livestock yields in the 'developed' countries; this has been very largely the result of technical improvements (i.e. a shift of the supply curve) and only to a lesser degree of more intensive production following on price changes (i.e. a movement along the curve). It is thus very difficult to relate changes in yields to price changes. Agricultural production in Germany in the last hundred years offers an example.[5] Cereal yields since 1870 show a fairly steady increase in the three periods 1881–1914, 1925–38, and 1950–59, the yearly rates of increase were 1·45 per cent, 1·34 per cent and 1·85 per cent respectively. In this period, however, the real prices of agricultural products changed very considerably. The period 1850 to 1914 was in Germany one of rising real agricultural prices. The ratio of agricultural prices to wholesale prices in general rose by one-fifth between the middle of the nineteenth century and

1914. German agricultural economists of the time, maintaining the views expressed earlier in the century by Ricardo, believed that his improvement in agriculture's terms of trade would continue, and lead to a continued increase in the intensity of production. But in the following periods the terms of trade worsened, whereas the increase in yields continued. Between 1904–14 and 1931–34 the price index fell by one-seventh, without causing any fall in yields. In the 1950s the real price of agricultural products seems to have fallen to an even lower level. During this period the real prices of some agricultural inputs fell—especially fertilisers—but this was not true of inputs in general.

In most developed countries, indeed, a noticeable acceleration in the rate of improvement in yields has set in since the Second World War, which is not connected with an improvement in prices (Fig. 35). At the same time the composition of inputs has changed at an unprecedented rate, because of the substitution of labour by machinery.

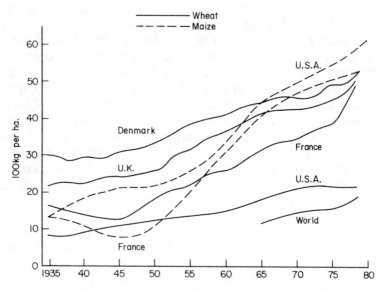

FIG. 35. Yields of wheat and maize, 1935–78

Source: International Wheat Statistics and FAO Yearbook.

The effect of these technical changes can be represented as a shift of the cost curves to the right and downward. In spite of the worsening of the terms of trade, average costs may well be lower, but only if production is increased. This is because modern farming techniques involve high total fixed costs—for machinery and buildings—which have to be spread over a large output if they are to be brought down to a low average figure. Thus the net effect of post-war changes has been to force some marginal farmers out of business, but to compel those who remain in production to produce more intensively than before.

International Comparisons
The conclusion that there is no simple relationship between the intensity of production and the level of farm prices is reinforced by comparisons between countries. International comparisons of gross output per acre cannot, of course, be made in national prices, since this would mean that a higher level of price support resulted in an apparently higher level of production. The various commodities must be valued at constant prices to make them comparable. The results of two such comparisons are given in Table 19, which gives estimates for 1955 and 1974. In 1955 the Netherlands and Belgium had the highest Gross Output per hectare in Western Europe, followed by Denmark, West Germany and Switzerland. The UK was in the next group, and in the group with the lowest production were the somewhat less developed countries. But producer prices in these countries at that time did not correspond at all closely to these output levels. The Netherlands and Denmark had the lowest prices, Switzerland the highest. Those of Germany, Italy, and Austria were relatively high, whereas those in the UK were in an intermediate position. In the bottom group, Irish prices were low, but Finnish high.

In 1974, the UK also occupied a middling position in terms of gross output per hectare, above France and Ireland, but well below Belgium, the Netherlands, Denmark and West Germany. The UK scored better in terms of gross output per worker, although it ranked below Belgium, the Netherlands and Denmark. These figures of output, reinforced by another study of net output per £100

TABLE 19

(a) Gross Output per Hectare in 1955 at Constant (1934–38) Prices

	Dollars
Netherlands, Belgium	+350
Denmark, West Germany, Switzerland	200–300
Austria, France, Italy, Norway, Sweden, UK	100–200
Finland, Greece, Ireland, Portugal, Spain	under 100

Source: Yates, P. L., Food, Land and Manpower in Western Europe, London, 1960, p. 156.

(b) Gross Output per Hectare and Worker, in 1974 at UK Prices

	per hectare £	per worker £
Belgium	805	9,741
Netherlands	550	8,775
Denmark	450	7,934
West Germany	414	4,756
Italy	357	3,396
UK	302	6,102
France	229	4,868
Ireland	152	2,917

Source: Doyle, C. J., 'A comparative study of agricultural productivity in the UK and Europe', JAE, September 1979.

of inputs,[6] suggest that, although British agriculture is fairly efficient compared with that in most Western Europe, its superiority is not as great as is sometimes imagined.

International differences can partly be explained by differences in climate and soil, but much of it is due to differences in the skill and knowledge of the farmers in the various countries. A great deal depends on the structure of agriculture and its position in the economy. For example, although the fall in prices on the world market at the end of the nineteenth century affected Britain and Denmark in the same degree, it produced different reactions. Whereas in the UK the result was a certain running-down of agriculture and a move to more extensive 'dog and stick' farming, the Danes reacted by developing new forms of bacon and dairy production, and were even able to conquer a large market in the UK.

An opportunity of isolating the effects of different price levels is provided when a national boundary crosses a uniform geographical region, and when the countries on either side of the boundary have differing price levels. Such cases exist on the boundary between Denmark and Germany, and between the Western Canadian provinces and the North Western states of the USA. In these two cases, Denmark and Canada have the lower agricultural prices. Studies which have been made in these two cases suggest that the Danish and Canadian farmers, by exploiting every opportunity for efficiency, and to some extent by harder work, have been able to make nearly comparable incomes in spite of lower prices. It is also noticeable that land prices are on the whole higher in the countries with higher agricultural prices, indicating the way in which agricultural price support tends—as the theory of rent would suggest—to bring about a rise in land values and thus ultimately benefit the landowner (who may or may not also be the farmer). There can come a point, however, when efficiency cannot make up for low prices, and this came in Denmark in 1961, when some—relatively modest—measures of price support were introduced.

'Backward Sloping' Supply Curves
The above discussion leads on to the question of whether, as is sometimes maintained, the supply of agricultural products in some cases reacts 'perversely' i.e. that the supply curve is 'backward sloping', so that a rise in price leads to a reduction in supply (Fig. 36). It is assumed that the farmer seeks to maintain a certain income, and thus works harder and produces more when prices fall. This 'income effect' offsets the 'price effect' and may thus be expected to be particularly important in the case of monoculture, or when applied to total output.

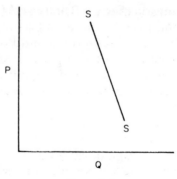

FIG. 36

Professor Kaldor has stated, without giving much evidence, that the supply curve for wheat is backward sloping[7] and Professor Allen suggested that there was statistical evidence for this in Canada, although his evidence was shown to be rather suspect.[8] In fact, it is hard to find any solid evidence at all for the phenomenon. Something of the type may occur in developing countries, where consumption on the farm accounts for a large proportion of total production. As the income elasticity of demand for food is high in such cases, the farmer consumes more when prices rise, and sells less. But even if this occurs, it is not a true backward sloping supply curve of the type postulated above (and it obviously does not apply in the case of non-edible products such as coffee, cocoa or cotton). Most alleged cases of backward sloping curves turn out to have ignored falls in the general price level, or the opening up of new land, or some other change producing a shift of the curve to the right.

If the hypothesis of 'perverse' supply curves were correct, it would mean that Britain could have raised production during and after the war by lowering farmers' pricess. The fact that the governments of the time in fact raised farmers' prices considerably shows that they believed the supply curve to be of the normal, forward sloping type. However, the hypothesis of the backward sloping supply curve is sometimes put forward by farmers organisations, although under conditions which inspire doubts as to its validity. For example, the British National Farmers Union argued in

1962, when an unmanageable increase in milk supplies was expected, that low prices would force producers to maintain their income by increasing output, and that only a substantial price increase could prevent a large increase in output.[9] In the following years, large numbers of producers went out of milk production, while total output remained at roughly the same level, as a result of increased output from those remaining. In 1965 the NFU foresaw the danger of a severe milk shortage, which could only be prevented by a substantial price increase. One cannot escape the suspicion that the backward sloping curve is only brought into the argument when it would serve to justify a price increase.

And yet there may be something in the idea. It is possible that some individual farms of a certain type may have a backward sloping supply curve, notably large farms with a low output per acre. In such cases it is possible that the farmer would react to lower prices by increasing his output. Admittedly, if output is at the optimal level at which marginal costs are equal to price, it will not be profitable to increase output in this way. But it is well known that because of lack of knowledge, uncertainty or indivisibilities in inputs, many farms are not producing at anywhere near this level. But even if some farms reacted in this way, this 'perverse' reaction would normally be more than offset by the normal reaction of other farms. For example, it is conceivable that a fall in milk prices would induce some milk farmers to expand production, but induce others to give up producing milk, as indeed has been happening in the UK, other European countries, and the USA, in recent years. Thus the aggregate supply curve for milk remains forward sloping, although it can, of course, be shifted by technical and economic changes.

A final reason why total agricultural production on the whole reacts 'normally' is that one (and perhaps the main) connection between price and output is by way of investment. Professor Cochrane argues that high prices provide the farmer with the liquid capital for investment and technical improvement, and also create a favourable climate for undertaking investment.[10] On the other hand, when prices are low, farmers are neither able nor willing to undertake investment. The farm is slowly run down, and the normal rise in output thus dampened. The experience of British agriculture in the depressions at the end of the nineteenth century and in the 1930s lends plausibility to this explanation,[11] and a statistical study of agricultural output in New Zealand points in the same direction.[12] It is certainly this type of 'income effect' that is important in farming in developed countries.

Broiler Production
It has already been mentioned that it is not the price by itself but the change in profitability (or relative profitability) in a particular branch of production that is decisive. If productivity and input prices remain constant as between enterprises, production will tend to move in the same direction as price changes; if wheat becomes dearer in relation to barley, the production of wheat will rise in relation to that of barley. But changes in productivity can more than offset price changes in their effect on profitability. American broiler production provides a striking example. Between 1947 and 1963 the producer price fell by more than half (Table 20). But, at the same time, food conversion improved so much that food costs per lb. of meat fell almost as much; the cost of chicks also fell. Thus the 'Index of Profitability' fell only slightly. At the same time, the increase in the size of broiler houses increased labour productivity. To a large extent, therefore, the rise in productivity accompanied, and indeed caused, the fall in price, so that both consumer and producer gained.

But the situation was not altogether so satisfactory. After 1960, output overshot demand and led to a fall in price which was not offset by an increase in productivity. Thus producers found themselves making lower total profits from a higher output, which they understandably resented. A tendency of this type for output to overshoot the mark, until adjustment takes place through a subsequent rise in demand, or a movement of some producers out of production, is typical in agriculture; in this case, however, it may have been exaggerated by the organisation of the industry. Broiler production had been organised largely by feed merchants anxious to secure outlets for their feed,

TABLE 20

Changes in Broiler Production in the USA

	(1)	(2)	(3)	(4)	(5)	(6)	(7)
	Feed	Feed Costs	Chick Costs	Cost Index Feed & Chicks	Pro- ducer Price	Profit- ability Index (5) ÷ (4)	Pro- duction
	lb.	cents	cents	1957–59 = 100			mill. lb.
1947	3·95	20·7	5·4	152	187	1·19	1,127
1950	3·33	16·4	5·1	126	154	1·22	2,415
1960	2·51	11·6	3·7	90	95	1·06	6,836
1963	2·47	11·9	3·1	87	82	0·94	7,200

Source: USDA, *Poultry and Egg Situation*, PES–228, November 1963.

rather than, as in the UK, by retail distributors. The feed merchants, not being directly concerned with marketing, were perhaps less conscious of the limits of demand than they should have been, and encouraged an excessively rapid increase in production. Contracting which comes from the side of the retailers—as is more usual in Great Britain—would seem less liable to this danger.

The Influence of Price on Individual Commodities
The relation between the costs of individual farms and the extensive margin of cultivation was discussed above. The same principles apply not only to agricultural production in general but to the production of individual commodities. When, as a result of a price fall, the production of a commodity falls, the first enterprises to go out of production are those with the highest (opportunity) costs. Production becomes more concentrated in those areas which, because of soil, climate or nearness to markets, are the most suitable. A good example is the extension and contraction of cereal production in England and Wales in

the last hundred years. Between 1870 and 1900 the wheat price fell by nearly a half. As the general price level also fell, the fall in real terms was not so great; nevertheless animal products, whose price fell by only one quarter, became more profitable, and the wheat acreage fell by roughly half. Wheras in 1870 the wheat acreage was fairly evenly distributed over the country, it became very concentrated in East Anglia at the end of the century. In recent years it has again become rather more dispersed. Barley shows an even greater contraction and expansion, although the post-1945 expansion has been concentrated on the Downs, indicating that technical changes can cause the supply contraction and expansion to be asymmetrical.

In addition to these geographical changes, the type of farm producing a given commodity can also be influenced by changes in prices and costs. In the early 1960s the number of milk producers in England and Wales fell sharply, although production remained fairly constant. The farms which went out of production were mainly either large farms or farms with very small numbers of cows. The large farms turned to other enterprises, while the farmers with small herds, had no real alternative to milk, either expanded or gave up altogether. At the same time, the remaining, mainly middle-sized farms increased their output. This process can be thought of as a mixture of rising and falling costs. While some farms give up production because the price has fallen below their costs, others expand their output and thus achieve a reduction in costs.

Empirical Studies of Supply Elasticity
The above discussion has been concerned with the micro-economic changes lying behind the response of supply to price changes. But increasing attention has been devoted in recent years to empirical studies of supply changes. Probably the first empirical investigation of the response of supply to price was a study on cotton which appeared in 1917 in the USA. It was based on a correlation between the cotton acreage in one year with the price of the previous year. Since that time, similar studies—based on a correlation between price series and production or acreage

series, with a time-lag—have been made for various products, but very convincing results cannot be said to have been achieved.

A different approach was indicated by the American economist J. D. Black in the 1920s, when he advocated the calculation of 'synthetic' supply curves based on the costs and expected reaction to price changes of a typical farm or farms.[14] This method has since been discussed theoretically many times, but rarely applied in practice. As in the calculation of demand elasticities, there are thus two methods of calculating supply elasticities:

(1) time-series analysis;
(2) cross-section analysis.

Whereas the first method is based on correlation between time-series, the second approaches the question from the point of view of the costs underlying supply; either by a study of the costs of a sample of farms, or by the construction on paper of a 'representative' farm, it seeks to calculate how farms would react to price changes, assuming the farmers' aim is to make maximum profits. There are grounds for doubting whether the 'cross-section' method can in practice be applied in any very rigorous way, but because of its usefulness as a theoretical model, we shall discuss it first.

Cross-section Methods: Enterprise Costs

The general supply theory assumes that firms have differing costs, and that they start production, or give it up, when the price rises above or falls below, these costs. The idea naturally arises, that information on the costs of individual farms, or groups of farms, would enable a supply curve to be constructed. However, the calculation of production costs for commodities produced on the same farm, and sharing some factors of production, raises theoretical as well as practical difficulties.

In the early years of the twentieth century, a number of German and American agricultural economists began to apply cost-accounting methods to agriculture, in the hope of obtaining costs for each enterprise, so that the farmer would know which were profitable and which unprofitable, and governments would know what an adequate price was for the product. This type of calculation was early on attacked by Friedrich Aereboe in Germany and J. D. Black in the USA, and by the 1920s it was generally accepted that it was an inappropriate approach (although in the UK, the Agricultural Economics Service produced figures of this type for many years).

The difficulty arises when factors of production such as labour or machinery are used in the production of several products. To allocate these costs to individual enterprises can produce misleading results. Take the case of a farm which produces milk and beef, and on which the total costs of milk production are calculated as x pence a gallon. Assume that the milk falls to $0 \cdot 8x$ p. a gallon, so that the milk enterprise shows an apparent loss, while the beef enterprise, on the same basis of calculation, shows a profit. This would indicate that it would pay to cut down milk production and expand beef production. But in fact this may not be the case. If the factors used in milk production (e.g. the farmer's own labour), cannot be reduced, then the loss of the milk receipts may well be greater than the increased income from beef. The calculation ought thus to be in terms of the changes in receipts and costs brought about by proposed change in the farm plan. Or in other words, the relevant cost of any product is the income foregone in an alternative enterprise—the 'opportunity cost'.[15]

Thus even if it were possible to ascertain the enterprise costs of every single farm—which is naturally impossible—it would still not be possible to deduce the supply curve from these costs. Some farms would continue to produce even when the price was below their 'cost' while others would give up production—in favour of even more profitable enterprises—when the price was still above their 'cost'. For these reasons, American attempts in the 1920s to calculate supply curves on the basis of enterprise costs were a failure. But the same method could, thirty years later, be put forward in Britain without any apparent qualifications.[16] The construction of 'synthetic' curves is not open to the same criticism. It consists in constructing for each farming area a representative farming system, from which the most profitable combinations of products at various prices can be calculated. (In recent years, linear programming has been used for this purpose.) This therefore yields a supply curve for the representative farm, from which, by taking into account the area of the region, a regional supply curve can be calculated. The total of supply curves for the various regions makes up the supply curve for the country; at the same time the regional distribution of production is indicated.[17]

A method of this type is theoretically attractive, but presents obvious difficulties in execution. Regions with farms of roughly the same size, and roughly the same farming system, are rare—even rarer in Europe than in North America. Countries can indeed be divided into agricultural regions, and these can be very useful for various investigations, but differences between farms are nearly always very great, so that it is difficult to speak of a 'representative' farm. Because of these difficulties, the method hardly seems capable of yielding any accurate results, although it may nevertheless give some indications of supply reactions. For example, in order to assess how far a rise in the cereal price would lead to increased production, an examination of the areas which could profitably be used for cereal growing—but are not so used at the moment—is perhaps the best method. Further, by comparing the financial returns from various crops in a certain area, it is possible to obtain some indication of the effect on production of changes in price relationships.[18] This is probably the most that can be expected from this approach.

Time-series Analysis
The other, and more usual, approach is based on a comparison of time series. Even here grave theoretical problems arise, as a result of the characteristics of the short-, medium-, and long-term supply curves. The short-term curve is usually represented as completely inelastic, although the supply can be altered in two ways; by storage or by marketing livestock sooner or later. When livestock markets are held weekly, a very short-term cobweb cycle can arise, in which light prices in one week

are followed by an increased supply in the following week. But in general the short-term supply is inelastic and subject to various irregular shifts. At the other extreme, it is also impossible to calculate a long-term supply curve, since if long time-series are used, the technical conditions will have altered so much during the period that it becomes impossible to draw any conclusions about the influence of price. For example, the nominal wheat price in the USA in 1960 was roughly twice as high as in 1910–1914, whereas the real price had fallen to about 70 per cent of the 1910–14 level. But it can certainly not be assumed that these prices of 100 and 70 are points on a long-term supply curve, since in the intervening period the technique of wheat-growing had been revolutionised by the combine-harvester.

Thus the only supply curves which can possibly be measured statistically are those for a medium-term period, in which the farmer has time enough to react to price changes but in which production methods do not change greatly. It is thus necessary for supply elasticities to refer to a specified period of time. One German investigation, for example, indicates a fairly good relationship for vegetables between price in one year and acreage in the next, with a supply elasticity of 0·2.[19] But for other crops it may well take several years of high or low prices to influence production, so that it may be necessary to correlate acreage with the prices in several preceding years. But in spite of statistical refinements, the results of such analyses have not been very satisfactory. One reason is that, when price support schemes are in operation, there is often very little change in real agricultural prices in the short medium term; and if there are no price changes, even the best techniques can say nothing about their influence.

Tree Crops

In the case of tree crops, such as most types of fruit, as well as coffee, cocoa and natural rubber, it takes longer to increase or reduce production—especially to reduce it—than in the case of annual crops. Production can be altered slightly in the short run by taking more or less care in harvesting, but in general the level of production cannot economically be altered once the trees are in fruit. Thus if production gets out of phase with demand, high or low prices can last a long time. Coffee is a product which, for these reasons, shows an irregular cycle of high and low prices. A study of prices and production in Brazil between 1870 and 1953 indicated that the time lag between the upturn in production and in prices varied from 2 to 10 years, with an average of 4·7 years. A correlation of the price and production rise in each cycle indicated elasticities of between +0·5 and +1·0.[20] The supply elasticity appears to be greater in Brazil than in the African coffee growing countries, because of higher wages and more alternative land uses. Coffee also provides an example of the 'irreversibility' of supply. Production only declines when prices have remained low for many years; this happened in 1940 after a decade of low prices. Conversely, it was the high prices after 1945 which stimulated planting and eventually produced the over-production which caused such problems for coffee producers in the mid-1960s. This period of low prices was followed by the better prices of the 1970s (and a severe frost in 1976 caused a short-lived price 'explosion').

Pigs and Poultry
In the production of pigs and poultry, the relationship between product price and feed price is decisive, since feed costs make up two thirds of total costs. According to experience in West Germany, an improvement in the pig/feed price relationship leads to an increase in the number of in-pig sows after a time-lag of 4 to 9 months.[21] The supply elasticity has been calculated as 0·45 per cent in the period 1951 to 1959, but only 0·23 per cent in the period 1959 to 1967, the decline being due to the increase in the size of enterprises. A supply elasticity of 0·23 per cent means that an improvement of 1 per cent in the pig feed relationship leads, after 4 to 9 months, to an increase of 0·23 per cent in the number of in-pig sows. Knowledge of this type can be used to make forecasts of pig slaughterings, and thus enable policies to deal with gluts or shortages to be prepared.

Similarly, in the USA, where there is a broiler cycle, the

relation between poultry-meat prices and the costs of feed and chicks gives a good indication of the production a year later. When the 'Profitability Index' (see Table 20) and the change in production a year later are shown on a diagram, they lie fairly closely along a linear function (Fig. 37). But it is only for pigs, poultry, and to a limited extent for vegetable crops, that it has been possible to calculate supply elasticities which stand the acid test of being able to forecast future production with any accuracy.

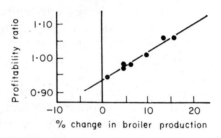

FIG. 37. Production response for broilers, USA

Source: USDA, The Poultry and Egg Situation, November 1963, p. 13.

Summary
Less success has been achieved in the empirical estimation of supply than demand elasticities. Indeed it is doubtful whether most of the elasticities which have been calculated are of any value at all for forecasting. The reason for the meagre outcome is that the supply curve is actually an array of curves, depending on the time period being considered; this array of curves is itself subject to large shifts, which cannot readily be forecast, as a result of technical progress. In spite of this 'operational' failure, the study of supply functions has tended to confirm the conventional assumption that output, after a time, reacts positively to price changes. There is little evidence of a 'backward sloping supply curve', although there can be a 'ratchet effect' in which price falls have little immediate effect on output, and depress output only in the economic 'long run'.

Notes

1 Nerlove, Marc, *The Economics of Supply*, Baltimore, 1958, p. 26 and 'Time-series analysis of the supply of agricultural products', in Heady, Earl O. *et al.*, *Agricultural Supply Functions*, Ames, Iowa, 1961, p. 31.

2 FAO, *The World Rice Economy*, Vol. II (Commodity Bulletin Series No. 36), Rome, 1963, p. 1.

3 Patton, H. S., *Grain Growers Co-operation in Western Canada* (Harvard Economic Series 32), Cambridge, Mass., 1928.

4 Henderson, H., *Supply and Demand* (Cambridge Economic Handbooks), Cambridge, 1932, Ch. 5.

5 Pentz, W., 'Die Steigerung der deutschen Getreideerträge', *Agrarwirtschaft*, Heft 4, 1960.

6 *The Efficiency of British Agriculture*, Centre for Agricultural Strategy, University of Reading, 1980.

7 Kaldor, Nikolas, *A Reconsideration of the Economics of the International Wheat Agreement* (FAO Commodity Policy Studies no. 1), Rome, 1952.

8 Allen, G. R., 'Whear farmers and falling prices', *The Farm Economist*, Vol. VII, no. 8, 1954, and Farnsworth, H. C. and Jones, W. D., 'Response of wheat growers to price changes', *The Economic Journal*, Vol. LXVI, 1956, p. 271.

9 National Farmers' Union of England and Wales, *Information Service*, Vol. 17, no. 1, 1963 and Vol. 20, no. 1, 1965.

10 Cochrane, W. Willard, *Farm Prices—Myth and Reality*, Minneapolis, 1958, pp. 46–50.

11 Orwin, C. S. and Whethan, E. H., *History of British Agriculture, 1864–1914*, London, 1964, pp. 240–88.

12 Philpott, B. P. and Steward, J. D., *Income and Productivity in New Zealand, 1921–56* (Technical Publication no. 17), Lincoln College, University of New Zealand, 1958, pp. 30–41.

13 Hallett, G., 'Konzentration und Spezialisierung in der Landwirtshcaft Grossbritaniens', *Konzentration und Spezialisierung in der Landwirtschaft* (Schriften der Gesellschaft für Wirtschafts- und Sozialwissenschaften des Landbaues, e.V., Band 2), Munich, 1965.

14 Cavin, James Pierce, *Economics for Agriculture: Selected Writings of John D. Black*, Cambridge, Mass., 1959, Part VII, p. 303.

15 This more sophisticated approach has come to dominate farm management analysis, even in the UK, where old-style, with arbitrary allocation of fixed costs, was fashionable for so long. The detailed techniques of modern farm management

analysis include linear programming; simpler methods based on it, notably programme planning and 'gross margin' analysis; and partial and total budgeting, which is a comparison of the change in costs and receipts for any proposed change in farm output or organisation. Although differing in their detailed approach and practical applicability, all these techniques are based on the marginal analysis, and thus the principle of 'opportunity cost'.

Professor Wiles, who has many shrewd things to say about agriculture, is on less firm ground when he says that farmers do not know their marginal costs, and so misjudge the correct level of output (*Price, Cost and Output*, p. 290); he is, perhaps, too much influenced by the older British books on farm accounting, which he so rightly trounces (pp. 121–2). It is in any case questionable whether any farmers ever read these books; the home-spun calculations of most farmers probably amounted in effect to equating marginal cost with price.

16 Holme, E., 'Estimating a supply curve', *JAE*, Vol. XIII, 1958/59, p. 67.

17 Mighell, R. L. and Black, J. D., *Inter-regional Competition in Agriculture*, Cambridge, Mass., 1951.

18 Jasny, Naum, *Competition among Grains*, Food Research Institute, Stanford University, California, 1939, pp. 560–77.

19 Arnsmeyer, Fr. W., 'Die kurzfristigen Auftriebs- und Preisschwankungen auf den westdeutschen Schlacht-schweinemärkten', *Agrarwirtschaft*, Sonderheft 2, Hanover, 1956.

20 Hopp, H., *Supply and Demand in relation to the Price of Coffee* (Foreign Agriculture Circular FCB 30–54), USDA, Washington DC, 16 December 1954, p. 15, and FAO, *The World Coffee Economy* (Commodity Bulletin Series no. 33), Rome, 1961.

21 Wöhlken, Egan, 'Analyse der zyklischen Veränderungen des Bestands an trächtigen Sauen', *Agrarwirtschaft*, August 1967.

Further Reading

Boussard, J. M., 'Les modèles d'offre en France: vue rapide et critique', *Economie Rurale*, July–September 1964.

Cowling, Keith and Gardner, T. W., 'Analytical models for estimating supply relations in the agricultural sector: a survey and critique', *JAE*, Vol. XV, no. 3, 1963.

Yates, Lamartine P., *Food, Land and Manpower in Western Europe*, London, 1960.

CHAPTER NINE

Distributive and Processing Margins

Farmers' Criticisms of Margins

In all countries, farmers complain that the margin between the prices they receive and the prices paid by consumers is too large, that the middle-man receives too much for his services. Whether or not this criticism is justified, it must be first be made clear that the mere size of the margin is not necessarily a guide to the efficiency of marketing. The smallest margin is when the farmer sells direct to the consumer, either by taking the goods to his home or by selling them at a weekly market. In this case the margin is nil, but the method is not necessarily efficient because:

(a) the farmer has to spend time taking the goods to market;
(b) the housewife has to spend time preparing the unprocessed and ungraded products.

With the increasing trend to specialisation in our economic system, there is a tendency for these functions to be undertaken by specialist intermediaries. For example, it was once common (and in many underdeveloped countries still is) for poultry to be sold live, so that the housewife has the laborious and unpleasant task of slaughtering, plucking and dressing. In modern table poultry production, these processes are carried out very efficiently in a slaughterhouse, so that the housewife merely has to cook the oven-ready bird. Even this function has now been taken over by 'chicken restaurants' where chickens roasted ready for eating can be bought. The provision of this type of extra service naturally tends (other things being equal) to increase the distributive margin, but this in itself is no sign of inefficiency.

Similarly, a concentration of production in particular regions leads to an increase in transport costs, which may, however, be more than outweighed by the reduction in production costs. For example, if West European apple production became concentrated in North Italy, the distribution costs would rise as a result of increased transport costs; nevertheless, because production costs were so much lower, the retail price might still be less than if the apples were grown near the consuming areas. The concentration of production into certain areas—and into large units—can sometimes reduce not only production but also collection costs; this is particularly true for milk and eggs. (In practice, production is hardly ever concentrated exclusively in one area, but there is today a distinct trend to greater regional specialisation.)

In order to go beyond such generalities and reach practical conclusions, it is necessary to have detailed and reliable figures or margins, and here the picture is very mixed. Figures of the distributive margins for agricultural products, and of their changes over time, are available in great detail for the United States, and in a less comprehensive form for some European countries, but for many underdeveloped countries, and even for countries such as France and Italy, only very fragmentary information is available. In order, however, to interpret correctly what information is available, one must distinguish between three differing measurements of the distributive margin:

(1) the distributive margin for a particular product, based on comparisons of prices at various stages of distribution;
(2) the margin of a particular group of distributors, based on a study of firms' trading accounts;
(3) the farmer's share of the retail value of a product, calculated from aggregate figures of the value of production and of retail expenditure.

The Margin for a Product
The total distributive margin is the difference between the price received by the farmer for the product as he sells it

TABLE 21

Breakdown of Milk Price in England and Wales 1977–78
(pence per litre)

	p.	p.
Retail price for 'Pasteurised Milk'	20·4	
Distribution margin		8·6
Distribution allowances		0·5
		9·1
Net return to Board for liquid milk	11·3	
Net return to Board for manufacturing milk	8·4	
Average return to Board	10·4	

Source: Federation of UK Milk Marketing Boards, *Dairy Facts and Figures 1978.*

and the price paid by the consumer for the product in its final form. The total margin usually consists of margins for several stages of distribution—assembly, processing, wholesaling, retailing—and in each case the margin is the difference between the buying and selling price of each distributor or processor. A part of this margin consists of profits and remuneration for the distributor, but the greater part usually consists of payments for wages, rent, transport, etc. Table 21 shows the retail and wholesale margins for milk in England and Wales.

But for most products it is extremely difficult to calculate margins in this way. Many products are sold in a variety of processed forms; cereals as various sorts of bread, cakes, spaghetti, etc.; meat as fresh meat, tinned meat, sausage etc. The retail prices of all these articles, which vary regionally and over time, are often not available. Prices at earlier stages of distribution are often available from public markets—e.g. fatstock markets—but the buying and selling prices of co-operatives, processing firms, wholesalers and retailers are rarely published. In consequence, it is often only for products—such as milk—where prices and margins are set by an official agency for which regular and reliable data on margins at all stages is available. For some countries, figures of retail margins for fresh meat are calculated and published regularly (e.g. for West Germany in the journal *Agrarwirtschaft*); these probably give a good impression of at least the changes in the size of margins.

The Distributor's Margin

The problems of calculating margins when foodstuff is retailed in a variety of forms can be solved only by a different approach, namely an investigation of the trading accounts of a sample of distributors. For example, information on retail butchers' total receipts and their expenditure for carcases enables the retail margin as a percentage of the retail value to be calculated. The fact that the butcher buys both beef and pork sides, and uses them to produce a wide range of fresh cuts and manufactured products, presents no difficulties. Some results of investigations of this type (for all food retailers) for the UK and West Germany are given in Table 22.

TABLE 22

Margins and Profits in Retailing

United Kingdom	1961	1976
Gross Margin as % of Turnover		
Total Retail Trade	24·9	27·0
Grocery and Provision Dealers	16·0	17·0
Other Food Retailers	24·2	25·1
Butchers	22·2	22·4
Greengrocers	20·9	21·1

West Germany 1960	Gross Margin as % of Turnover	Profit as % of Turnover
Total Retail Trade	26·4	7·3
Food Retailers	18·6	5·1

Source: Report on the Census of Distribution and Other Services 1961, HMSO, 1964; Business Monitor, 1976: Retailing, HMSO; Umsatz, Kosten, Spannen und Gewinn des Einzelhandels in der BR Deutschland in Jahren 1958, 1959, und 1960, Opladen, 1963.

In both countries the average margin for food retailers is lower than the average for all retailers. This is probably because the turnover of food products is faster than that of other products. Nevertheless the fact speaks well for the efficiency of food marketing in these countries. Investigations giving distributive margins of this type have been made of the German bakery trade,[1] British vegetable distribution,[2] and the British meat trade.[3]

The Farmer's Share of the Retail Value

The third approach to margins is to calculate the farmer's share of the retail value, as calculated from aggregate consumption and production figures. Taking the value of sales of the national farm (a), the total retail value of agricultural products (b), the retail value of imports (c), and the farm-gate value of exports (d), the farmer's share is $a - d/b - c$.

Calculations of this type indicate that the farmer's share in the USA, after falling in the 1950s, has levelled off at around 40 per cent. The same fall, followed by a levelling-off in the 1970s at around 46 per cent, is shown for West Germany. The earlier fall reflects the higher handling costs resulting from the concentration of population in urban centres, as well as more preparation and packaging. (See Table 23.)

The three types of figures which have been discussed—the margin for a particular product, the distributor's margin, and the farmer's share of retail value—measure different things and give different information. Taken together, they are capable of complementing each other and casting light on the subject.

Long-term and Short-term Changes

In considering the level of distributive margins it is necessary to distinguish between two aspects:

(a) The general level of margins, and long-term changes over years or decades, reflecting basic changes in wages, competition, productivity or marketing methods.

(b) Short- and medium-term fluctuations extending over

TABLE 23

The Farmer's Share of Retail Expenditure

	Cereals	Eggs	Fruit and Vegetables	Meat and Meat Products	Milk and Milk Products	Total
USA						
1963	17	—	25*	54	43	38
1975	19	—	27*	59	49	42
1978	14	70	26*	56	51	39
West Germany						
1966/67†	17	86	41	52	53	50
1970/71	16	85	33	48	57	46
1977/78	14	81	40	49	60	47

*Fresh and processed. The 1979 figures were: fresh fruit 28·4, fresh vegetables 31·6, processed fruit and vegetables 18·5.
†Not completely comparable with subsequent years.

Source: Agricultural Statistics, 1976, USDA, p. 448. Agrarbericht der Bundesregierung, 1979, Materialband, p. 103.

days, weeks, months, or even a year or two, which are a consequence of temporary price changes, mostly of a rise or fall in producer prices as a result of fluctuations in production.

These two aspects raise quite different issues. The first is concerned with the general height of margins, and the accusation often made in this connection is that the margins are permanently too high as a result of inefficient methods or excessive profits. The second is concerned with short-term reactions; the criticism often made in this connection is that, by keeping their margins inflexible, or even widening them when prices fall, the distributors throw the whole burden of the price fall onto producers. This second criticism does not therefore necessarily imply that the general level of margins is too high; it is concerned with fluctuations in producers' and distributors' receipts. We will deal with the two aspects in turn.

The General Size of Margins: International Comparisons
The mere size of the margin is in itself no indication of efficiency or inefficiency. It can only be said that a margin is too high if the remuneration of the distributors is exceptionally high or if there is reason to believe that costs could be reduced by means of a reorganisation of the distributive system. It is in costs rather than profits that the greatest savings can be achieved, since, as can be seen in Table 22, profits—at least in developed countries—account for a fairly small part of the margin and, expressed as a return on capital, are rarely higher than in other branches of distribution or in other occupations. It is also to be noted that the largest items in the total distributive margin are processing and retailing. Farmers' criticism is often directed at margins between the farm and the wholesale level—dealer's margins etc.—but these do not usually account for a major part of the total distributive margin.

In any country there are two main factors which determine the absolute level of the distributive margin:

(1) the general wage level;
(2) the productivity of processing and distribution.

Over time, these two factors tend to act in opposite directions. With economic progress there is a rise in wages, but also a rise in the efficiency of processing and distribution, which partly or wholly offsets the effect of rising wages. Consequently, countries with the lowest wages do not always have the lowest margins. Table 24 gives some results of a survey of meat margins in West European countries. It can be seen that the total distributive margin for beef was over twice as high—in absolute terms—in Italy as in Norway, and that the countries with the highest margins were not always those with the highest wages. In

TABLE 24

Distributive Margins for Beef in various Countries

Total Margin for Beef* 1955–57 (per 100 kg carcass weight)		Earnings per hour in Mining and Manufacturing 1956		Margin expressed in no. of man/ hours	
(1)		(2)		(1) ÷ (2)	
US $				man/hours per 100 kg.	
Italy (Milan)	35·60	Sweden	0·92	Italy	107·9
Switzerland	35·20	Norway	0·75	Austria	61·5
Belgium	34·14	Switzerland	0·73	France	61·0
France	33·55	Denmark	0·68	Belgium	61·0
Sweden	29·00	Belgium	0·56	Germany	57·4
Germany	26·98	France	0·55	Netherlands	53·5
Denmark	24·38	Ireland	0·50	Switzerland	48·2
Ireland	23·59	Germany	0·47	Ireland	47·2
Netherlands	22·99	Netherlands	0·43	Denmark	35·9
Austria	22·76	Austria	0·37	Sweden	31·5
Norway	15·44	Italy	0·33	Norway	20·6

*Excluding consumption tax.

Source: Mittendorf, H. J., *Marketing and Distribution Margins for Livestock and Meat in OEEC Countries*, Paris, 1959, Tables 6 and 9.

fact, the country with the highest margin—Italy—had the lowest wages rates, whereas the country with the lowest margin—Norway—had almost the highest. When the margin is expressed in terms of hourly wages (using wages in manufacturing for want of information on those in retailing), the differences in efficiency are striking; the figures range from 107·9 man hours in Italy to 20·6 in Norway. (The UK would probably be somewhere in the middle.) The very high efficiency of the Scandinavian countries appears to be the result of the dead-weight marketing system and an efficient system of retailing, in which the co-operative societies maintain a high level of competition.

The extent to which improved methods can offset higher wages rates becomes even clearer when comparisons are made with underdeveloped countries. In 1959, for example, the total margin for chickens, expressed in US dollars, was just under 50 per cent greater in the USA than in Bangkok.[4] But the chickens in the USA were sold oven-ready, whereas in Bangkok they had head, feet, feathers and entrails intact. And money wages rates in the USA were naturally many times those prevailing in Thailand. As a percentage of the retail price, the margins in the two countries were almost exactly the same, at just under 50 per cent. An even more striking comparison is that between the distributive margin for eggs in Denmark and Turkey in 1959. Although the retail price was almost identical, the total margin in Turkey accounted for 60 per cent of the retail price as against 23 per cent in Denmark.

Development of Margins in the USA
The trend of distributive margins in the USA over the last half century—the only country for which information over such a long time-span is available—reveals the same factors underlying differences between countries at different stages of development. During such a long period the general price level has altered considerably, so that the two most meaningful measures of the distributive margin are:

(1) the absolute margin expressed in real terms, i.e. divided by general index of retail prices;

(2) the margin as a percentage of the retail price of the product.

There is the further problem that the decline in direct marketing causes the rise in the total marketing cost to be greater than the rise in the cost of goods sold through the normal wholesale-retail channel. Thus for purposes of judging the efficiency of the marketing system, it is best to take the margin of goods sold through retailers. Even here the switch from cheaper, unprocessed foodstuffs to foodstuffs with higher retail margins—such as meat—causes a rise in the average margin. The best guide to the change in the retail margin (although not in the total cost of marketing) is thus the real cost of marketing for a constant selection of goods sold at retail.

As can be seen from Fig. 38, the real marketing costs in the USA for a 'market basket' of foodstuffs sold through retailers has remained roughly constant since the early 1920s. This means that over this period the increase in the productivity of food distribution was equal to that of the economy as a whole—a very considerable achievement, considering the difficulties of mechanising distribution.

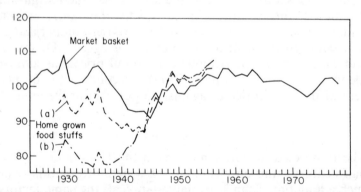

FIG. 38. Real marketing cost per unit of food, USA
(1947/49 = 100)

Source: Schmitt, Gunter, 'Die Handels- und Verarbeitungsspannen bei Nahrungsmitteln', *Berichte über Landwirtschaft*, Sonderheft 171, 1959, p. 70.
Market basket 1965–78 estimated by the author.

The productivity increase in food distribution and in the economy as a whole did not, however, always proceed in the same tempo. From 1935 to 1945 the development of the chain-stores and self-service led to a fall in real marketing costs. After the war, however, in a period when real wages were rising sharply, and when the increase in the productivity of distribution was apparently no longer so great, the real costs of marketing rose again.

The two broken curves in Fig. 38 show the development since 1929 of the marketing costs of (a) all domestic foodstuffs sold through retailers, (b) all domestic foodstuffs sold through all marketing channels. Because of the change in food consumption and the decline in direct marketing, these curves—and especially the latter—show substantial rises since the 1930s, but this is no reflection on the efficiency of marketing.

The experience of the United States suggest, therefore, that over long periods of time there is not necessarily any 'law of increasing margins'; improvements in efficiency of distribution can offset rising wages. In Western Europe, countries such as the United Kingdom, West Germany, and the Scandinavian countries have, in the 1950s and early 1960s, gone through the same 'super-market revolution' that occurred in the USA some years earlier, and have almost certainly, experienced a fall in average marketing costs in real terms.

Margins for Meat

A tendency for margins to rise is nevertheless discernible in the more developed European countries for products whose preparations involve a good deal of labour—especially meat and bakery products. The figures for retail margins for meat (Table 25), although they must be very cautiously interpreted, suggest that there has been a significant widening in Germany since 1957. Some critics detected a similar development in Britain in the 1960s, but the evidence is conflicting.[5] The available figures on butchers' trading accounts do not indicate widening percentage margins, and the most detailed recent investigations clear the meat trade of most charges of inefficiency. The Price Commission (which produced some

TABLE 25

Retail Margins for Pork in West Germany 1953–1979
(DM per kilogram)

	Wholesale Price of Carcases (December)	Retail Price (December)	Retail Margin (excl. turnover tax; 12 month average)
1957	3·09	4·16	0·69
1961	3·24	4·70	0·92
1963	3·84	5·58	1·05
1964	3·31	5·07	1·36
1966	3·75	5·63	1·25
1979	4·10	7·44	2·84

Source: Agrarwirtschaft monthly statistics.

useful investigative reports in the course of its more questionable price-fixing role) concluded in 1975 that 'the trade operates in a competitive environment and [that] profits—and prices—are not unreasonable'.[6] Another study pointed out that the discussion of margins had distracted attention from the important structural change which was taking place.[7] The traditional system based on auctions and public slaughterhouses was giving way to a more vertically integrated system based on deadweight marketing. The wholesale side was becoming dominated by large producer-controlled or private companies, the retail side by supermarkets. The trade was highly competitive and percentage margins had remained steady for a long time (although there was some seasonal 'smoothing' of prices).

Retail Milk Delivery
The cost of milk distribution raises special problems. The UK differs from most countries in having a regular milk delivery to the doorstep. This system is of great convenience to the housewife, since it relieves her of carrying home milk from the shop, and with a total retail

margin of no more than 30 per cent of the retail price, it is carried out remarkably cheaply. It is clear, however, that as wages rise, the cost of delivery will also rise, unless substantial labour economies can be achieved. The largest economy could be made by delivering on alternate days, which would reduce delivery costs by nearly half. A system of this type is possible if housewives have refrigerators—as is increasingly the case. Delivery on alternate days, previously advocated for the US, has been proposed for the UK.[9]

Until now, the home delivery of milk in the UK has been protected by restrictions on the ability of supermarkets to undercut the delivered price. The supermarket chains were in 1980 seeking to challenge this 'restrictive practice' and it was clear that if they won the competitive freedom they sought, it could be the beginning of the end of the milkman. This is a contentious issue on which economists should not disguise their value judgements. The author's view is that the milkman, like chemists and village shops, contributes to the 'quality of life'. Of course, if he becomes *too* expensive he will not survive, but a case can be made for a modest degree of protection from supermarket competition. The whole question of the *satisfaction* which people get from economic activities has tended to be ignored in economics, but it is receiving increasing attention.[10]

Competition and Distributive Margins
Competition plays an important role in the determination of margins. Except in the few cases where they are fixed by an official body it is, in the last resort, competition between distributors which determines margins. In the short run, official or unofficial agreements between distributors, or 'conventional' mark-ups, may govern the level of retail prices. But if one distributor is in a position to lower margins, either by accepting a lower profit margin or by adopting new cost-cutting methods, he can enforce a general reduction in margins. The number of food retailers who have gone out of business is sufficient evidence that the competition in this branch of distribution is hard and effective. Similarly, in the collection and

processing of agricultural products in many countries, private firms face strong competition from farmers' co-operatives.

Although no one familiar with developments in food retailing in Northern Europe and North American would deny that competition in this field exists, and that it is effective, it is not easy to define it. Certain popular, and even certain academic, concepts of competition do not adequately explain the facts. For example, the mere existence of a large number of firms (normally given as a necessary condition for 'perfect competition') is no guarantee that margins will be kept to a minumum, nor is it true that the existence of a small number of firms ('imperfect competition') leads to unnecessarily high margins. One might almost say that the reverse is the case. Thus France, with its many independent retailers, has, until recently, higher margins than Germany or the UK. (The situation in 1980 was changing, as France acquires a more concentrated retail pattern.) Again, the margins on liquid milk are, compared with other European countries, extremely high in Belgium, where the retailing is handled by large numbers of small dairies.[11]

The Mediterranean countries in particular offer many examples of large numbers of small retailers or wholesalers whose philosophy, or at least practice, is 'low turnover, high margins' instead of the 'high turnover, low margins', which is more the rule in North-West Europe (reflected in the fact that Spanish oranges are cheaper in Britain than in Spain!). In many Mediterranean countries the distributor lacks the managerial knowledge, capital and perhaps the inclination to adopt more efficient modern methods, cut margins, attract more custom, and drive his competitors out of business. The average costs curves of the individual firms are, at the current level of throughput, still sloping downwards, a situation which we have already encountered in agricultural production. This situation is, however, basically unstable; at some stage more enterprising and ambitious firms arise, who begin to cut margins and squeeze out their competitors. This process, of which the beginning can already be seen in France and Italy, can give rise to 'small shopkeeper' problems similar to the 'small farm' problems of agricultural production (e.g. the 'Poujadist' movement in France).

The countries in which (in terms of wage costs) food retailing margins are lowest have certain characteristics in common. There is strong competition between a relatively small number of large retailing organisations. These organisations can be either private 'chains', which are predominant in the USA and the UK; 'voluntary chains', which are particularly well developed in Germany; or consumer co-operatives, which play an important role in Scandinavia. The retailing organisations all possess sufficient capital and 'knowhow' to handle all classes of foodstuffs, and to extend their influence back along the distributive chain by undertaking wholesaling and even processing. At the other end of the distributive chain—in the collection of produce from farms—there exists in all these countries competition between co-operative and private organisations, and a tendency for local units to link up into wider organisations, so as to facilitate the concentration into fewer and larger plants often rendered necessary by technical progress. A concentration of this type is taking place among grain elevators in the Canadian prairies, dairies in Denmark, and slaughterhouses in the UK, to name only a few examples.

A policy of relying on competition in distribution to hold down margins cannot therefore consist merely of an attempt to maintain the maximum number of firms. There are often situations in which a reduction in the number of firms is necessary, if margins are to be kept to a minimum. This does not mean, on the other hand, as some British economists argued after the War, that competition in distribution is undesirable.[12] There are admittedly certain exceptional cases—such as the collection of milk from farms—in which official control seems necessary in order to achieve rational organisation. For most of food distribution, however, competition between firms large enough to make full use of modern methods has shown itself capable of developing very effective distribution systems. The most effective guarantee of competition is perhaps the existence of co-operative organisations— either farmers' or consumers' co-operatives—alongside private firms. Under these conditions there is little danger of the firms acting in collusion to maintain excessive margins. The success of co-operative organisations depends primarily on those who manage them, but government policy can at least ensure that no financial or legal obstacles are laid in the way of co-operatives—or indeed private firms—who wish to enter new fields of distribution.

A second way in which the government can strengthen competition is in the field of consumer enlightenment. The theory of competition (and of demand elasticities) assumes that consumers are able to compare the price and quality of competing goods. This is no doubt to a large extent the case, but there are practices which make it more difficult; for example, when meat prices are not marked, when the net contents of packets ar not given, or when packets are issued in a confusing range of sizes. Regulations that meat prices be displayed in butcher's shops, and that goods have to be sold in standard sized packages with clearly marked contents, are examples of ways in which the state can ensure that the consumer is given the information he needs in order to buy rationally.

Short-term Fluctuations in Margins
So much for the general level of margins. The second criticism mentioned above is concerned with short-term fluctuations in margins, especially retail margins. The criticism is that retail prices follow the movements of producer prices either sluggishly or not at all, so that the fluctuations in producer prices are consequently greater than they would otherwise be. In order to clarify the relations between producer price, retail price and margins, the possible behaviour of margins will first be examined in purely theoretical terms.

There are theoretically five ways in which margins can alter when the producer price changes. The margin can be:

(1) inverse;
(2) constant in absolute terms;
(3) under-proportional;
(4) proportional;
(5) more than proportional.

The differences between the five forms is made clear in the upper part of Table 26 and in Fig. 39.

(1) An inverse margin is one which falls in absolute terms when the retail (or the producer) price rises (and vice versa). As a percentage of the retail price the margin falls even more sharply. A margin is inverse, for example, if the retail price remains unaltered when the producer price changes.

(2) A constant absolute margin remains constant in money terms, when the retail price changes. As a percentage of the retail price, it falls when the retail price rises, although not as sharply as in case 1.

(3) An under-proportional margin lies between cases 2 and 4. That is to say, it rises in money terms as the price rises, although not sufficiently to maintain a constant percentage.

(4) A proportional margin remains a constant percentage of the retail price, and in money terms rises as the retail price rises.

(5) A more-than-proportional margin rises not only absolutely but even relatively, as the retail price rises.

The relation between producer and retail prices with the five types of margins is shown in the lower half of Table 26. When the retail price rises, the rise in the producer price is largest in the case of the inverse margin and smallest in the case of the more-than-proportional margins. The rise in the case of the constant absolute margin is larger than in the case of the proportional margin. This means that, when the margin is constant in absolute terms, changes in retail prices produce greater fluctuations in producer prices than when it is proportional.

To put it another way, a fall in the producer price will, in the case of a proportional margin, lead to a proportionately similar fall in the retail price; the fall in the retail price will be progressively smaller if the margin is under-propotional, constant or inverse. Fluctuations in producer prices resulting from fluctuations in supply are therefore less readily passed on to retail prices when the margin is proportional than when it is fixed, and even less when it is inverse. And the less the change in producer prices is

TABLE 26

Types of Distributive Margin

Retail Price	Type of Margin									
	Actual Margin					Margin as % of Retail Price				
	Inverse	Constant	Under Proportional	Proportional	More than Proportional	Inverse	Constant	Under Proportional	Proportional	More than Proportional
20	10·0	10·0	10·0	10·0	10·0	50·0	50·0	50·0	50·0	50·0
30	9·0	10·0	13·5	15·0	16·0	30·0	33·3	45·0	50·0	55·0
40	8·0	10·0	16·0	20·0	24·0	20·0	25·0	40·0	50·0	60·0
50	7·0	10·0	17·5	25·0	32·5	14·0	20·0	35·0	50·0	65·0

Retail Price	Producer Price					Producer's Share				
	Inverse	Constant	Under Proportional	Proportional	More than Proportional	Inverse	Constant	Under Proportional	Proportional	More than Proportional
20	10·0	10·0	10·0	10·0	10·0	50·0	50·0	50·0	50·0	50·0
30	21·0	20·0	16·5	15·0	13·5	70·0	66·6	55·0	50·0	45·0
40	32·0	30·0	24·0	20·0	16·0	80·0	75·0	60·0	50·0	40·0
50	43·0	40·0	32·5	25·0	17·5	86·0	80·0	65·0	50·0	34·0

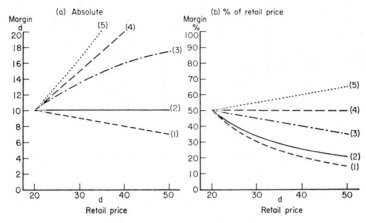

FIG. 39. Types of margin

Source: Schmitt, p. 120.

transmitted to retail prices, the greater it must be to have the same effect on demand. A given change in supply will thus have the smallest effect on producer prices when the margin is more-than-proportional and the greatest when it is inverse.

The effect of changes in supply on price can be illustrated by drawing demand curves for producer and retail prices on the assumption of various margins (Fig. 40). When the margin is constant in absolute terms, the vertical distance between the two curves will at all points be the same, if an arithmetical scale is used (top left). The price elasticity of demand is in consequence lower at the producer than at the retail level, especially at low prices. This can be illustrated by drawing the curves with a double logarithmic scale (top right); the elasticity at the producer level ranges from 0·8 to 0·3 whereas the elasticity at the retail levels is unity throughout. When the margin in proportional, the vertical distance between the curves on an arithmetical scale declines with a fall in price (bottom left). On a double logarithmic scale the slope of the curves, i.e. their elasticity, is at all points the same (bottom right).

In the example given in Fig. 40, therefore, the demand curve at the retail level is the same in both cases, but the

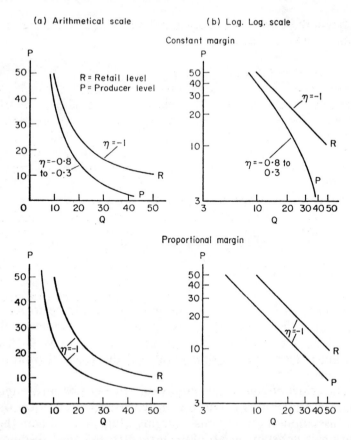

FIG. 40. The influence of distributive margins on the price elasticity of demand

demand curve at the producer level is very different. In the case of the fixed absolute margin, the elasticity at the producer level at a price of 20 is approximately 0·5, and the price flexibility, therefore, 2·0. This means that a 10 per cent rise in production leads to a 20 per cent fall in price. In the case of the proportional margin, the elasticity at the same price is 1·0 so that a 10 per cent rise in production leads to only a 10 per cent fall in price. If, on the other hand, production sinks, the rise in price will be greater with a fixed margin. Price fluctuations resulting from fluctuations in production will therefore be larger with a fixed than with a proportional margin, and larger still with an inverse margin.

The Actual Behaviour of Margins

These are then the theoretical possibilities. How do margins in fact behave? It is difficult to generalize, firstly because the information available is limited, and secondly because margins do not always behave according to a regular pattern. The first point to be made is that retail prices do on the whole—after a slight time-lag—follow wholesale prices: prices at least are not rigid. As far as margins are concerned, American data suggests that most are under-proportional; in absolute terms they fall slightly when producer prices fall, but not as much as would be necessary to give a proportional margin.[13] The same appears to be broadly true of fruit and vegetable margins in Britain and Germany.[14] The margin falls in absolute terms as prices fall, although it rises as a percentage of the retail price. However, there is a difference between the various types of produce. The cheaper vegetables have more nearly a constant absolute margin, whereas some expensive varieties have proportional or even over-proportional margins.

These results can be explained by reference to the characteristics of (a) retailing costs, (b) the price elasticity of demand at the retail level. A retailer's total costs—rent, labour etc.—are mostly fixed, and within limits do not vary with the amount of produce sold. When supplies increase and wholesale prices fall, the retailer will reduce his retail price and increase his turnover. It is a reasonable assumption, however, that he will expect his net receipts (gross margin times sales volume) to increase with the increase in sales, or at least to remain constant. If the price elasticity of demand at the retail level is unity, and the retailer applies a proportionate margin, then his net receipts will remain constant. If the price elasticity is less than unity—which is the case with many products—then a proportionate margin will lead to a fall in net receipts with increasing turnover. Only an under-proportional margin will maintain constant net receipts. If there are any costs which vary with throughput—wastage, extra staff etc.—then the margin will have to move still nearer to a fixed absolute margin if net receipts are to be maintained.

It is thus easy to understand that, given 'imperfect competition', underproportional margins will emerge, partly as a result of conventions among traders as to what constitutes a 'normal' margin. The existence of such conventions does not exclude the possibility of competition. As Alfred Marshall pointed out in his discussion of pricing in manufacturing industry:

There is in each trade and in every branch of each trade, a more or less definite rate of profits on the turnover which is regarded as a 'fair' or normal rate. Of course these rates are always changing in consequence of changes in the methods of trade; which are generally begun by individuals who desire to do a larger trade at a lower rate of profit on the turnover than has been customary, but at a larger rate of profit per annum on their capital. If however there happens to be no great change of this kind going on, the traditions of the trade that a certain rate of profit on the turnover should be charged for a particular class of work are of great practical service to those in the trade.[15]

The behaviour in the short run of meat margins seems, however, to differ from that of other products. When wholesale prices fall (e.g. beef prices in the autumn) the retail prices are reduced, but not by the same absolute amount; that is to say, the margin rises. Conversely the margin falls when prices rise. The margin is therefore inverse. Butchers tend to average out price changes over the course of the year, and between different types of meat; when beef prices are high they take lower margins on beef and make up by taking higher margins on pork, and vice versa. This practice is defended by butchers on the ground that consumers prefer steady to fluctuating prices. It means, however, that fluctuations in producer prices are greater than they would otherwise be, and most independent observers tend to feel that it would be preferable if retail meat prices followed wholesale prices more closely.

Summary
The 'stickiness' of retail prices varies from product to product. For fruit and vegetables and eggs, retail prices

seem to respond to changes in wholesale prices after a fairly short time-lag; the margin may be larger in percentage terms when producer prices are low but not in absolute terms. Retail prices also respond more quickly to changes in producer prices when the way from producer to retailer is fairly direct rather than through several independent distributors. It is thus possible that the development of vertically-integrated distributing chains will produce greater flexibility in retail prices. The state can assist this process by measures such as the publication of information on prices. On the whole, however, the behaviour of retail margins is, from the distributors' point of view, not unreasonable, and it seems probable that a certain degree of stickiness in prices, or under-proportionality in margins, is something which the agricultural industry will have to live with. The most effective way of reducing these fluctuations is to reduce the fluctuations in supply which give rise to them.

Notes

1 Ackermann, Klaus, 'Die Entwicklung der Backspannen unter dem Einfluss von Betriebsstruktur Kosten und Konkurrenz', *Agrarwirtschaft*, Sonderheft 8, 1959.

2 *Committee on Horticultural Marketing* [Runciman Committee] *Report*, HMSO, Cmd. 61, London, 1957, pp. 23–9, 157–67, 171.

3 *Committee of Inquiry into Fatstock and Carcase Meat Marketing and Distribution* [Verdon-Smith Committee] *Report*, HMSO, Cmnd. 2282, London, 1964, Chs. XIII, XIV, pp. 102–18, 218–45.

4 Stewart, G. F. and Abbott, J. C., *Marketing Eggs and Poultry* (FAO Marketing Guide no. 4), 1961.

5 Houston, George, 'Meat marketing margins in Britain', *JAE*, Vol. XV, 1963, p. 2.

6 Price Commission, *Prices and Margins in Meat Distribution*, HMSO, London, 1975.

7 Palmer, C. M., *Distributive Margins for Meat in Great Britain*, Agricultural Economics Unit, University of Exeter, 1975.

8 Bressler, R. G., *City Milk Distribution*, Harvard, 1952.

9 Davies, J. L., *An Inquiry into Milk Distribution Methods in England and Wales*, HMSO, London, 1966.

10 Scitovsky, T., *The Joyless Society*, Oxford, 1976.

11 Milthers, A., *Marketing and Distribution Margins for Milk and Milk Products in OEEC Countries* (Documentation in

Food and Agriculture, 1960, Series no. 24, EPA-Project no. 285), Paris, 1960. Introduction by Professor Plate, pp. 133–6.
12 Hall, M., *Distributive Trading: An Economic Analysis*, London, 1948.
13 Schmitt, Gunter, 'Die Handels- und Verarbeitungsspannen bei Nahrungsmitteln', *Berichte über Landwirtschaft*, Sonderheft 171, 1959, p. 125.
14 *Committee on Horticultural Marketing* [Runciman Committee] *Report*, HMSO, Cmnd. 61, London, 1957, and Lenz, D., 'Die Handelsspannen bei Gemüse und Obst und ihr Zusammenhang mit der Preisbildung', *Agrarwirtschaft*, 1959, p. 296.
15 Marshall, Alfred, *Principles of Economics*, eighth edition, London, 1920, p. 617.

Further Reading
Dijk, G. van, *Price Formation and Margin Behaviour of Meat in the Netherlands and the Federal Republic of Germany*, Wageningen Agricultural University, Neths., 1978.

PART III

Problems of Agricultural Policy

CHAPTER TEN

Agricultural Price Policies

Government intervention in the agricultural industry—as indicated in Chapter 1—can be divided into:

(a) price (and income) policies;
(b) marketing policies;
(c) structural policies.

These three types of policy will be analysed in turn in subsequent chapters, before their combined operation in the European Economic Community, in the 'Third World' and at a wider international level, is discussed. Such a discussion is bound to be based, at least implicitly, on a view of the nature of economics and politics. Some economists (in the words of a critic) 'proffer policy advice as if they were talking to a benevolent despot who stood at their beck and call'.[1] They begin by analysing the defects of an uncorrected market system and go on to explain that the state intervenes to correct these defects, implicitly assuming that the state possesses perfect knowledge, that policies decided at a high level are in fact implemented on the ground, and that political and administrative processes are free from all the defects of real-world market processes. A similar view implicitly underlies almost all descriptions of national agricultural policies produced by governments for international organisations, which give the impression that the policies adopted represent the best of all possible worlds. If only it were so! An independent observer must conclude that the agricultural policies adopted by governments in recent decades, although sometimes doing good, have sometimes done grave harm to producers or consumers; examples include the shortages and human suffering caused by forced collectivisation in 'centrally planned' economies, the 'urban bias' of many 'less developed' countries and the burdensome and disruptive surpluses of the EEC. A salutary corrective to the 'enlightened despot' school has been provided by the 'economics of politics' school, which stresses that—in agricultural or any other type of policies—politicians and administrators acquire 'empire-building' interests of their own, which do not necessarily coincide with the public interest, and that political and administrative systems have defects (inefficiency, ignorance, inertia, nepotism) at least as noteworthy as those of market systems. This school can also be criticised for over-simplification. It tends to attribute to politicians and administrators a ruthless Machiavellianism which is as unrealistic as the assumption that they are selfless servants of the public good. It does, however, emphasise the important point that some political and administrative arrangements are better calculated than others to make politicians' and administrators' 'private' interests coincide more closely with those of the population in general. We will assume in our discussion that *both* an uncorrected market mechanism *and* state intervention have defects; that any successful agricultural system requires both; and that it is the task of economists to investigate the most satisfactory 'mix' of the two systems.

Stabilising Prices or Raising Them?
State intervention in agricultural price formation is usually said to be designed to 'stabilise' prices, but 'stabilising' is often a euphemism for 'raising' or—less fre-quently—'lowering'. Stabilising means raising prices when they are abnormally low and lowering them when they are abnormally high. If they are 'stabilised' at a 'peak' or a 'trough' level, they are raised or lowered as well as stabilised; this has very different economic consequences. Broadly speaking, the effect of price policies has been to hold food prices *up* in the developed countries and to hold them *down* in the 'less developed' countries (in the supposed interests of the urban population). In international negotiations, the aim of the major exporters

of primary products has been to both stabilise prices and raise them.

The aim of price stabilisation as such is mainly to prevent undesirable fluctuations in farmers' incomes. The aims of price raising, on the other hand, can be extremely diverse. In the past, the aim was often to maintain the agricultural population, either because rural people were considered the backbone of a country's infantry, and a 'reliable', conservative element in politics, or because it was thought desirable to give as many people as possible the advantages of an allegedly healthy country life. This aim has today, in practice if not always in mythology, been abandoned in nearly all developed countries. A different aim of price support, theoretically at least, is that of maintaining a certain level of production. The reason for maintaining production has in the past been the fear that food supplies could be cut off in time of war. A somewhat different reason, which is perhaps more relevant today, is that political disturbances could cut off supplies, or that a country could lay itself open to political blackmail if it depended for its food supplies to too large an extent on distant countries.

A different 'strategic' argument is that production should be maintained in anticipation of a developing world food shortage. This development was widely expected in Britain after the Second World War, and only a very few economists such as Mr Lamartine Yates correctly predicted that the shortages on the world markets would be overcome by the early 1950s.[2] Experience, however, has shown that surpluses produced in developed countries as a by-product of a price support policy are not helpful to less developed countries and can sometimes—notably in the case of sugar 'dumping' by the EEC—do grave harm to poor and vulnerable countries. A final argument for maintaining agricultural production is that this helps to deal with a tendency to run into a balance of payments deficit. This argument has been particularly stressed in Great Britain, which has a relatively high dependence on food imports and has also suffered from recurrent balance of payments problems.

Although many of the arguments for maintaining the

level of agricultural production are open to question, there is probably some justification for the widespread feeling that too great a dependence on imports is unwise. It cannot be assumed that food supplies on the world market will always remain plentiful and cheap, and it must be frankly admitted that no one can say with confidence what supplies and prices of foodstuffs on the world market will be in ten or twenty years time. Events have too often, since the time of Malthus, falsified the prognoses of eminent economists for them to be able to claim any great certainty for their long-term forecasts. It is true that events have generally falsified prophecies of shortage, but it is by no means certain this must always be the case. As Professor Cochrane has written: 'The finest of lines separate the conditions of too little and too much in agriculture'.[3] The sudden appearance in recent years of China and the Soviet Union as large purchasers of cereals on the world market shows how rapidly the situation can change.

Agricultural policies, therefore, should not be based irrevocably either on the hypothesis that surpluses and low prices on the world market will continue, or that shortages and high prices will develop. They should be flexible enough to react either to surpluses or to shortages, according as the situation develops. This implies, among other things, that ample stocks should be maintained of the easily storable agricultural products—cereals, sugar, dried milk, etc. Substantial stocks in the hands of public authorities act as a buffer between production and consumption, and give production a breathing space in which to develop according to long term trends. They also reduce short-term price fluctuations, which can be disturbing for production and for price stability in both importing and exporting countries—specially the latter. They can also, when situated in the country itself, be used by developing countries to meet food shortages caused by harvest failures, and thus remove a threat which often has a laming effect on the development plans of these countries.

Probably the most important reason for price support, however, is to maintain neither the farming population nor agricultural production but farmers' incomes. The tendency, in the developed countries, of production to outstrip demand—aggravated in some West European countries by competition from lower-cost suppliers—gives rise to an income disparity between agriculture and other occupations, which price support helps to reduce. The argument for price support—or rather income support—in these circumstances is on grounds of equity.

The Results of State Intervention
Whatever the reasons for its adoption, agricultural price support means a transfer of income from the non-agricultural to the agricultural sector; it also means, in some cases, that the level of agricultural production will be maintained at a higher level than would otherwise be the case. This is contrary to the free trade doctrine, based on the theory of comparative costs, that a country should concentrate on the production of those things it produces relatively cheaply, and import those which it produces relatively expensively. But even apart from the 'strategic' reasons why countries may be willing to sacrifice some of the advantages of international specialisation, there are other reasons why countries may not wish to allow complete free trade in agricultural products. For example, as modern welfare economics has stressed, any conclusions on whether a country is better or worse off under one economic policy or another cannot ignore the distribution of income. It is therefore perfectly legitimate to depart from free trade if it involves an unacceptably low level of agricultural incomes. This is not to say that agriculture can, or should, be given complete protection from the effects of economic change or overseas competition. It is economic pressure which generally brings about structural change; economic pressure may thus be needed to initiate the agricultural adaptation which in the long run is the only solution to low farm incomes. But even if the aim is to achieve structural change, so as to make support unnecessary, agriculture may still require support for the transitional period, like other 'problem' industries. The peculiarity of agriculture is that structural changes take an exceptionally long time—often a generation or more. Thus

the distinction between transitional and permanent support is not always clear-cut.

Because of the difficulties in agricultural adjustment, it is not always possible to rely completely on the market price mechanism. As one fairly liberal economist remarked in a different connection: '. . . particular maladjustments of large magnitude and crucial importance may remain, after global equilibrium has been restored. Whenever such maladjustments exist, the short-term equilibrium price may diverge widely from the long-term equilibrium price; and real difficulties and problems may arise for which the ordinary price mechanism affords no adequate solution . . . In such conditions, regulation and deliberate direction may be useful and sometimes indispensable. To anyone concerned in a responsible capacity with the problems that arise, the later proposition at least is obvious common sense. I deplore the fact that it is necessary to argue it among professional economists'.[4] Probably the most reasonable attitude to take towards agricultural price support is that it cannot in all circumstances be ruled out as economically nonsensical, but that it is excessive if it seriously hinders desirable changes in farm structure. It is therefore a matter of finding the right level and type of price support.

Types of Price Policy
Some of the main types of agricultural price policy are outlined in Table 27. Policies designed to stabilise prices rather than raise their general level significantly include buffer stocks and policies which set a minimum 'floor' price. Buffer stock schemes operate by building up stocks when supplies are plentiful and running them down when supplies are scarce, thus raising prices in time of glut and lowering them in times of scarcity. A 'floor' price, on the other hand, can be established either by means of short-term supply control, by which supplies are held back from the market in times of glut, or by a deficiency payments scheme with the guaranteed price set at a low level in relation to normal market prices. Import restrictions or levies, which are applied only when prices are unusually low, fall into the same price-stabilising category.

TABLE 21

Characteristics of Some Agricultural Programmes

Programmes	Nature of Adjustment	Allied Problems	Farm Price		Retail Price	Cost Burden
			Level	Stability		
(1) *Import Restriction* Tariffs, import levies, import quotas.	Restriction of imports restricts total supply and raises price.	Restriction on international trade. Possible retaliation.	Higher in short run.	Possibly more.	Higher.	Consumer and foreign supplier.
(2) *Deficiency Payments*	Price system functions, but producer prices raised to 'fair' level by direct payment.	Heavy exchequer cost. Admistratively complex.	Raised.	More.	Probably lower.	Taxpayer and foreign supplier.
(3) *Buffer Stock Scheme*	Lower supply in glut raises price; increased supply during shortage lowers price.	Deciding right buying and selling prices.	On average roughly unchanged.	More.	On average roughly unchanged.	Taxpayer or producer and consumer.
(4) *Short-term Supply Restriction* Support buying with diversion or destruction. Minimum marketable grade provisions.	Lower supply raises price in short run.	Price must be set low, otherwise surpluses accumulate.	Fractionally raised.	More	Slightly higher.	Taxpayer or producer (levy).
(5) *Permanent Supply Restriction.* Acreage or marketing quotas; licensing of producers.	Lower supply raises price permanently.	Restriction on farm decision-making. Ossification of production pattern if quotas not saleable. Complex administration.	Raised.	Possibly more.	Higher.	Consumer.
(6) *Curtailing Inputs* 'Soil Bank'; attracting labour off land.	Decreased inputs; decreased output; increased price.	Substitution of other inputs can offset result.	Depends on output change.	No more.	Depends on output change.	Taxpayer.
(7) *Price Discrimination*	Higher price in market with less elastic demand.	Complex administration. Encourages long term rise in output if prices pooled. Only applicable in certain cases.	Raised.	More in less elastic market.	Raised in one market, lowered in the other.	Some consumers.

The aim of stabilising prices is generally to stabilise receipts, which fluctuate mainly as a result of fluctuations in supply. The relationship between fluctuations in supply and in receipts will depend on the price elasticity of demand at the farm gate. If the elasticity is less than 1·0, receipts will fluctuate inversely with supply and, if it is 0·5, receipts will vary exactly in inverse proportion, e.g. a 10 per cent rise in supply will lead to a 10 per cent fall in receipts.[5]

But stabilising prices will not stabilise income. If the price is held constant, while supply fluctuates, receipts will fluctuate in proportion to supply, i.e. just as much as if the price were uncontrolled, with an elasticity of −0·5, although in the opposite direction. To stabilise receipts (and thus, assuming unchanged costs, net income) when supply increases, prices must fall to such an extent that PQ remains constant; in other words, the movement must be along a demand curve of unitary elasticity. If supply increases by 25 per cent, the price must fall by 20 per cent.

Other types of policy are concerned with raising the general level of producer prices. This can give rise to problems, and the higher the level of price support, the greater are the problems raised. Policies that do not seek to raise the price level, but merely reduce instability, or put a floor on the market, give rise to the least problems, and can be most unequivocally recommended. When price policies go beyond this objective, the most important point is the *level* of protection; the method adopted, although important, is secondary.

The *methods* of price support fall into two groups—methods that affect market prices, and subsidies. All methods that work through market prices are based on the principle that a decrease in the supply coming on to the market raises the price, and an increase lowers it, the extent of the price rise or fall being determined by the price elasticity of demand. A subsidy can be either used to reduce the cost of agricultural inputs, such as fertilisers, or to increase the total price received for farm products. In the second case, the subsidy can take the form of a fixed payment per unit of output—which obviously has little price stabilising effect—or it can be based on the deficiency payments principle, under which the state makes up the difference between a guaranteed price and the average market price. In both cases, the cost of agricultural support has to be borne by *someone*, but subsidies are borne by the taxpayer, whereas policies which raise the market price are borne by the consumer. Consumer and taxpayer are, of course, to some extent the same person.

Of the various methods of price support, deficiency payments have considerable attractions. The system allows freedom of trade and marketing, and gives an indication of the cost of agricultural support (both in aggregate and for individual commodities) in the annual budgetary expenditure. But deficiency payments are only feasible in certain circumstances. The number of farmers must be small enough, and their educational standard high enough, to allow satisfactory administration, and the budgetary cost has to be tolerable. It admittedly makes no difference from the point of view of resource allocation whether a given level of producer is maintained by deficiency payments or the support of market prices; however, deficiency payments make demands on the public purse, and this is in practice not bottomless. The budgetary cost will be lower if a country imports a large proportion of its supplies, or if the commodity concerned is a minor one, than in the case of a major commodity in which a country is more or less self-sufficient.

If the budgetary cost of deficiency payments is substantial, the 'open ended' nature of the commitment can be an embarrassment to governments. An unexpected fall in market prices will cause a rise in the cost of the payments, which disturbs financial planning. It was for this reason that British governments in the early 1960s introduced various measures to limit the cost of deficiency payments. Thus the import quotas for bacon introduced in 1963 had the effect of holding up the market price of bacon and limiting the expenditure on the deficiency payments for pigmeat. At the same time, 'standard quantities' were laid down for various products; if production exceeded this amount, the guaranteed price was reduced accordingly.

Supporting Market Prices

The alternative way of supporting farmers' prices is to support the market price. If imports are prohibited, or excluded by high transport costs, the market price can be raised by restricting domestic supplies. This can be done by imposing quotas on individual producers, or by a public trading agency buying up a proportion of the output and keeping it off the market, either through non-commercial disposals or by prohibiting its use as food. Non-commercial disposals (e.g. of EEC 'intervention butter' to schools, etc.) is effective only if commercial sales are not correspondingly reduced. The more usual method is to ensure that the produce is not used for food; potatoes, cereals or skimmed milk can be confined to animal feeding by prohibiting the retail sale of potatoes of below a minimum size, or by dyeing any of the products a startling colour; surplus wine can be distilled into alcohol. Of course, if this kind of intervention comes to be used regularly, as distinct from times of occasional glut, one may reasonably question the economics of the system. A French economist has calculated that it would be more efficient to use rickshaws than to grow wine, distil it into aclohol, and add it to petrol as a motor fuel! This criticism would seem to apply to the 1979 proposal of the EEC Commission that alcohol produced from surplus wine, etc. should be subsidised sufficiently to enable it to undercut the price of synthetic alcohol.

When imports are possible, raising the market price involves one or more of the following, in addition to intervention buying: import tariffs or variable import levies, export subsidies, import quotas. When a country (or an economic union) is a heavy net importer, it is fairly easy to maintain prices, either by means of a deficiency payments scheme (if this is feasible) or by maintaining market prices through import tariffs or levies. But as a country nears or exceeds self-sufficiency, price support becomes more difficult and expensive—as the EEC has discovered.

A special form of supporting market prices is price discrimination. This is used particularly for milk—in the UK by the Milk Marketing Boards (Chapter 5). Provided that the degree of price discrimination is not too great, the system has virtues in the case of milk: it enables a reasonably steady price to be maintained in spite of seasonal gluts. But if the pooled price, and output, is raised too much, the system will gradually undermine itself, as the quantity of milk used for manufacturing (and after a point, sold at subsidised prices) rises.

'Production' Subsidies

In addition to deficiency payments and market price support, there are 'production' subsidies. These take the form of subsidies for various inputs, e.g. fertilisers, subsidies for certain operations such as land reclamation, and payments related to numbers of livestock, such as the British Hill Cow and Hill Sheep Subsidies (which are designed to assist marginal farming regions). Some of these subsidies originated after the War, when an increase in output was being encouraged almost irrespective of cost. Others seek to encourage cultivation practices which are desirable on long-term grounds, but which may not be profitable in the short term—e.g. a subsidy for ploughing up permanent grassland, and then a subsidy for growing beans as a break crop, which were paid until recently in the UK.

The *rationale* of this type of subsidy is a divergence between short- and long-term profitability. Some farming practices reduce soil fertility, the classic case being the American 'dust bowls' of the 1930s, and some (although not all) scientists are worried that the specialised methods being adopted in European agriculture may be lowering soil fertility and causing an increase in plant diseases. But problems of this type have been caused more by ignorance than the pursuit of short-term profit; at least when there is a stable pattern of family farming, farmers have never been inclined to adopt 'soil mining'. The main need—both in temperate and tropical agriculture—is for agricultural scientists to keep long-term effects firmly in mind when developing new higher-yielding systems, and to publicise the principles of good, modern husbandry, once they are established. Many studies, both in developed and less developed countries, have shown that farmers are extremely shrewd in adopting the techniques best suited to the conditions—financial and social, as well as physical—in which they operate.

There are, however, some situations in which 'social' costs diverge from 'private' costs, and in which a subsidy to cover this 'externality' may lead to an economically more optimal pattern of production. With the growing concern for 'ecology' in developed countries, and the reduced need for agricultural production on marginal land, there is an increased role for the state both to acquire marginal land and manage it on a non-commercial basis, and to use subsidies for 'ecological' purposes. But a great many production subsidies, especially in the UK were devised in an era of scarcity, and have harmful rather than beneficial 'social' effects. It would seem desirable to encourage the preservation of what is left of natural habitats, but subsidies are still being paid to drain marsh-lands, plough up moorlands, etc.

A final category of subsidies are those explicitly designed to maintain farmers' incomes rather than production, or even to *reduce* production: e.g. the provisions in the USA whereby, in certain years, farmers who keep some cereal acreage fallow are paid for doing so. This is not necessarily as topsy-turvy as it might seem. If there is a *temporary* glut of a product, and it is desired to maintain the production structure and not impoverish the farmers by allowing a very sharp price fall, then (after buffer stocks have reached the maximum feasible level) a 'set-aside' policy can make sense. The American programmes since the War seem, in retrospect, to have been justified. The problem is to know whether a current surplus is temporary or permanent.

In cases in which the aim of subsidy policy is explicitly social—i.e. supporting farm income during a period of structural change—the simplest and most effective way would simply be to pay farmers an annuity. Such payments would not have the unwanted effects of price support on production. They have occasionally been proposed, but rarely implemented. Politicians probably feel that an unashamed income transfer would be harder to justify to the electorate than price or 'production' subsidies.

Theoretical Analysis of Price Support
The effects of a subsidy can be illustrated by the use of a supply and demand diagram in the way illustrated in textbooks of general price theory.[6] The effect of a subsidy—ignoring imports for the moment—is to shift the

supply curve (based on the market price) downwards. The subsidy—if a fixed amount per unit—will represent the vertical distance between the two supply curves. The intersection of the new supply curve and the demand curve represents the new equilibrium point which, if both curves are elastic, will be at a lower price and a higher level of production than before. In this case, the price received by the producer will be higher than the equilibrium price in the absence of the subsidy, but not by the full extent of the subsidy. The extent of the change in market price and production will depend, however, on the elasticities of supply and demand; the lower the elasticities, the less market price and production will change. If the elasticity of supply is zero, market price and production will remain unchanged, and the farmer will receive the full benefit of the subsidy. If the elasticity of demand is zero, the market price will fall by the amount of the subsidy, and the farmer will receive the same total price as before. Since, however, the elasticities of agricultural supply curves vary with the length of time involved, the situation is likely to be different in the short and the long run. In the short run, the farmer is likely to receive the full benefit of the subsidy; in the longer run, production is likely to increase, so that the market price falls.

This analysis, however, assumes a fixed subsidy per unit and ignores the effect on imports. If a subsidy of the 'deficiency payment' type is employed, the producer price will be maintained irrespective of movements in the market price. The result, still ignoring imports, is represented in Fig. 41. The equilibrium market price is P_1. Setting a guaranteed price of P_2 will, after time for adjustment, cause output to rise to Q_2 and the market price to sink to P_3. The distance ab represents the deficiency payment per unit, and the shaded area the total deficiency payment.

When imports are brought into the picture, the result of setting a guaranteed price above the previous market price can be represented in Fig. 42, in which Sd represents domestic supply and Si the supply of imports. The sum of these two supply curves gives the total supply curve $SD + i_1$ and the intersection of this curve with the total demand curve D gives the market price Pm_1 and the quantity Q_3. At

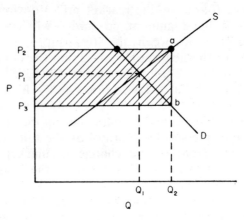

FIG. 41

this price, home production is Q_1. Establishing a guaranteed price of Pg raises home production to Q_2. Adding Q_2 to the curve of Si yields a new total supply curve $Sd + i_2$. The intersection of this curve with the demand curve produces the total supply Q_4, and imports are represented by $Q_4 - Q_2$. The shaded area represents the total deficiency payment. The proportionate change in domestic production naturally depends on the proportionate price change and the elasticity of domestic supply. For any given rise in domestic production, the fall in market price will be less, the higher the elasticities of demand and of the supply of imports. The fall in market price will also be less, the smaller the ratio of home production to total supplies.

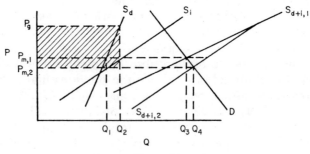

FIG. 42

A rise in the guaranteed price will increase the total subsidy, because a higher subsidy per unit has to be paid on a larger output. However, if the subsidy rises beyond a certain level, there will usually be political pressure for its reduction. This can be achieved either by reducing the guaranteed price or by raising the market price by means of import controls. A subsidy may nevertheless benefit farmers by causing an increase in production and squeezing out imports. Thus its effect on production is virtually the same as a policy based on supporting the market price, although it is sometimes argued that farmers do not have the same confidence in a producer price maintained by subsidies as in an equivalent market price. The main difference, however, between a given producer price maintained by means of a subsidy and one maintained by support of the market price is that, with the subsidy, the market price would be lower, and hence total consumption slightly higher.

Whereas a deficiency payment, if anything, lowers the market price, a tariff will raise it. However, the extent of the price rise depends on the elasticity of supply of imports. If this is high—as will be the case if the supplying country has many alternative markets—the internal price will be raised by nearly the full amount of the tariff. Home production will be expanded, according to the elasticity of supply, and imports correspondingly reduced. If the elasticity of supply of imports is low, e.g. when there are no alternative markets, the import price will be depressed by the imposition of a tariff, and the internal price raised less. In this case, the tariff has the effect of 'taxing the foreigner'.

A variable import levy differs from a tariff in that it is not fixed, but altered so as to maintain a given internal price. There is thus no possibility for the supplying country to get under the tariff wall by accepting a lower price. The effect on home production will depend solely on the elasticity of domestic supply, while the reduction in imports will depend on the increase in home production and the decline in total consumption (according to the demand elasticity). An import quota also raises the internal price, according to the elasticity of demand. In this case, however, the supplying country, instead of the importing country's exchequer, will reap the benefit of the higher price. Thus the imposition by the UK of import quotas for butter in 1962 was done at the request of New Zealand; it had the effect of raising the receipts of those countries who were granted quotas.

When domestic supply is highly elastic, an attempt to maintain a level of prices above the equilibrium level, whether by subsidies or support of the market price, is likely to prove unsuccessful in the long run. This is particularly noticeable in the case of pig, poultry and egg production, which, given a supply of cereal feeding stuffs at a constant price, can be expanded without excessive difficulty and without running up against rising costs. In these cases, the equilibrium price will be determined by the cereal price and the costs of efficiently converting cereals into meat or eggs; any attempt to hold the producer price significantly above this level is (in the absence of production quotas) likely to lead to unmanageable surpluses, which thus force a reduction in the level of support. This happened in the case of eggs in the UK in the late 1950s and early 1960s, when a level of guaranteed prices which yielded above-normal profits to the more efficient producers led to a great increase in production. Self-sufficiency was reached and even exceeded. This meant that egg exports were being subsidised, which aroused protests from traditional egg exporters. The British Government sought to limit production to the needs of the home market and successively reduced the guaranteed price.

West Germany during the late 1950s had the reverse problem. A relatively high cereal price, combined with free entry for egg imports, rendered egg production unprofitable. It was only when a levy was imposed on egg imports, to bring egg prices into line with the high German cereal price, that egg production became possible on a commercial scale.

Buffer Stocks
The classic method of price stabilisation for agricultural products is buffer stocks,[7] of which the first reported case is

described in the Book of Genesis (Chapter 41); Pharaoh, showing considerable confidence in Joseph's interpretation of his dream, built granaries to store one fifth of the grain harvest in the seven fat years to use in the seven lean years. This was apparently one of the more successful buffer stock schemes, mainly because the buffer stock manager knew the exact length of the periods of glut and scarcity in advance, an advantage not possessed by his successors.

In the modern world, there are many state agencies which hold stocks of agricultural products, but these stocks are generally held in connection with price-support or marketing policies; they are not pure buffer stocks, although they sometimes function as such. A type of buffer stock policy is, for example, operated by the Canadian Wheat Board, which has to sell its wheat at the current world market price, but can build up stocks when supplies are exceptionally heavy or international demand exceptionally poor, and run them down when supplies are light, or demand strong. International buffer stocks have often been proposed as a means of reducing fluctuations on world commodity markets, but a scheme of this type has in fact never been set up for agricultural products, mainly because the countries concerned have never been sufficiently united to accept a common policy. The only international stock scheme which has operated continuously for several years has been the International Tin Agreement. It has had somewhat mixed fortunes, having periodically exhausted its funds when attempting to hold prices up, or its stocks when attempting to hold prices down.

The difficulties of the tin scheme illustrate one of the main problems of a buffer stock, namely judging the long term price trend correctly. If the prices at which the buffer stock buys and sells are based on an under-assessment of the long term price trend, the stock will always be selling, and will eventually be exhausted. If the prices are based on an over-assessment of the long term trend, the buffer stock will always be buying, and will eventually break down when stocks become unmanageably large.

A buffer stock evens out the price, but does not

necessarily mean that producers receive exactly the same average price as they would have done in its absence. Apart from the costs of storage, receipts may be higher or lower according to the characteristics of the demand curve.[8] Let us take the case in which fluctuations are in supply rather than in demand (the most usual case) and ignore the costs of operating the scheme. Let us first assume that the demand curve is elastic.

If demand is above unity, i.e. elastic, marginal revenue will be positive (Fig. 43(a)). This follows from the formula $MR = P(1 + 1/\eta)$. Let us assume that in two periods the supply is Q_2 and Q_1, producing prices of P_2 and P_1. If a quantity $Q_2 - Q_1/2$ is not stored in the first period and put on the market in the second, the supply in both periods will be Q. Total revenue is represented by the area under the MR curve. Thus the move from Q_1 to Q causes a rise in total revenue equal to the shaded area A, while the move from Q_2 to Q causes a fall in total revenue equal to the shaded area B. As A is obviously greater than B, there is a rise in total revenue.

But if demand is inelastic, it follows from the formula for MR that MR is negative. Thus if the $\eta = -\frac{1}{2}$, $MR = P(1 - 1/\frac{1}{2}) = -p$. In this case of a constant elasticity under unity, the MR will be a mirror image of the D curve (Fig. 43(b)). As in this case MR is negative, the move from Q_1 to Q causes a *fall* in total revenue equal to the shaded area A, and the move from Q_2 to Q causes a *rise* in total revenue equal to the shaded area B. There is thus a fall in total revenue as a result of stabilization.

However, it does not need to be assumed that the elasticity is constant. When a market is saturated, and storage is impracticable—as can happen with horticultural products—the farm-gate elasticity drops sharply at low prices. Thus a straight line demand curve (Fig. 43(c)) can be quite a realistic case. Indeed, most empirically derived farm-gate demand curves are of this type.[9] The elasticity of the demand curve in Fig. 43(c) is at all points less than unity, but declines as the price falls; the MR curve slopes downward in the normal way, although it is negative. When the MR curve is of this type, a stabilisation scheme will cause a rise in total revenue equal to B, and a fall equal to A, which obviously means an increase in total revenue.

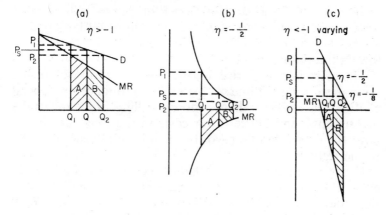

FIG. 43

Thus a buffer stock can either raise or lower producers receipts, according to the characteristics of the demand curve. If the elasticity is below unity and constant, a buffer stock scheme may reduce total revenue. But if the scheme is operated so as to put a 'floor' on the market at very low prices, where the elasticity falls off sharply, then the scheme is likely to increase total revenue.

The Dutch Price Insurance Scheme

Another type of price policy which is stabilising, rather than price-raising, in effect is the price insurance scheme operated in conjunction with the Dutch vegetable auctions—the *Veiling*. This scheme was introduced to deal with the gluts that occasionally occur in vegetable production, which can produce wholesale prices that are not merely low, and to some extent passed on to the consumer, but so low that they cease to cause any appreciable expansion in demand and bring producer prices down to almost zero. Under the Dutch scheme, a low minimum price is set, below which product is withdrawn from sale and either disposed of to schools etc., or in the last resort destroyed. The producers concerned are compensated at the minimum price, and the finance is obtained from a small levy on all produce sold. The price is set at a level which is not intended to cover costs of production, but merely to provide some compensation. Since the scheme is self-financing, there is a virtual guarantee that the general level of prices will not be seriously affected. Thus if an auction finds that larger sums are being paid out than are being obtained from the levy, it lowers the minimum price.

The existence of a price 'floor', even at a level well below the normal range of market prices, can influence producers' confidence, make them more willing to undertake investments, and hence lower costs in the long run. It can have the effect, in other words, of shifting the supply curve to the right.

If a minimum price scheme ceases to be locally controlled and self-financing, there is the danger that the minimum price will be set at a level which begins to affect significantly the average price received. Thus the minimum price scheme adopted in the horticultural policy of the Common Market is financed partly out of the general Agricultural Guarantee and Guidance Fund. Under these circumstances, there is a danger that the minimum price will encourage the production of surpluses.

Post-War Support for British Agriculture
Leaving aside the complexities of agricultural subsidy methods, there is the more basic question of the level of agricultural price support. British experience since 1945 illustrates the difficulty of striking the right balance in this respect. In 1947, in the immediate aftermath of a balance of payments crises caused by making sterling convertible prematurely, a policy of agricultural expansions was decided on. To this end, guaranteed prices were raised substantially, and a wide range of production grants introduced. In the mid-1950s it became clear, however, that at least one of the assumptions on which the programme had been based—that food supplies on the world market would become scarcer and dearer—was not being realised, and a discussion began on the future course of agricultural policy. Even among economists, there were differences of emphasis. Professor Austin Robinson, on the grounds that Great Britain would have great difficulty in exporting enough to pay for essential imports, advocated the encouragement of a substantial increase in agricultural output by means of price supports.[10] Economists of the

TABLE 28

UK Agricultural Income and Output

Year	Net Farm Income at Current Prices* (3 year moving average) £ million	Net Product at Constant Prices†	Labour Productivity‡
1970	617	100	88
1972	784	111	102
1974	934	114	109
1976	1200	90	93
1978	1255	118	118

*Net income of farmers after (historic cost) depreciation.
†Value added at constant prices (1975 = 100).
‡Gross output, less inputs, at constant prices (1975 = 100).
Source: Annual Review of Agriculture, Cmnd. 7812, HMSO, London, 1980.

'Aberystwyth School', on the other hand, questioned the economic value of subsidised increases in output, and emphasised the need to concentrate public funds on easing the problems of transition faced by marginal farmers.[11]

In the 1960s and 1970s the real price of many products fell, and yet output continued to rise, with signs of some faltering in the late 1970s (see Table 28). At the same time, considerable streamlining took place, notably in poultry and egg production. It would therefore seem that some of the earlier arguments for raising prices were overdone. And yet, in the late 1970s, the pendulum seems to have swung from one extreme to the other. Whereas in the post-War period government policy may have been to support agriculture somewhat uncritically, in the 1970s it often seems to have been concerned solely with the consumer's interest in low prices (even within the constraints of EEC policy). Perhaps the best conclusion is that both extremely high and extremely low prices are inimical to the development of an efficient agricultural industry. Extremely low prices may lead to dereliction, which is later regretted, together with unacceptably low levels of farm income, whereas high prices can perpetuate inefficient forms of production. Moreover, the considerable range of efficiency in the industry has to be considered, with the incomes of some marginal farms treated as an aspect of social rather than food production policy. If the author may quote himself, the following conclusion is perhaps still valid, and not only for British agriculture:

Some degree of protection for British agriculture may be desirable; its level, however, should be judged by the more efficient rather than the less efficient farms, marginal farms being treated separately, with measures designed ultimately to withdraw resources from conditions in which they cannot be profitably employed.[12]

Notes
1 Buchanan, J. B., 'From private preferences to public philosophy', *The Economics of Politics* (Institute of Economic Affairs, Reading, Series no. 18), London, 1978, p. 4.
2 Yates, Lamartine, P., 'The international framework', in Bateson, F. W. (ed.), *Towards a Socialist Agriculture*, London, 1946.
3 Cochrane, Willard W., *Farm Prices—Myth and Reality*, Minneapolis, 1958, p. 54.
4 Henderson, Sir Hubert, 'The price system', *The Economic Journal*, December 1948.
5 When $\eta = -0.5$, the demand equation is $Q = kP - \frac{1}{2}$
 $\therefore P = (k^2/Q^2)$
 The relationship between proportionate changes in Q and PQ is then $d(PQ)/dQ(Q/PQ)$ which can be shown to equal -1.
6 Boulding, K., *Economic Analysis*, fourth edition, London, 1966. Vol. 1: Microeconomics, pp. 207–11.
7 Harbury, C. D. and Tyszynski, H., 'Notes on commodity agreements and price fluctuations', *The Economic Journal*, 1951, and Porter, R. S., 'Buffer stocks and economic stability', *Oxford Economic Papers*, Oxford, 1950.
8 Bateman, D. I., 'Buffer stocks and producers' income', *JAE*, Vol. XVI, no. 4, 1965.
9 Shepherd, G. S., *Agriculture Price Analysis*, fifth edition, Iowa, 1963, p. 172.
10 Robinson, E. A. G., 'The problem of living within our foreign exchange earnings', *Three Banks Review*, March 1953; 'The problem of living within our foreign exchange earnings further considered', *ibid.*, March 1954; 'The future of British imports', *ibid.*, June 1958.

11 Nash, E. F., *Agricultural Policy in Britian: Selected Papers*, edited by G. McCrone and E. A. Attwood, Cardiff, 1965, and McCrone, G., *The Economics of Subsidising Agriculture*, London, 1962.
12 Hallett, G., 'The economic position of British agriculture', *The Economic Journal*, September 1959.

Further Reading
FAO, *An Enquiry into the Problems of Agricultural Price Stabilisation and Support Policies*, Rome, 1960.
Tracy, M., *Agriculture in Western Europe*, London, 1964.

CHAPTER ELEVEN

Structural Policies

Agricultural structural policies are those designed to encourage changes in the size or organisation of farm enterprises; to alleviate the hardship or disruption caused by such changes; or to find ways of retaining non-financial social benefits which are in danger of being lost in the unrestrained operation of market forces. Structural policies are not peculiar to the agricultural industry. All industries are subject to a continuous process of change, reflecting changes in economic variables, social attitudes or technology. This process is sometimes slow, presents no serious problems to managers, and attracts little attention outside the industry. But from time to time rapid and drastic changes occur, which force themselves on the attention of public and politicians because of the number of livelihoods and interests they affect. It then becomes necessary for politicians to take a view of the changes being experienced, and of the ways in which public policy might seek to influence them.

Examples of public policy on structural change outside the agricultural industry include policy towards the contraction of the British cotton industry before and after the Second World War, the contraction of coal mining in many European countries in the 1950s, the consolidation of the independent British motor industry into British Leyland, the reorganisation of the British steel industry under the British Steel Corporation, and the (possibly) sweeping impact of the silicon chip. On some of these issues it is possible to reach tentative conclusions. Public policy was sometimes well judged and successful; it sometimes did more harm than good. In the agricultural industry, dramatic changes occurred during the 'transformation of traditional agriculture' which took place in the 'developed' countries in the nineteenth century or earlier, and which is taking place today in the less developed countries (see Chapter 14). The framework of public policy within which these changes occur can profoundly influence the course they take. Changes are also taking place, however, in the agriculture of developed countries, and it is with these that the present chapter mainly deals. In developed countries, structural policy in the broad sense covers:

(1) The adaptation of farm structures to changes which necessitate larger (full time) farms, fewer farmers, and possibly a contraction of the cultivated area.
(2) The wider social and environmental consequences of (1).
(3) The special case of farm fragmentation in regions which have not undergone an enclosure movement.

Structural policy is linked with price and income policy, which is largely necessary because the agricultural industry cannot adjust itself rapidly enough to technical change. The question therefore arises of how far the state should assist change in the structure of agriculture, and of how the available finance should be allocated between structural and price support policies. The four possibilities are:

(a) no structural policy and no price support;
(b) structural policy but no price support;
(c) a combination of structural and price policies;
(d) price support but no structural policy.

Before 1939, many Continental countries adopted policy (d) but have since the war gradually switched to (c). The UK can be said to have followed (a) until 1931 and (d) subsequently, because of its relatively good farm structure. Denmark followed policy (b) until the 1960s when it also switched to (c). It is sometimes argued that price support inevitably reduces economic pressure on farmers and thus the incentive to undertake structural change. If the aim is to bring about an improvement in the efficiency of agriculture, so that it can eventually do without support then, it is argued, the less money spent on price support, and the more spent on the encouragement of structural change, the better (at least, as long as the imputed interest charge on the capital cost of structural improvements is less than the consequent saving in price support). From the long term point of view there is some truth in this argument. The more efficient structure of farming in the UK, Denmark and the Netherlands—compared with, on the whole, France, Germany and Italy—is at least partly the result of greater exposure to internationl competition in the nineteenth and early twentieth centuries. But when agriculture is already undergoing rapid change as a result of the pressure of modern industry, it is not so certain that some degree of price support will significantly slow down the rate of change. In the post-1945 period, the proportion of the total population engaged in agriculture, and the actual numbers, have been falling in nearly all developed countries at a more rapid rate than at any previous time, as a result of industrial demands for labour and the mechanisation of agriculture (Table 29). The falls have been largest in those countries which previously had a relatively high proportion of their population in agriculture, but which today have widespread and expanding industries—notably West Germany. Of the countries listed, only Greece showed a rise in the agricultural labour force before 1962, resulting from a high birth rate and slow industrialisation, but this was reversed after 1962. Under these conditions a moderate level of price support is unlikely to slow down the rate of structural change substantially.

A strong 'pull' from industry for agricultural labour is an essential requirement for improving the efficiency of agriculture, and without it the scope for any structural reform is limited. But it may not be enough simply to rely on the industrial demand for labour to bring about reform. The obstacles to structural change are often so great that, in the absence of official assistance, little happens except that the young men leave the farms; when the fathers die, whole areas are abandoned, even when, with a better structure, they could be farmed profitably. This is a very real danger in some Mediterranean countries. It can, of course, be argued that this breakdown of the old structure

TABLE 29

Agricultural Labour Force as % of national
Labour force

	1950	1962	1978
UK	5·6	4·0	2·7
Belgium	11·1	6·9	3·4
Netherlands	14·3	9·9	5·8
Sweden	19·4	10·6	5·6
Switzerland	16·5	11·1	5·6
Germany	24·7	13·5	4·6
Denmark	24·9	19·1	7·7
France	28·2	20·7	9·5
Norway	30·5	21·6	8·5
Austria	33·0	23·2	10·1
Italy	39·9	28·0	12·5
Finland	45·0	35·0	14·5
Ireland	40·9	36·0	22·0
Spain	49·8	41·9	18·9
Portugal	49·7	44·2	27·6
Poland	56·6	47·8	32·0
Yugoslavia	60·0	48·0	39·8
Greece	48·2	53·4	38·8

Source: FAO, *Whither European Agriculture?*
Rome, 1964, p. 29. FAO Production Yearbooks.

should be encouraged, that the land can subsequently be
resettled with a modern pattern of farms. But a crudely
mechanical view of this type overlooks the often deplorable
social consequences of disrupting the social fabric of a
region. The view that economic progress must have priority
over all other considerations has been well represented in
British economic thought, from Adam Smith to the
advocates of economic growth in the 1960s, and yet many
examples of the unfortunate consequences of this view can
be seen in Great Britain. The ruthless way in which the
Industrial Revolution was carried through in Great Britain
left scars on the British landscape and in British society

from which the country is still suffering. Countries which had their industrial revolution later—such as Germany and the Netherlands—were able to avoid many of the British mistakes. And although a very poor country cannot afford to sacrifice the maximum possible increase in real income, a more wealthy country can. Moreover, as the agricultural labour force shrinks, the economic gains from further reductions become correspondingly less.

In planning structural change in agriculture, a distinction must therefore be drawn between the ideal structure, which is the end goal of public policy, and the speed with which it is desirable to achieve this structure. Limits are set to the speed of structural change by the extent to which it is physically possible, economically sound, and socially desirable. There are two limits to the rate of movement out of agriculture which is desirable in the narrowest economic sense. Firstly, such a change is not merely a matter of a different labour organisation; it involves considerable investment in new machinery, farm buildings, roads etc. To scrap overnight the greater part of the existing stock of capital equipment—so long as it still has a useful life—and replace it with new, would not always be economically justified by the saving in running costs. Secondly, it cannot be taken for granted that the contribution to economic output of labour released from agriculture will always be as high per man as that in other sectors of the economy. Middle-aged or elderly farmers or farm workers will rarely be in a position to undertake more than unskilled labour, and will therefore contribute little to economic output. If, indeed, there are at the time no possibilities of employment for them in the neighbourhood where they live, they will contribute nothing to economic output. If, on the other hand, they have to leave their home in the village and move to an industrial centre, this will often necessitate additional expenditure for new housing and other facilities—not to mention the personal hardship often involved.

Furthermore, in assessing the most desirable rate of movement out of agriculture, the long term consequences for the distribution of industry and population must not be overlooked. It is becoming clear in many countries that the concentration of population in conurbations brings many social and economic costs with it—long journeys to work, traffic congestions etc. At the same time the depopulation of certain rural regions—besides being arguably a cultural loss—also involves economic costs, in that the sparseness of the population makes the provision of such public services as roads, railways and drainage very costly. Many countries have therefore accepted a policy of encouraging the development of industry in the smaller towns in agricultural areas, and some have achieved considerable success.

These regional problems cannot be solved by permanently maintaining the agricultural population at an unnecessarily high level; other employment opportunities must be provided. On the other hand, it may, from this point of view, be no bad thing that the rate of movement out of agriculture is less than the maximum possible, since the development of industry outside the main centres is a gradual process. When the annual movement of labour remains within certain limits, it is easier to provide employment in their home area for at least a good proportion of those leaving the land; they are otherwise forced to leave their homes and move into a distant city, with all the social disruption and long-run economic problems that this brings with it.

All these considerations do not mean that the movement out of agriculture is undesirable or is necessarily proceeding too fast. They simply mean that the question whether the rate of movement in any particular country or region is too slow, too fast or about right, must be considered in light of the implications for the agriculture of the country or region and the employment possibilities for the people involved. The aim of agricultural policy in countries where agriculture is being put under pressure by the growth of industry must therefore be to ease the transition to a new equilibrium both by relieving excessive hardship through price and income policies and by encouraging structural change by an appropriate structural policy.

Land Reform
Structural policy can be divided into three main types; land reform, consolidation and amalgamation. 'Land reform' has come to have the rather specialised meaning of the

breaking up of large estates and their division among people who were previously either tenants or hired labourers. This type of policy is generally the outcome of a period in which estates have been neglected by absentee landlords, and the motives behind it are often more political than agricultural. There are various examples in tropical countries; in Western Europe the most notable cases have been in Ireland, under the various Land Acts, and in the Italian South (the *Mezzogiorno*) after 1945. When the size of farms created under a programme of land reform is large enough to yield a reasonable income, and farmers are provided with adequate sources of capital, technical assistance and marketing arrangements, the results can be very satisfactory. But when there is a lack of alternative employment, and hence pressure of population on the land—as there generally is in the somewhat backward regions where land reform is undertaken—there is a danger of creating units which are far too small to be economic. In such cases the results can range from disappointing to disastrous. In the south of Italy, for example, many of the tiny smallholdings carved out of the large estates since 1945 have proved so uneconomic that they have been abandoned by their farmers. On the other hand, where irrigation has made possible intensive horticulture, and thus a higher output, the new holdings have proved successful.

A land reform of sorts was also carried out in Eastern European countries after the Communist take-over, although in most cases this was merely the prelude to a regrouping of the land into co-operative or state farms. Later, in view of the obvious weaknesses of collective farming, some countries, notably Poland, abandoned collectivisation and gave the land back to the farmers. In general, land reform is no longer an issue in developed countries, and the problem is not that of breaking-up agricultural units but of consolidating farms and making them larger.

Consolidation and Amalgamation
The need for consolidation and amalgamation—and the cost of carrying it out—depends on the state of the farm

structure. Some West European countries—such as West Germany, France and Italy—have in many regions a system of fragmented holdings dating from medieval times. The farmsteads are situated in the village, and the farmer travels out to the scattered pieces of land he owns, often too small for mechanisation and situated considerable distances from each other. One 50-acre farm in West Germany, before it was consolidated, consisted of 283 separate pieces of land! At the same time, the farmsteads in the village are often too cramped to provide either proper housing for the farm family or adequate housing for the livestock. When conditions of this type are present, it is virtually impossible for any individual farmer to improve the condition of his farm: change can only come about through a public programme for arranging an exchange of land between farmers. The scattered strips belonging to each farmer can in this way be consolidated into a single block, or at least several largish blocks situated not too far from each other. It is then possible to build a new farmstead in the middle of the consolidated land. Britain is fortunately very largely free of excessive fragmentation.

The second stage of structural development, once a reasonable degree of consolidation has been achieved, is amalgamation. At this stage, governmental intervention is not so essential as it is for consolidation, since amalgamation can, and does, take place merely as a result of economic pressure. In the 1950s, for example, the average size of a farm in the USA rose from 211 to 300 acres without any government encouragement (Table 30). Nevertheless, just as there is a good case for financially assisting the contraction and modernisation of the cotton industry and coal mining, so there is a good case for assisting desirable changes in the structure of farming. In fact, there are special grounds for doing so, since changes in the layout of agricultural land raise peculiar problems. A non-viable small farm may, for example, become vacant at a time when neighbouring farmers are unable or unwilling to buy it. It is for this reason that in several other European countries—notably France, Sweden and Ireland—public boards have been set up to buy unviable small farms when they come onto the market, in order to amalgamate them

TABLE 30

Changes in Farm Size

	Change of average size of holding 1950–60 1960–77		Average size of holding 1977
	%	%	hectares
France	+10	+ 52	26
Belgium	+21	+ 61	15
Canada	+28	+ 47	223
Denmark	+ 4	+ 52	24
West Germany	+19	+ 29	15
Netherlands	+22	+ 67	15
Ireland		+ 20	21
Sweden	+12		
Switzerland	+10		
UK	+12	+134	66
USA	+41	+ 33	162

Source: OECD, *Low Incomes in Agriculture*, Paris, 1964, pp. 64, 65; Statistical Yearbooks.

with other farms when this becomes possible. Thus in France the problem of fragmentation and small size have been tackled since the early 1960s by the SAFER(*Sociétés d'Aménagement Foncier et d'Etablissement Rural*).[1] These are public corporations, financed by the state, possessing powers to buy and sell land in order to improve farm structure. They have no powers to compel sale, but if land is offered for sale, they have a pre-emptive right to purchase it. They can thus amalgamate small farms, hold pieces of land until they can be taken over by neighbouring farms or divide up land and dispose of it to adjoining farms so as to increase their average size.

The farm structure of a country or region depends largely on the period at which the farms were laid out, and in general the earlier this period, the less suited is the structure to modern conditions. Thus the scattered strip farming still found in many areas of continental Europe is the outcome of the medieval open-field system. At the other extreme, the New World of North America and Australasia has farms laid out in more modern times, which are therefore larger and more efficient. But even in these countries there are considerable differences between regions, reflecting the date of colonisation. The farms of Quebec or New England, laid out in the eighteenth century, are on a European scale, whereas the Canadian prairies, colonised in the late nineteenth century, were laid out in rectangular blocks of a quarter square mile (160 acres) with each farmer receiving one or two 'quarters'; farms of three or four 'quarters' have subsequently become common. Britain was unusual among European countries in that, as early as the eighteenth century, common land was enclosed by private landlords who created a pattern of farms which was, and to a large extent has remained, the most efficient in Europe. In the late nineteenth century a similar process was undertaken in Denmark, and spasmodic efforts were made in most other European countries, but serious programmes of farm consolidation were for the most part started only after the Second World War.

All countries have found that, with the passage of time, the standard for the minimum viable size of family has had to be increased. The farms laid out in Denmark at the end of the nineteenth century were generally of 40–50 acres, and this structure, combined with very efficient plant and animal production made Danish agriculture for many decades among the most efficient in Europe, and even the world. But in recent years it has become clear that this size of farm has become too small for modern conditions. Under the pressure of the cost-price squeeze and the movement of population out of agriculture, a process of amalgamation has begun, although it is still hampered by outmoded laws which, in order to protect the small farmer, make amalgamation difficult.

In some countries farms have been laid out which were too small from the beginning. In West Germany, for example, the farms laid out under the earlier post-1949 amalgamations were of 20–25 acres. It was later realised that this was too small and the size was increased to 45–50 acres. Even these farms are clearly too small in the light of modern agricultural techniques, and will probably have to be amalgamated in the next generation. The Netherlands have had similar experiences, and there are agricultural economists who question the wisdom of taking two bites at the cherry in this way. However, once consolidation has been carried out, a process of amalgamation does at least become possible, whereas when farms are fragmented nothing at all can be done.

Part-time working can sometimes help to solve the small farm problem. This is particularly noticeable in West Germany, where industry is very dispersed, so that many farms which were once full-time units, but which as such would nowadays be hopelessly uneconomic, are run as part-time enterprises. If it is feasible, and if the families concerned are prepared to accept the work involved, part-time working is a thoroughly satisfactory system. There are, however, limits to its applicability, and it does not obviate the need for an increase in the size of those farms which will continue to be run as full-time concerns.

Structural Policy in Great Britain
In Great Britain relatively little attention was, until recent years, paid to structural problems, because of the relatively good structure bequeathed to their ancestors by the eighteenth century enclosers. Within a largely unchanged structure, it has been possible for productivity to rise by means of a reduction in the once exceptionally large force of hired workers (Tables 31, 32). But with steady improvement in agricultural techniques, the structure of British farming became more and more in need of reform, and indeed considerable changes began to be carried out in the 1950s and 1960s by progressive farmers and landlords without any official intervention. The idea that this process should be encouraged by official action, for long advocated only by a few academics crying in the wilderness, was explicitly accepted as government policy in the Agriculture Act of 1967.

A White Paper introducing the Bill calculated that, of the 455,000 agricultural holdings in England and Wales, roughly half were too small to provide a full-time living, but did not have to do so because their farmers had other

TABLE 31

Agricultural Workers in England and Wales (000)

	Farmers	Family Workers	Full Time Hired Workers	Part-Time Workers	Total
1851	249	112	1,268	79	1,708
1911	229	115	688	154	1,186
1931	248	81	539	130	998
1947	270	549		228	1,047
1961	306	447		88	841
1978	234	43	134	54	539

Sources: *Agricultural Statistics*; Population Censuses, *Farm Economist*, Vol. VIII, no. 4, 1955; MAFF, Press notices.

sources of income.[2] A quarter were viable full-time units. Another quarter—i.e. about 110,000—were being run as full-time farms but were too small, under modern conditions, to be viable units. In order to assist the amalgamation of these small full-time farms, an Agricultural Land Commission was set up and empowered

TABLE 32

Agricultural Holdings over 1 acre in England and Wales

	Number (000)	Average Size (acres)
1870	450	55
1913	434	60
1939	361	72
1951	377	68
1960	345	74
1977	194	121

Source: Ministry of Agriculture, *Agricultural Statistics—England and Wales*.

to buy farms offered for sale, in order to carry out amalgamations and reshape agricultural units. This proposal came shortly after a Conservative government had abolished the existing Agricultural Land Commission, which had since the War managed state-owned agricultural land.

The hostility of the Conservative Party to any state ownership of land appears to date from the Crichel Down affair, when a civil servant resorted to improper methods in order to ensure that some land which had been acquired by the state during the War was not returned to its owner.[3] This affair profoundly shocked Conservative opinion; on the other hand the Labour Party's sympathies appeared to be on the civil servant's side. There appears to be a need for a less doctrinaire approach on both sides, in which it is recognised that the buying up of some agricultural land by the state can be used to improve farm structure, and in some cases to provide land for recreation, without there being any question of the state's acquiring permanent ownership of a large proportion of the country's agricultural land.[4]

Other provisions of the 1967 Agriculture Act provide grants for farm amalgamation, and pensions to elderly farmers who sell land for amalgamation schemes. The scheme for pensioning off farmers is modelled on that adopted in the Netherlands. It should not be thought, however, that when the very small farms have been amalgamated, the problem of farm structure will have been settled. Technical progress will continue to increase the size of business that can be managed as a family farm, and pressure on farms which are now regarded as viable will develop. The reform of farm structure is not therefore to be a once-for-all question, but a continuing process of which the end cannot be foreseen.

Specialisation

Together with an increase in the size of farms, there is in modern agriculture a marked tendency towards specialisation. This development has been made possible by the introduction of artificial fertilisers and pesticides, which make elaborate rotations and mixed farming less necessary than in the past. And it has been made necessary by the increasing mechanisation of farming; the cost of machinery for four or five enterprises will normally be much higher than if the farmer concentrates on one or two.

Unfortunately, high British rates of death duties and Capital Gains Tax are beginning to make it difficult for a farmer to pass on a large farm to his son. Fiscal policies are thus working against structural policies.[5]

Specialisation has been carried furthest in North America and Australasia. In New Zealand, for example, farms specialise according to the conditions of the region, in the production of fat lambs, or milk, or store lambs. But in recent years specialisation has increased considerably in British agriculture. There is also considerable specialisation in Denmark, the Netherlands, and the Paris basin of France; in other parts of Western Europe the development is not so far advanced. It is noticeable in the figures in Table 33 the number of producers in the enterprises listed has fallen by a considerably larger proportion than the total number of holdings given in Table 32, thus indicating increasing specialisation. The last two columns indicate the extent to which production is concentrated on very large producers. The concentration is particularly marked in the case of poultry; on the other hand, herds of dairy cows have increased in size all round, without the emergence of exceptionally large herds.

Specialisation is largely a matter of internal farm management. Governmental policy, however, must be based on a correct assessment of the trend towards specialisation, if mistakes in investment are to be avoided. For example, price-support policies and the recommendations of the advisory services led in the 1950s in Great Britain to many small poultry keepers increasing their egg production, even when they were remote from both markets and cheap cereal supplies. With the development of large units in the 1960s, many of these smaller producers had to give up. A more far-sighted policy would not have encouraged a type of production with such poor prospects.

Marginal Farming Areas

Marginal farming areas present special problems for structural policy. These are areas which, because they are in hills or uplands, or because of the soil or climate, suffer

TABLE 33

Concentration in Agricultural Production in England and Wales

	Year	No. of Producers (000)	Crop Area or Livestock Nos. (000 acres or 000 head)	Share of the largest 5,000 and the largest 5% of produce in total production	
				5,000	5%
				%	
Wheat	1948	124	2,188	29·8	33·1
	1961	68	1,731	37·9	30·5
	1975	38	2,422		
Dairy Cows	1955	141	2,476	14·5	18·4
	1960	123	2,556	15·2	17·5
	1975	63	2,422		
Pigs	1948	185	1,626	35·6	44·7
	1961	110	4,579	39·0	40·8
	1975	35	6,337		
Hens	1948	293	19,638	15·0	27·6
	1961	213	35,363	29·1	41·1
	1975	59	38,815		

Source: Britton, D. K., and Ingersent, K. A., 'Trends in concentration in British Agriculture', *JAE*, Vol. XVI, no. 1, June 1964; MAFF, Press notices.

from relativley high costs of production. For purely historical reasons, such areas often suffer the dual handicap of poor soil and small farms. When farms are large, however, low yields can to some extent be offset by extensive production methods—such as hill sheep farming—but with rising cost of labour, even farms of this type are coming under pressure from the more productive lowland farms.

As outlined in previous chapters, the contraction or expansion of extensive margin depends on the cost-price relationship in agriculture, which again depends on the relationship between supply and demand. In most developed countries, the expansion of production on the more fertile areas has in recent years been so great that there has been a tendency for the extensive margin to contract. This contraction has often been hindered by special subsidies for farming in these areas; in Britain by grants for land reclamation in hill farming areas or by the Hill Cow and Hill Sheep subsidies, in the Netherlands by higher producers prices for farmers on sandy soil. These subsidies are based partly on the belief that it is socially desirable to maintain farm population in these areas, partly on the idea prevalent in the immediate post-war period, that it was necessary to obtain the maximum agricultural output from all areas, almost regardless of cost. A contributory factor in Britain was the belief, propagated by agronomists such as Sir George Stapledon, but since found to be too optimistic, that technical improvements, such as the use of new strains of grass, could offset the natural disadvantages of hill areas.[6] An increasing body of expert opinion is beginning to question the wisdom of seeking to maintain hill farming in its present form. It is clear that fundamental changes are already taking place in hill areas, and it is arguable that subsidy policy should assist the transition to a more satisfactory pattern of land use, rather than attempting to maintain full-time commercial farming under inevitably disheartening conditions.

Recreational Use of Land

Potentially the most important use for the upland areas is for recreation. Already in many of the upland areas of

Europe there is an increasing flow of visitors from the towns seeking fresh air and exercise in natural surroundings, and with the increase in real incomes and car ownership, the numbers are going to increase enormously. It has until now been customary to regard recreation as at best a side-issue compared with the serious business of agricultural production. However, non-agriculturalists account for 96 per cent of the population in the UK and over 90 per cent in most European countries North of the Alps, and the figure is rising fast. The recreational needs of this vast majority are not unimportant, nor, given modern democracy, can they be ignored. Moreover, the uplands offer one of the best areas for preserving natural flora and fauna which, with the increasing 'industrialisation' of farming techniques, is declining in the lowland farming areas. British subsidies for the reclamation of hill land have often resulted in heather moors of considerable natural interest and beauty being ploughed up to produce poor, weed-infested pastures which without the subsidies would have been hopelessly unprofitable. It would be a more rational use of resources to obtain the increased production from more intensive cultivation of the lowlands and to retain moors for recreation, scientific study and rough grazing.

An increasing emphasis on the use of marginal farming areas for recreation does not mean turning them into deserts, and depriving the inhabitants of their livelihood. Recreation can be combined with forestry, and even with agriculture of an extensive type, especially if receipts from farming are supplemented by those from tourism itself. But if serious attention is to be devoted to recreation, changes will have to take place in British subsidy policy. A state organisation such as the Forestry Commission can run at a loss, and can legitimately do so in order to provide recreation and beauty, but private landowners cannot be expected to sacrifice profitability for the well-being of the public. Subsidies to agriculture and forestry should therefore compensate owners for doing so. In the Netherlands, tax concessions to woodland owners are conditional on their opening their woods to the public, and Britain could well follow this example. Similarly, instead of giving grants to hill farmers to plough up moorland, the Government could give them grants not to do so.

The problem of recreation and 'amenity' in the lowlands is somewhat different from that in the uplands. The lowlands are where most of the food is produced and where the requirements of serious farming will have to prevail, even though these need not completely exclude other considerations. The long-settled countryside of Europe is deeply influenced by the work of past generations, and this historical influence will not vanish overnight. Nevertheless, even the countryside of Britain and other European countries is now being changed by modern farming techniques, and is moving towards the pattern best suited to twentieth-century farming. What this means can be seen in the American Middle West or Australia, and it is not altogether attractive—large fields bounded by fences, and no public access.

This landscape is very different from what most British people think of as 'country', and which they tend to consider natural and unchanging. But the British countryside is not natural; it was created, largely by the enclosers of the eighteenth century. Their work was a magnificent achievement in country planning and multiple land use. It gave Britain not only a farm layout which remained relatively efficient for over a century, but also a countryside which, with its hedgerows, field paths, country houses and parks, possessed a unique beauty and provided recreation—walking, hunting, shooting—to the relatively small numbers of people who sought it.

Under the impact of modern agricultural technology, however, this traditional British countryside is vanishing. Farming is becoming more intensive, hedgerows are being bulldozed, field paths being closed and barbed wire springing up to keep the public out. A reduction in agricultural price support would do little to arrest this process since, on good land, intensive techniques would be profitable even at lower prices. This 'dehumanisation' of the countryside is proceeding at a time when the demand by townspeople for recreation in the countryside is increasing, and the growth of car ownership is making access to the countryside easier.

One reaction to this problem may be termed the

'blanket preservationist', which seeks to keep footpaths open, stop the destruction of hedgerows, and generally slow down the rate of change. Such an approach can serve to publicise the dangers in what is happening, and modify some of the more ruthless developments. But in view of the economics of modern farming, and the difficulty of making a good living at it, any policy designed to oppose the adoption of economical farm layouts is likely to be fighting a losing battle.

A policy likely to be more successful might be termed one of 'selective preservation'; this would seek to preserve, at public expense, islands of landscape beauty in the midst of industrialised farming. This does not mean, however, that farming areas have to be written off as mere agricultural factory sites. They can be made to serve an invaluable recreational purpose provided that the public is kept out of the actual cultivated area. Lanes or paths can pass through cultivated areas while being separated from them, so that they do not interfere with farming operations, while public authorities can acquire small woodland areas and manage them primarily for the purpose of public recreation. West Germany, for example, provides many excellent examples of the recreational use of woodlands in the vicinity of towns. Indeed, West Germany provides today probably the best example of the way in which the countryside of a densely populated nation can be planned to provide recreation.

If the lowlands are to be used both for efficient food production and recreation, there will have to be segregation between the two uses, analogous to the segregation between cars and pedestrians needed in towns. It will have to be a countryside in which areas of intensive cultivation, from which the public is excluded, are dotted with woodland areas open to the public, some of which can be used as a screen for parked cars. The wooded recreation areas can be linked by paths or lanes open to walkers and farm vehicles but closed to cars. In this way, the public will be able to enjoy the countryside without interfering with the farmer's livelihood (and without being run over). The cost of acquiring and managing the recreational areas and footpaths will have to be borne by public or charitable authorities; the farmer or landowner can, for the most part, no longer be expected to bear this cost as a public service. (At the same time, the public will have to be trained to use the countryside in a civilised way, without scattering litter and smashing things up.) Some of these ideas have begun to receive official approval in Britain; the idea of 'country parks' was mooted in a White Paper of 1966, and the idea has since made steady, if slow, progress.[7]

Employment in the Countryside
Another area of discussion centres on two seemingly contradictory trends. On the one hand, there is a movement of professional people from the cities into rural areas, reversing (in a small way) the great rural–urban migration which took place in the developed countries in the nineteenth century and is taking in the developing countries today. On the other hand, there are growing complaints that rural communities are suffering from a decline in essential services. Shops, public houses, schools and bus services close down because—by modern standards—there is insufficient business to render their provision economic. Young people go to the towns for education and entertainment, and ultimately move there for employment, leaving behind an ageing and unbalanced population with an uncertain future.

One of the problems is that, for reasons of economics or convention, many public services come in large 'packages'. With the decline in the agricultural labour force, and in many traditional kinds of rural industry, the local population can fall below the 'threshold' for the provision of services. Possible policies to deal with this situation include special subsidies (at least as a transitional measure); joint services to reduce costs, e.g. the post bus; and some rethinking of conventional ideas about minimum sizes of public services. (There is, independently of any 'external' effects, surely a need to reconsider whether, in the secondary schools of several thousand pupils or the 'regional' hospitals which are the main achievement of post-War British education and health policy, the managerial diseconomies of scale do not far outweigh any economies of scale.) However, the best answer is probably enough non-agricultural employment to ensure that basic services, whether public or private, will continue to be provided. This raises questions of what used to be called 'town and country planning'. Some countries have encouraged small-scale industry in rural areas (e.g. Switzerland and parts of southern Germany). British policy, on the other hand, has been ambiguous. The Scott Report on rural land use—one of the three war-time reports on which post-War policy is said to have been based—was, apart from the Note of Dissent by Professor Dennison, hostile to 'urban' employment in rural areas.[8] This attitude seems to have prevailed in some, although not all, rural areas of the UK. In any event, these new problems of the countryside—which are emerging in nearly all developed countries—necessitate new policies if the countryside is not to become highly efficient in food production, but visually and socially a rather unattractive place.

Summary
Changes in farm structure can sometimes occur spontaneously, but at other times state intervention may be needed to remove institutional constraints or to guide structural change into socially acceptable paths. In developing countries, structural policies can include breaking up large estates, undertaking enclosure movements, and easing the transition from a subsistence to a mainly commercial agriculture. In developed countries, they include the consolidation of fragmented holdings, the encouragement of consolidation, the withdrawal of marginal land from cultivation, and policies to ensure that the countryside continues to provide recreation as well as food. An underlying issue is the provision of non-agricultural employment to offset the fall in the agricultural labour force and so maintain a sufficient population to enable communal services to be maintained.

Notes
1 Butterwick, M. and Rolfe, E. N., 'Structural reform in French agriculture—the work of the SAFERS', *JAE*, Vol. XVI, no. 4, 1965.

2 HMSO, *The Development of Agriculture*, Cmnd. 2738, London, 1965.
3 *Public Inquiry ordered by the Minister into the Disposal of Land at Crichel Down*, HMSO, Cmnd. 9176, London, 1954.
4 Hallett, G., *The Economics of Agricultural Land Tenure*, London, 1960, Ch. 8.
5 Clayton, D. *et al.*, *Capital Taxation and Land Ownership in England and Wales*, University of Reading, 1967.
6 Stepledon, R. G., *The Land: Now and Tomorrow*, London, 1935, and *The Hill Lands of Britain*, London, 1937.
7 *Leisure in the Countryside*, HMSO, Cmnd. 298, London, 1966; *Report of the Land Use Study Group, Forestry. Agriculture and the Multiple Use of Rural Land*, 1966, and *The Structure of Agriculture*, 1966.
8 *Report of the Committee on Land Utilisation and Rural Areas* (Scott Report), HMSO, London, 1942.

Further Reading
Clout, H. D., *Agriculture Macmillan Studies in Contemporary Europe*, London, 1971.
OECD, *Structural Reform Measures in Agriculture*, Paris, 1972.
Shoard, Marion, *The Theft of the Countryside*, London, 1980.
Tweeten, L., *Foundations of Farm Policy*, Lincoln, Nebraska, 1970, Chs. 12–14.
Whitby, M. C. and Willis, K. G., *Rural Resource Development*, London, 1978.
Yates, Lamartine, P., *Food, Land and Manpower in Western Europe*, London, 1960.

CHAPTER TWELVE

Marketing Policies

Marketing is an integral part of the agricultural industry, except in the case of subsistence agriculture. Produce has to be collected from farms, processed, graded and transported *via* various channels to the consumer. A wide range of types of enterprise undertake these functions, including independent merchants, farm co-operatives, and 'agribusinesses' based on processing or retailing. The 'normative' question with which the student of agricultural policy is concerned is 'What is the appropriate role of the state in marketing?' He would, however, be well advised to start with a different question, 'What are the political forces which impel governments to intervene in marketing?' Most of the pressure for intervention in the currently developed countries has come from farmers' organisations, although in some developing countries it has been prompted by a nationalistic reaction against foreign enterprises, or merchants of alien racial origin.

Farmers' Complaints against 'Middlemen'
The pressure from farmers for state intervention is understandable in view of the peculiar position of agriculture. Farmers feel that they are the tail of the economic dog, and can receive severe price jolts from changes in the rest of the economy. Moreover, the middleman is the intermediary through whom these jolts are transmitted. The farmer, in an industry characterised by perfect competition, naturally feels vulnerable in a world of oligopoly, and seeks some measure of 'countervailing power'. This can be done by the farmers themselves setting up marketing agencies. The classic form has been the co-operative; these play an important, sometimes even a

dominant, role in several countries. Denmark's emergence as an exporter of bacon and dairy produce in the late nineteenth century was based on co-operative marketing agencies, and in the 1920s the co-operatives founded by Western Canadian farmers wrested control of grain exporting from private merchants.[1] An alternative form of organisation is a limited liability company formed by a farmers' organisation, such as the Fatstock Marketing Corporation in the UK, the main founder of which was the National Farmers' Union. The emergence of farmer-sponsored participants in the market process has the usual advantages of new competition in shaking up possible complacent organisations, together with the indirect benefits of raising the status and self-confidence of farmers, and educating them in marketing issues. Although there is a long history of such participation in the market by farmers' organisations, it has recently been put in a new context by the emergence of 'contract farming'. Large retailing organisations, seeking regular supplies of uniform quality, have engaged in vertical integration, making contracts with organisations all the way back to the farmer.[2] 'Contract farming' to some extent reduces the uncertainty and instability of 'perfect competition' but it does raise the possibility of the farmer becoming little more than an employee of a large 'agribusiness' firm—which is indeed the situation in some tropical countries. Hence the continuing attraction of a system in which the contract is with a co-operative organisation rather than with the individual farmer.

An alternative to the co-operative approach, which is based on voluntary membership, is for the state to give farmers' representatives a statutory monopoly in marketing, or certain aspects of marketing; this method was widely adopted in the UK, the USA and some European countries in the 1930s. In many of the developing countries 'co-operative' marketing organisations have been set up which in effect are controlled by the government. As Professor Mellor points out, 'Under such circumstances, the membership tends to be quiescent, contributing little of managerial talent, local know-how, or even a guard against corruption. As a result, corruption and inefficiency are common, further reducing local interest in the co-operative'.[3]

However, the problems which have induced farmers either to participate in the market, or to press the government to give statutory powers to their representatives, have not been mainly marketing problems. When farmers face merchants who give them prices which are inadequate to provide a satisfactory income, there is an understandable tendency to blame the 'middleman' for taking too much of the final price, and to seek a solution through some kind of marketing policy. But these problems usually arise because prices are temporarily low following temporary over-supply, or because the scale of output of many farmers is insufficient to yield them a normal income, or because farmers in one region or even country are uncompetitive with those of another region or country. In other words, farm income problems usually reflect price or structural problems, rather than marketing problems, and so cannot effectively be tackled through marketing policies.

Types of Marketing Policies
There are, however, more directly justifiable forms of state intervention in marketing. These can be classified as:

(1) measures to maintain competition or control monopoly;
(2) measures to improve the functioning of markets;
(3) measures to foster economic or social progress.

Category 1 can take the form of:

(a) 'trust busting';
(b) encouraging new competitors to enter the market;
(c) providing 'countervailing power'.

'Trust busting' has been pursued particularly in the USA: a Congressional investigation into charges of collusion among meat-packers was partly responsible for the Sherman Anti-Trust Act of 1880. Probably more important, however, has been legislation which has removed obstacles to the formation of co-operative marketing organisations (or, perhaps, given co-operatives privileges). Agricultural marketing in the USA today is, in terms of the number of organisations involved, more concentrated than it was in the 'robber baron' era after the Civil War. On the other hand, farmer co-operatives play a major, in some fields a predominant, role, and there is certainly 'workable competition'.[4] But there are more subtle ways in which government policy can increase, or sometimes unintentionally reduce, competition. For example, there has recently been a decline in the number of independent butchers in the UK, obtaining their meat from public slaughterhouses; they have given way to vertically integrated supermarkets.[5] This trend may to some extent be inevitable. However, it has been furthered by the rather brutal and monolithic type of urban renewal practised in the UK, which has destroyed independent butchers' shops and made it difficult for new ones to be created.[6] (Moreover, British taxation policies have arguably been less favourable for small, as against large firms, than in other countries; the proportion of small firms is certainly lower in many comparable countries.)[7] Market structures and the nature of competition can thus be influenced by policies remote from competition policy or agricultural marketing policy as generally understood.

Improvements in the functioning of markets (apart from changes in competition) fall into three main categories. There are, firstly, those aspects on which the consumer is not able to make an informed judgement; notably the enforcement of hygienic standards. An extension of this approach is in the field of dietary education. It has been argued that the state should supplement the urgings of 'diet reformers' and dentists, that people in Western countries should adopt a more fibrous diet, that supermarkets should cease to place sweet racks by the check-out points, etc. In the same category are functions such as devising and enforcing grading standards (in so far as this is necessary to enable consumers to make rational choices. The pursuit of tidiness, uniformity and etymological purity can, however, become something of an obsession with administrators, and be pushed too far. It is hard to see what consumer interest is served by, for example, two recent EEC directives that Oregon sugar peas and thousands of other varieties of vegetable seed may no longer be sold by seedsmen, and that a fish known for generations in the fish-and-chip trade as 'rock salmon' must be described as 'dogfish'.)

A second type of policy consists of publicly sponsored research in marketing. There is not quite the same case for publicly sponsored research in this field as there is in agricultural production, since marketing organisations can, and do, undertake research themselves. However, the kind of basic research carried on in the USA by the 'land grant' Universities, which has underlain the remarkable achievements of US agriculture since the 1940s, has also covered the technical aspects of marketing, which are sometimes closely linked with production techniques.[8]

A third category of policies are those designed to improve marketing when a country's agriculture is losing ground to imports because of poor marketing, or to win export markets. It has often been argued that British agriculture, lulled into a false complacency by having a large market on its doorstep, has failed to process and present its products well, and so has lost ground to foreign suppliers—Danish bacon producers or even French growers of 'Golden Delicious' apples. In such cases, national governments are inclined to seek to ginger up the marketing system. Similarly, the aggressive marketing of a country's food exports is as important in influencing trade flows as 'comparative costs' (tariffs and subsidies permitting).[9] This international marketing can be undertaken by farmers' co-operatives—as Denmark—or by private firms, but it can be assisted by government sponsorship of food fairs, etc. Carried to extremes, such competitive national intervention could be economically harmful; at the moment, however, any dangers of this kind pale into insignificance compared with the economic harm done by the more extreme kinds of agricultural protection carried out in the name of price support.

There is thus an important role for the state in agricultural marketing, deriving from two general grounds for state action. There is firstly the provision of:

those public institutions and those public works which though they may be in the highest degree advantageous to a great society are, however, of such a nature that the profit could never repay the expense to any individual or small number of individuals, and which it therefore cannot be expected that any individual or small number of individuals should erect or maintain.[10]

A quite extensive programme of hygienic controls, research and the provision of market information can be justified on this principle of Adam Smith's.

The second ground for state action concerns competition policy in the broadest sense—of the kind that the West Germans call *Mittelstandspolitik* (small business policy). It may, for example, be desirable, on both social grounds and grounds of marketing efficiency, to encourage a significant role for farmers' co-operatives by tilting the balance of advantage, if anything, in their favour. Whether farmers' organisations should be given monopoly powers is a different question, more concerned with price policy than with marketing efficiency; as with any monopoly, the possible benefits to farmers have to be weighed against the possible disadvantages to consumers.

On the other hand, the popular idea that agricultural marketing is peculiarly inefficient, and that any and every government intervention will achieve large economies for the benefit of farmers or consumers, is hardly borne out by experience. Most of the problems which have led farmers to criticise 'middlemen' do not have their origins in marketing inefficiency, and cannot effectively be tackled by marketing policies.

The British Marketing Boards
In the aftermath of the depression which began with the Wall Street crash of 1929, farmers in Britain and some other countries came to believe that the cause of the disasters experienced by agriculture lay in the arrangements for marketing their products. In Britain the outcome was the Agricultural Marketing Acts of 1931 and 1933, which established marketing boards as, in most cases, monopolistic selling agencies for agricultural producers. This development was part of a general turning away from liberal economic policies which characterised the 1930s. However, the fact that the marketing boards were given

more extensive powers than comparable bodies in most other democratic countries, and were—for the most part mistakenly—seen as a means of improving marketing efficiency, rather than raising and stabilising producer prices, was probably connected with the relative backwardness of co-operative agricultural marketing in Great Britain. Although the co-operative movement had originated in Great Britain—with the 'Rochdale Pioneers' in 1844—it had never developed in agricultural marketing as it did in countries such as Denmark, Germany, Sweden, Canada and the USA. The system of marketing through dealers and auctions was therefore subject to attacks which would probably have been more restrained—and for which there might have been less cause—if the private traders had been in competition with co-operatives. In the 1920s, a series of reports on agricultural marketing published by the Ministry of Agriculture, the 'Economic Series', combined useful description with less well-founded criticisms of the cost of marketing (i.e. of margins) and a not too well thought out advocacy of 'orderly marketing', which was conceived as the answer to all problems.[11] At the same time, theories of imperfect competition were used by some economists to suggest that competition in general did not work at all satisfactorily; these theories fell on receptive ears at a time when the existence of heavy unemployment made it clear that the economic system was not in fact working very well. This was then the background to the Agricultural Marketing Acts.

The Acts gave producers the right to submit a scheme for regulating the marketing of their product; once it came into force all producers had to comply with its provisions, unless exempted by the Act. The procedure to be followed in setting up a marketing board is laid down in the 1931 Act, with some modification by the 1949 Act; all the provisions are consolidated in the 1958 Agriculture Act.

Farmers' representatives (which normally means the National Farmers' Union) can submit schemes for a single commodity to the Minister of Agriculture, covering any part or the whole of Great Britain. The Minister must give notice of submission of the scheme, and objections may be made in writing to him. The Minister can then suggest modifications of the scheme to the original promoters, while serious objections are considered at a public enquiry. After agreement has been reached on the purpose and terms of the scheme, the Minister must bring the scheme before Parliament. If, or rather when, approved by Parliament, a poll of producers is taken, and unless two-thirds of the registered producers controlling two-thirds of the product of those voting support it, the scheme fails. If the scheme receives the requisite support, it comes into full force. When the scheme is finally approved, any minority of producers of the commodity affected, even though not in favour of the scheme, have to use the facilities and marketing channels provided.

By 1938, schemes had been introduced for hops, potatoes, pigs, bacon and milk. The schemes for pigs and bacon broke down, however, and were abandoned. Finally, in 1949, a third Agricultural Marketing Act was passed to allay the fears that producer marketing boards might work to the detriment of consumers. Under this Act, if the Minister considers that any act or omission of the Board is contrary to the public interest, he may direct it to change its policy.

What a Board Can Achieve

The Marketing Boards fall into two categories— compulsory trading Boards empowered to buy from farmers all produce offered for sale (or to control its sale), and non-trading Boards whose function is to regulate supply. The Wool, Hops, Milk and Egg Marketing Boards are examples of the first, the Potato Marketing Board of the second. (The Egg Marketing Board was wound up in 1972.) The underlying purpose of both types is to serve the interests of producers, and farmers look upon them as a means of raising farm-gate prices. It needs to be examined whether this view is justified.

In theory, a Marketing Board with statutory powers can improve the price received by the farmer (or by some farmers at the expense of others) in four ways; by raising the retail price; by reducing distributive margins; by preventing discrimination between producers, thereby ensuring that all producers receive the same price for the same products; or by imposing restrictions on the more successful producers in order to help the less successful. These principles apply equally well to comparable statutory marketing organisations in other countries.

Raising Retail Prices
The first method is simply to raise the wholesale and hence the retail prices. It is often assumed in farming circles that a Marketing Board will automatically enable this to be done; that, once farmers can 'speak with one voice' they will be able to obtain a higher price. But this can be done only if supply is restricted. If the supply increases, in the absence of change in demand, the price will fall; if the supply is decreased, the price will rise. Farmers sometimes argue that the price of motor cars and other industrial products is not affected by supply and demand. A firm producing motor cars they argue, sets a price to cover its cost and give a comfortable profit; why should not a Board do the same for farmers? The answer is that the power of a firm to set prices is based on its power to regulate supply. When the demand for cars falls off, firms tend to reduce production and maintain prices, or develop lower-priced models. If they continue to produce as many cars as before, they could sell them only by reducing prices.

This may suggest that agriculture might be justified in adopting similar tactics by restricting supplies, but the difficulties are much larger than in manufacturing industries, because of the large number of producers. Moreover, total supplies include both home production and imports, so that imports must also be limited if an attempt is to be made to raise prices. In the absence of controls on imports, restriction of home production is unlikely to have a significant effect on prices. On the other hand, the control of imports will by itself raise the prices received by home producers.

It should be added that the principle that a price rise depends on supply control applies to the general level of prices. There is some evidence that a marketing board, of the trading type, can prevent the complete collapse of prices which sometimes occurs when there is a sharp fall in demand or increase in supply. In these circumstances, a general demoralisation of the market can cause producer prices to fall temporarily to levels not justified by the general demand and supply position, especially when there are several stages in the distributive chain. By holding back supplies temporarily, and working on trade 'confidence', a trading board may be able to prevent this type of market collapse. But so can a non-monopolitic producer-controlled organisation. There are many cases in North American and Western Europe in which large farmers' co-operatives have been able to prevent a price collapse in exactly this way.

Supplies coming onto the market can be controlled in two ways: by setting limits to the production of individual farms—by means, e.g., of quotas for hops, sugar beet, and potatoes—or by price discrimination. Price discrimination is used by the Milk Board when it charges a higher price in the liquid than in the manufacturing market, and by the Potato Board when it restricts supplies for human consumption—by setting a minimum riddle size or through support buying—and diverts the remainder to animal feed. Price discrimination, however, can be practised profitably only in exceptional circumstances. There must be two or more distinct markets for the product, with differing price elasticities of demand and it must be possible to keep the market separate. These requirements are met *par excellence* in the case of milk, for which they are clearly defined liquid and manufacturing markets. By close supervision of a comparatively small number of creameries, the Board can ensure that the two markets are kept separate, and can profitably charge higher prices in the liquid market.

For other products, price discrimination is more difficult, and the power of a Marketing Board to influence prices is often limited. The British Egg Marketing Board—like many Continental egg marketing co-operatives—broke and froze eggs at times of glut and disposed of them to cake manufacturers. This method can stabilise prices and raises them slightly. In cereals, a Board can hold stocks and run them up or down to stabilise prices, but can only raise prices by withdrawing supplies from the home market and exporting them at a loss or otherwise disposing of them. A meat Board can store meat for short periods, although the cost of cold storage (and the deterioration of quality) imposes limitations.

But in none of these cases is a trading monopoly essential

to stabilise prices. A government support-buying organisation can intervene in the market to prevent severe falls in prices, as with cereals, butter and other products in the USA, Canada and most Continental European countries. In Britain, the Potato Marketing Board, although not a trading monopoly, engages in support-buying of this type.

Reducing Distributive Margins

The second way in which a marketing board may, in theory, be able to improve the price received by farmers, is by reducing distributive margins. As mentioned earlier there is a widespread—even if not very soundly based—belief that, as a result of high costs or profits, wholesale and retail margins for foodstuffs are too large. But a Board could reduce margins at any stage of distribution only by participating in that stage of distribution and effecting economies in it. Thus a Meat Board which bought animals from farmers, slaughtered them and sold the carcases to retailers might—if the previous system were inefficient—be able to reduce the margin for this stage of distribution, which in Britain accounts for about 14 per cent of the retail price of beef. But it would have no effect on the retail margin, which accounts for about 25 per cent. The only way in which it could do so would be by setting up shops of its own, although it is very doubtful if these would prove more efficient than private traders.

In the event, it is difficult to find cases in which British Marketing Boards have improved the efficiency of distribution, except in the case of the Wool Marketing Board. The rationalisation of milk collection from farms was undertaken by the wartime Government, not by the pre-war Milk Board, and the streamlining of the distributive system that has taken place in recent years for poultry, eggs, vegetables and to some extent meat has been the work of enterprising retail firms, local co-operative groups of farmers, and in some cases large individual producers. The Marketing Boards have on the whole been more concerned with maintaining prices than reducing distributive margins, but this is understandable in view of their constitution. They represent producers—enterprising and unenterprising, profitable and unprofitable—and they usually wish to remain on good terms with distributors; an organisation in this position is not well placed to bring about radical improvements in distribution.

Moreover, any economies in distribution which could be obtained by a Marketing Board could equally well be obtained by a voluntary farmers' organisation. If a farmers' co-operative can market more efficiently than its competitors it will either squeeze them out of business or force them to become equally efficient. Thus the reduction of distributive margins is not dependent upon the creation of a statutory marketing monopoly. In fact, a producer-controlled, but non-statutory marketing agency may do better than a board, in that a board may be hampered by the least progressive sections of the industry.

Whether it is achieved through co-operatives or boards, any improvement in the efficiency of marketing is naturally desirable, but it cannot be assumed that producers will necessarily obtain great benefits from it. Producers have an interest in seeing that their product is being marketed as efficiently as possible, when they are in competition with suppliers in other regions or countries. But the actual gains to producers from improved distributive efficiency may prove disappointing, in that the gains may be largely passed on to consumers.

A reduction in the distributive margin has theoretically the same effect as a reduction in a sales tax. That is to say, it can be represented as a fall in the supply curve, leading to a new equilibrium price at the retail and farm-gate level. If the elasticities of demand and supply are numerically equal, the benefits will be shared between consumer and producers. If the elasticity of supply is less than that of demand, the benefit will go mainly to producers; if it is greater the benefit will go mainly to consumers. The latter case seems to be the more usual one for foodstuffs. In Fig. 44 the intersection of demand curves at the retail and farm levels (D_r and D_f) and supply curves at the retail and farm levels (S_r and S_f), produces an equilibrium retail price (P_1) and an equilibrium farm-gate price (P_4). A halving of the distributive margin now causes the retail supply curve to fall to S_r^1 and the demand curve at the farm level to rise to

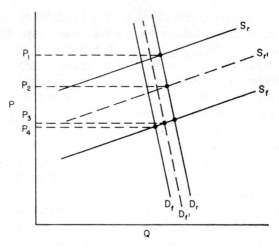

FIG. 44

D_f^1. This makes the retail price fall from P_1 to P_2, but the farm-gate price only rises from P_4 and to P_3, a smaller rise, even proportionately, than the fall in the retail price.

Preventing Discrimination between Producers
The third way in which a marketing board can theoretically help producers is by removing discrimination between them. When there are monopolistic elements in marketing, or ignorance among producers about prices, some producers may be offered less than others for similar produce. A marketing board can ensure that all are treated equally, after allowing for transport costs. It can even go further and pool transport costs, so that all producers receive the same price; the Egg Board, disbanded in 1972, paid the same price whether the eggs came from Cornwall, Middlesex or the Orkneys. Such an arrangement can be criticised for encouraging an uneconomic pattern of production although, as the remote areas are generally relatively poor, it may be defensible on grounds of equity.

As with distributive margins, however, discrimination between producers can also be prevented by farmers themselves, in that producer marketing organisations can enable farmers to avoid being exploited by local monopsonistic buyers. Farmers selling cattle can, for example, compare local auction prices with those of co-operative (or private) organisations buying on a deadweight basis. In Great Britain in recent years, competition of this type seems to have reduced market imperfections considerably. Prices differ slightly from one livestock auction to another, but there is little evidence of serious exploitation of farmers.

Restricting the more Successful Producers
The fourth way in which a marketing board can help a particular group of farmers is by imposing restrictions on the more successful producers in order to help the less successful. For example, the general tendency for the size of farm business to increase, and for small producers to be squeezed out, leads farmers adversely affected to demand restrictions on the larger producers. The Egg Marketing Board, for example, imposed a contract scheme which slowed down the growth of the largest producers.

The Egg Marketing Board attracted considerable criticism from both consumer groups and the more competitive producers. As discussed below, the current of opinion was moving against tightly monopolistic trading boards and in favour of boards with a more supervisory role. In accordance with the report of a reorganisation committee, the Eggs Board was wound up in 1972 and replaced by a non-trading Eggs Authority.[12]

Milk Pricing
The system of milk pricing operated by the Milk Marketing Board possesses certain peculiarities deserving special mention. Price discrimination combined with pooling of the receipts means that the price received by the producer for marginal production is higher than the market price of the extra milk. For example: if the price received by the Milk Marketing Board for liquid milk is 40p. per gallon, the price for manufacturing milk 20p., and the pool price received by the farmer 33p., it will pay individual farmers to expand production if their marginal costs are under 33p., a gallon. However, this increased produciton will be sold for 20p., which will tend to lower the pool price. If conditions remain unaltered, a system of price

discrimination of this type therefore tends to cause a fall in the pool price towards the level of marginal production costs.

In the late 1950s, the pool price was steadily reduced by increases in production that had to be used for manufacturing; as a result, the Government at one time proposed a change in the pooling system. The 1961 Price Review White Paper[13] stated: 'The need is to devise some modification of the pooling arrangements under the milk marketing schemes, which have the effect of obscuring from producers the consequences of producing more than can be sold profitably'. This implies that there should be some form of two-price system under which the producer would be paid a high 'liquid' price for the first so many gallons of milk produced, and a lower 'manufacturing' price for the rest. A system of this type would preserve the effect of price discrimination in raising the average price received, while avoiding the encouragement implicit in the pooling system, since farmers would receive the price which the marginal product actually fetched.

In the event, nothing came of the proposal, but the ways in which it might have been implemented are, nevertheless, worth examination, since the situation that produced it could recur. The quotas of high-priced 'liquid' milk could be allocated among farms in various ways: in particular, they could be based on production in a base year, or be the same for all farmers. And they could be saleable or non-saleable. If quotas were non-saleable, and determined by production in a base year, their imposition would tend to ossify the pattern of milk production; in the long run, this would reduce efficiency. If the same quota were set for all farms, the effect would be to force larger producers out of production and establish a pattern of small herds; this would reduce efficiency even more. However, if original quotas were allocated to base year production, and then made saleable, as has been done for hops under the Hops Marketing Board, many of these disadvantages would be avoided. Farmers who wished to expand could do so at a price, while farmers on marginal dairying land might be more ready to give up production if they could obtain a 'golden handshake' from the sale of their quotas. The price of the quota would reflect the value of the increased gallonage to the buyer.

It is, in fact, a general principle that, if production quotas are imposed, the price of the quotas will rise to a level at which marginal producers buying quotas make 'normal' profits, after including the cost of buying the quota in their expenses. If the quota is not saleable as such, but goes with the land, then the land will rise correspondingly in value. Or if a milk quota is attached to the herd, as has been done in some countries, then the herd will rise in value. It is only if the allocation of quotas is purely arbitrary that their value will not become embodied in a saleable asset. Such an arrangement is invidious, and rarely implemented, unless the quotas are so generous in relation to demand that their allocation is largely a formality.

The attaching of quotas to some physical asset such as land is a circuitous way of making them saleable, and there is little to be said for it. If production quotas are to be imposed at all, making them saleable is the economically least unsatisfactory arrangement. The sale of quotas can conveniently be undertaken by the issuing authority. For example, the Hops Board in Britain is ready to purchase quotas and resell them; in effect, it acts as a broker. The system appears to work quite well.

In the case of milk, a two-tier price system based on quotas, as envisaged in the 1961 Price Review, could be defended as a means of limiting output if supply were tending to seriously outstrip demand. This has periodically tended to happen in Western Europe, in spite of sharp falls in the number of dairy enterprises. Between 1960 and 1978, the number of milk producers in England and Wales fell from 151,625 to 64,723, but the number of cows remained virtually unchanged and, because of higher yields, milk output rose by 38 per cent. In the 'Nine' EEC countries over the same period, the number of cows also remained virtually unchanged, and output rose by 33 per cent.[14]

The Future of Marketing Boards
It has been suggested above that there has, in the past, been some confusion in Great Britain as to what a

Marketing Board can achieve. The Marketing Boards were put forward in the 1930s as a way of improving agricultural marketing, but they have not, on the whole, achieved significant results in this direction. This does not mean that the setting up of the Boards in the 1930s was not justified. In conditions of low and unstable farm incomes, the Boards were in some cases—although not all—able to raise and stabilise farm incomes. The Milk Marketing Board did this by means of price discrimination, the Hops Marketing Board by means of supply control. The Milk Board, moreover, has done good work in fields such as advertising and quality control, for which a Board is not strictly essential. Thus although some of the Boards—notably the Milk Board—have considerable achievements to their credit, the fact remains that the Agricultural Marketing Acts of 1931 and 1933 were passed in a hurry and under the influence of confused economic ideas. It later came to be realised that there were objections to the type of Marketing Boards set up, and attempts were made to change the system. It came to be widely felt that it was in principle wrong to grant price fixing powers to a body which only represented producers. Thus, on the report of an investigatory committee, a Milk Industry Bill was introduced in 1937 which would have transferred price-fixing powers to a Board representing producers, distributors and consumers.[15] However, the Bill was opposed by an alliance of the Milk Board and small dairymen opposing compulsory pastuerisation, and was withdrawn.

From about 1938 onward, however, there has been a tendency to favour the setting-up of commissions representing various interests rather than of the old type of producer-controlled Board. Thus although Boards were created after the War for wool and eggs, the proposal to set up a Meat Board has been regularly turned down by British Governments. On the ending of Ministry of Food control of agricultural marketing in 1954, the Conservative Government rejected the National Farmers' Union's application for a meat marketing board, and allowed complete freedom of entry in meat trading (with producers' prices supported by a deficiency payments scheme). The

National Farmers' Union responded by setting up a trading company of its own—the Fatstock Marketing Corporation—competing with private traders. Although the National Farmers' Union had strongly criticised decontrol, and the Labour Opposition had forecast catastrophic consequences, the free market worked on the whole very well, in spite of some teething troubles with the deficiency payments scheme.

In 1956, the Bosanquet Commission, reporting on the pig industry, came down against a monopolistic producer-controlled marketing board and recommended instead a Pig Industry Development Authority[16] representing various interests and with limited marketing powers. This was subsequently set up, although with less powers than proposed by the Commission. In 1964, the Verdon-Smith Committee, presenting the most comprehensive post-1954 examination of meat marketing in Great Britain, also advised against a marketing board, and proposed extending the principle of the Pig Industry Development Authority to the whole livestock industry.[17] This was later done, through the Meat and Livestock Commission set up by the 1967 Agriculture Act. In 1972, as mentioned above, the Egg Marketing Board was replaced by a supervisory Eggs Authority.

There has also been a trend in the post-war period to establish greater political control over the existing marketing boards. The power to set liquid milk prices, taken by the government in the War, has not subsequently been returned to the Milk Marketing Boards. At the same time, there has been a revival of interest in recent years in co-operative marketing (in particular 'group' marketing), which had previously been neglected in Britain.

With Britain's entry into the EEC in 1974, the future of the Marketing Boards seemed for a time to be in doubt. The marketing agencies in the other member countries did not possess the nation-wide monopoly powers which the British Boards, in theory, possessed; hence the British Boards were viewed in some circles as a 'distortion of competition'. However, after some scrutiny by the Commission, the existing Boards were implicitly accepted. They must, however, implement prices guaranteed under the Common Agricultural Policy, and the removal of barriers to imports (e.g. of milk) will inevitably reduce their effectiveness.

Although the existing Boards are likely to remain, the future will probably be characterised more by commissions, representing all the main interests, and exercising general supervision over marketing, than by the traditional type of producer-controlled Board. There is also likely to be strong competition between large marketing organisations—either producer-controlled organisations reaching forward from the farms towards the consumer, or organisations set up by retail firms reaching back from the retail outlet towards the farm. A system of this type, which combines general supervision of the marketing process with competition in the everyday business of marketing, is likely to serve the public interest better than either completely uncontrolled competition or a tightly organised monopolistic system.

Summary
Farmers regularly complain about the 'middleman', alleging that he takes too large a share of the retail price. However, these complaints usually reflect structural problems which cannot be corrected by marketing policy. Farmers, however, are justified in their belief that, because of the atomistic nature of the industry, they are in a vulnerable position, and should engage in vertical integration. This has been accomplished in many countries through co-operative marketing organisations. There is also a role for the state in establishing the framework within which marketing takes place. In Great Britain in the 1930s, farmers sought to solve their problems through the creation of monopolistic marketing boards. Those which have survived are likely to remain, but the tendency in recent years has been towards organisations of a more supervisory kind.

Notes
  1 Patton, H. S., *Grain Growers Cooperation in Western Canada*, Cambridge, Mass., 1938.
  2 *Report of the Committee of Inquiry on Contract Farming*, HMSO, London, 1972.
  3 Mellor, J. W., *The Economics of Agricultural Development*, New York, 1966, p. 342.

4 Clark, J. M., 'Towards a concept of workable competition', *American Economic Review*, 1940, p. 241.

5 Palmer, C. M., *Distributive Margins for Meat in Great Britain*, Agricultural Economics Unit, University of Exeter, 1975.

6 Hallett, G., *Urban Land Economics: Principles and Policy*, London, 1979, Ch. II.

7 Bannock, G., *The Smaller Business in Britain and Germany*, London, 1976.

8 One example is the tomato harvester, developed largely by the University of California. This was developed in conjunction with a thick-skinned tomato which can be picked mechanically. The two inventions together have allowed tomato production—at least for processing—to do without the large numbers of seasonal Mexican workers previously employed. At the same time increased yields, in the face of a market which has ceased to expand, have had the effect of squeezing out many smaller producers and canneries, leaving the field dominated by a few agribusinesses like H. J. Heinz, together with large farm co-operatives. The extension of mechanisation to other crops was in 1979 being challenged in a lawsuit on behalf of the farm-workers' union. This alleged that, in developing the harvester, the University of California acted contrary to its charter by developing a machine which increased private profits and was against the public interest because it destroyed jobs (shades of the Luddites!). Perhaps it could be argued that California, as a plantation economy next to a developing country, should have concentrated on 'intermediate technology'. However, if this lawsuit were to succeed, it could mean the end of virtually all agricultural research, because any new invention initially increases the profits of those who first adopt it.

9 As an example of the importance of marketing in the broadest sense, one might mention that Iran has in recent years become a substantial market for Danish cheese. The traditional Iranian cheese is a white cheese made from sheep's milk. The Danes produced a virtually identical cheese made from cow's milk and built up substantial exports during the latter years of the Shah's regime. Whether this trade will survive the 'cultural revolution' is uncertain, but the episode indicates the importance of discovering and meeting new demands—as well as the continuing enterprise of Danish farmers.

10 Smith, Adam, *The Wealth of Nations*, Bk. V, Ch. 1, Pt. III.

11 Ministry of Agriculture and Fisheries, Economic Series ('Orange Books' on marketing), 1925 onwards, and

especially *Milk: Report of the Reorganisation Commission for Great Britian* (Economic Series no. 44), 1936.

12 *Report of the Reorganisation Commission for Eggs*, HMSO, Cmnd. 3669, London, 1968.

13 *Annual Review and Determination of Guarantees*, HMSO, Cmnd. 1311, London, 1961.

14 Milk Marketing Board, *EEC Dairy Facts and Figures*, Thames Ditton, annual.

15 *Report of the Committee of Investigation for England on Complaints made by the Central Milk Committee and the Parliamentary Committee of the Co-operative Congress as to the Operation of the Milk Marketing Scheme 1933*, HMSO, London, 1936.

16 *Report of the Reorganisation Commission for Pigs and Bacon*, HMSO, Cmnd. 9795, London, 1956.

17 *Committee of Inquiry into Fatstock and Carcase Meat Marketing and Distribution: Report*, HMSO, Cmnd. 2282, London, 1964.

Further Reading

Allen, G. R., *Agricultural Marketing Policies*, Oxford, 1959, Chs. 7, 9, 10, 11.

Bateman, D. I., 'Agricultural marketing: a review of the literature of marketing theory and of selected applications', *JAE*, Vol. XXVII, no. 2, 1976.

Kohls, R. L. and Downey, W. D., *Marketing of Agricultural Products*, fourth edition, New York, 1972.

Morgan, D., *Merchants of Grain*, London, 1979 [a study of the US export-marketing corporations].

Price Commission, *The Marketing of Eggs*, London, 1974.
　Final Report on Fruit and Vegetables, London, 1974.
　Prices and Margins in Poultry Distribution, London, 1975.

Warley, T. K. (ed.), *Agricultural Producers and their Markets*, Oxford, 1967.

Whetham, E. H., *Agricultural Marketing in Africa*, Oxford, 1972.

Whetstone, L., *The Marketing of Milk* (Monograph 21), Institute of Economic Affairs, London, 1970.

Whetstone, L., *The UK Dairy Industry since 19701* (Monograph 21 Supplement), Institute of Economic Affairs, London, 1975.

CHAPTER THIRTEEN

Population and World Food Supplies

To put the question of population and world food supplies into perspective, let us begin with a brief account of the views of Thomas Robert Malthus (1766–1834), who is best known for his *Essay on the Principle of Population as it affects the Future Improvement of Society*, first published in 1798. He later expanded this short essay into a huge tome packed full of information about everything from the 'large number of academic bachelors in China' to 'the system of M. Condorcet with respect to the indefinite prolongation of human life'.

Malthus was not the first to discuss the question of population growth and food supplies, which, as he points out, was discussed by Aristotle, but he gathered together the views of previous writers; his work attracted considerable attention, and notoriety, at a time when Britain was entering the period of rapid population growth, similar to that which the developing countries have experienced since the Second World War. Malthus begins:

In an inquiry concerning the improvement of society, the mode of conducting the subject which naturally presents itself is:

(1) to investigate the causes which have hitherto impeded the progress of mankind towards happiness; and
(2) to examine the probability of the total or partial removal of these causes in future.

The principal object of the present essay is to examine the effects of one great cause intimately connected with the very nature of man; which, though it has been constantly operating since the commencement of society, has been little noticed by the writers who have treated this subject. The cause to which I allude is the constant tendency in all animated life to increase beyond the nourishment provided for it.

He suggests that this principle applies to humans as well as animal life, and lays down two postulates, to which most physiologists would probably still subscribe:

(1) Food is necessary to the existence of man.
(2) The passion between the sexes is necessary, and will remain nearly in its present state.

Population, unless checked in some way, will tend to increase in a geometrical progression (doubling every 25 years) while food production is likely to rise less rapidly, possibly in an arithmetic progression (i.e. 1, 2, 3, 4, . . .). This divergence gives rise to checks which either increase deaths or reduce births, and can be either 'human' or 'natural'. Human checks are infanticide or the

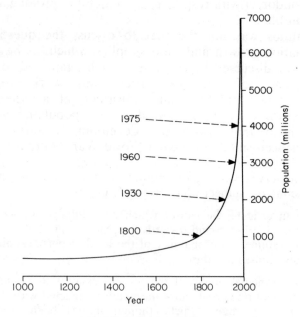

FIG. 45. World population growth

postponement of marriage. Natural checks are starvation or disease. Having painted this gloomy picture of population pressing on the means of subsistence, Malthus considers what can be done. He rejects infanticide on moral grounds. Contraception is not discussed, apart from an obscure reference to 'improper arts'; in any case the techniques of the time were crude in the extreme. He concludes that the only alternative to misery is the general adoption of late marriage ('unaccompanied by irregular gratification'), and that the economic system should not do anything to encourage the growth of population. In spite of having failed to provide any very convincing solution to the dilemma, Malthus ends on a note of hope:

It would indeed be a melancholy reflection that, while the views of physical science are daily enlarging, so as scarcely to be bounded by the most distant horizon, the science of moral political philosophy should be confined within such narrow limits, or at best be so feeble in its influence, as to be unable to counteract the obstacles to human happiness arising from a single source. But however formidable these obstacles may have appeared in some parts of this work, it is hoped that the general result of the inquiry is such as not to make us give up the improvement of human society in despair. The partial good which seems to be attainable is worthy of all our exertions; is sufficient to direct out efforts and animate our prospects.

Ever since Malthus, the debate has raged between those who predict disaster if there are any more mouths to feed and those who believe that human ingenuity will always find a way out. Malthus's fears for Britain seemed to be belied by the steady growth of prosperity in the Victorian era, while in the 1920s the decline in the birth rate led to exaggerated talk of 'race suicide'.

Malthusian fears have been revived by the rapid growth of population in the developing countries, resulting from a drastic fall in the death rate, resulting mainly from modern medicine and hygiene, without as yet a corresponding fall in birth rates. Although these countries are going through the same 'demographic transition' that European countries went through in the nineteenth and early twentieth centuries, the problems are in some way greater.

Population growth rates are higher than they ever were in Europe, and there are no large reservoirs of uncultivated land, like the North American prairies. The question concerning food supplies is: can agricultural production be raised sufficiently to both feed more mouths and also provide a better diet in parts of the world where it is inadequate, until the time when (hopefully) population stabilises? The associated question is: how far should family-planning programmes be supported, and a reduction in population growth supported? The arguments for seeking to limit population involve, of course, issues other than food, such as the quality of life on earth. Moreover, the factors influencing family size are complex, involving the status of women, the economic and social system, and religious and cultural attitudes.

Let us begin with the question of actual nutritional standards. Many people have an idea at the back of their minds that 'two thirds of the world is starving' without being able to say precisely how they obtained this information. It is an illuminating story.

In 1950, the Director-General of FAO (Food and Agriculture Organisation of the UN), Sir John Boyd-Orr, wrote a sombre article in an American magazine which included the passage 'A lifetime of malnutrition and actual hunger is the lot of at least two-thirds of mankind.'[1] This seemingly authoritative assessment soon reached the status of one of those things that everyone knows. Sir John (later Lord) Boyd-Orr never gave the source of this information, but its origin has been convincingly explained by an American authority on world food supplies (in the best book on the subject up to the 1950s).[2] The figure of two-thirds is that given in 1952 in the FAO's 'food balance sheets' for the percentage of the world's population living below a 'target' level of nutrution (in terms of calories and protein, including animal protein). However, even by the time Lord Boyd-Orr published this figure, these 'food balance sheets' had been withdrawn by FAO. The 'target' figures were largely based on the average diet of Western Europe and the USA, and it began to be realised in FAO that such a diet might not be necessary for health—even in the 'developed' countries, let alone in the rest of the world.

The reasons have been trenchantly explained by Dr Colin Clark.[3] There is considerable medical evidence that people in the developed countries eat too much. There is also no evidence that meat is an essential part of the human diet. If people like it and can afford it, well and good, but that is no reason for saying that those who eat little or no meat (sometimes for cultural reasons) are starving or even under-nourished. Food requirements vary according to body weight and the ambient temperature. In tropical countries, calorific requirements are substantially less than in temperate or cold countries. Calculations of desirable nutritional levels therefore require a more sophisticated approach than that originally adopted by the FAO.

In the 1960s the FAO steadily distanced itself from the suggestion that two-thirds of the world was starving, and in 1975 it published a far more scientific study, based on 1970 data. The conclusion was that 16 per cent of the world's population (outside China) was suffering from malnutrition, in terms of energy/protein supply. In the developed countries, only 3 per cent were in this category, whereas the figure for the developing countries was 25 per cent. Figures for starvation, in the strict sense of severe loss of body weight, are more tentative, since famines occur periodically and in different places; the expert consensus appears to be that in recent years it may have fluctuated between 1 and 2 per cent of the world population. It should be added that some of the most severe famines, such as those in Kampuchea and Uganda in the late 1970s, have been man-made.

The world food situation in 1970 clearly left much to be desired. Any such calculation must be subject to a wide margin of error, but a given percentage of the population undernourished may have secondary effects; persistent malnutrition in childhood may affect mental development. The latest projections indicate a slight rise in *per capita* food consumption in the developing countries by 1985.[4] The forecast for calories per day is 2,414 (as against 2,265 in 1972–4) and the forecast for protein is 63·1 grammes (as against 58·6). There will be slight increases in the consumption of wheat, rice, meat, milk products, fats and oils, and sugar. The conclusion would seem to be that,

TABLE 34

Estimated Number and Percentage of People with Insufficient Protein/Energy Supply by Regions (1970)

Region	Population Billions	Percentage below lower limit	Number below lower limit Millions
Developed regions	1·07	3	28
Developing regions*	1·75	25	434
Latin America	0·28	13	36
Far East	1·02	30	301
Near East	0·17	18	30
Africa	0·28	25	67
WORLD[1]	2·83	16	462

*Excluding Asian centrally planned economies.
Source: FAO, State of Food and Agriculture 1975.

although most of the world is not starving, there are serious problems of undernourishment in most of the developing countries. Moreover, because of their rapidly rising populations, these countries have to run in order to stand still.

The Growth of World Food Supplies
Estimates of world food supplies are published annually by FAO. For some countries these must be very wild estimates, but the broad changes indicated are probably correct. Total food production has increased dramatically since 1950, and it has increased more rapidly in the developing countries than in the developed countries. But because the increase in population has been so much more rapid in the developing countries, the rise in *per capita* food consumption has been less. In some countries—and in Africa as a whole—there has been little or no increase in

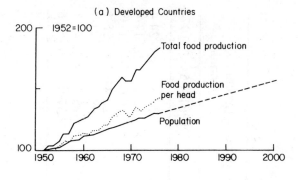

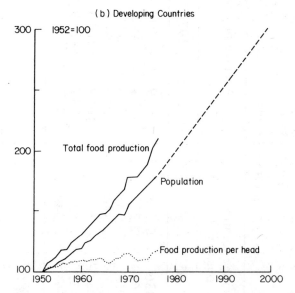

FIG. 46. Food production and population

Source: FAO, *Production Yearbook*.

food consumption *per capita* since the early 1960s, and any
faltering in production, due to bad harvests, can reduce
supplies to a dangerously low level. As one writer
commented in 1974:

In general, the Third World is not drifting towards famine, but
neither is it advancing rapidly to a state of abundance and
adequate nourishment.[5]

TABLE 35
Nutrition Levels

Region	Average calories per day		Average protein per day (grammes)			
			Total		Animal	
	1961–65	1974	1961–65	1974	1961–65	1974
World	2,436	2,568	65·9	69·0	21·8	24·4
Africa	2,165	2,212	55·9	56·3	11·1	11·4
Asia	2,068	2,233	53·8	57·8	10·0	11·9
South America	2,460	2,560	67·0	66·3	28·4	28·1
USA	3,345	3,504	101·8	104·3	68·8	71·7
Japan	2,551	2,835	73·2	85·9	25·5	41·1
UK	3,396	3,349	94·3	91·7	57·0	56·6

Source: FAO, *Production Yearbooks.*

Estimates of Total, Urban and Rural World Population; 1850–2000

Year	Population (millions)			Percentage Urban	Annual growth rates (%)		
	Total	Urban	Rural		Total	Urban	Rural
Currently more developed regions							
1850	352	40	312	11·4	0·6	1·9	0·4
1900	575	150	425	26·1	1·1	2·8	0·6
1950	857	459	398	53·6	0·7	1·9	0·3
1975	1,132	784	348	69·3	1·1	2·1	0·5
2000	1,360	1,090	270	80·1	0·7	1·3	1·0
Currently less developed regions							
1850	910	40	870	4·4	0·5	0·5	0·5
1900	1,075	70	1,005	6·5	0·3	1·3	0·3
1950	1,644	258	1,386	15·7	1·1	3·2	0·8
1975	2,836	772	2,064	27·2	2·2	4·4	1·6
2000	4,984	1,908	3,078	39·0	2·2	3·6	1·6
World							
1850	1,262	80	1,182	6·3	0·5	1·2	0·5
1900	1,650	220	1,430	13·3	0·6	2·3	0·4
1950	2,501	717	1,784	28·7	1·0	2·3	0·6
1975	3,968	1,556	2,412	39·2	1·8	3·1	1·2
2000	6,254	2,997	3,257	47·9	1·8	2·6	1·2

Source: UN Population Conference, 1974.

International Trade

In the world food situation, international trade plays a role, although a smaller role than is often imagined. Cereals dominate world food trade, but only around 10 per cent of world production has been exported in recent years. Imports of cereals are virtually indispensible for some countries which could not feed themselves, or only at enormous cost, and periodic imports are important for a larger number of countries, including the USSR, which experience large fluctuations in crop yields. But in all the large developing countries cereal imports are a very small proportion of total production.

The post-War period has seen a tendency for North America—and particularly the USA—to become the dominant world supplier. Whereas before 1939 the USA was only one among several countries exporting cereals, it has now become predominant in both wheat and feed grains. There has also been a change in the pattern of imports. Whereas before 1939 Western Europe was the main importer, its place has increasingly been taken by a range of Communist and Third World countries (and Japan). The imports of individual countries have fluctuated enormously, and some developing countries which were becoming increasingly dependent on imports in the 1960s, such as India, have since been able to become more self-sufficient. However, Asia, Africa, Latin America and the USSR constituted the main importers of cereals in the late 1970s.

TABLE 37

World Cereal Production and Exports, 1979

Cereal	Production (million tonnes)	Exports (million tonnes) World	Exports (million tonnes) US
Wheat	420	76	35
Coarse grains	732	101	71
Rice	374	12	2

Source: International Wheat Council.

At the beginning of 1980, the world grain market was assessing the implications of President Carter's decision to ban grain exports to the Soviet Union, following its invasion of Afghanistan. It seemed doubtful whether the ban could be made completely effective. In addition to the lack of enthusiasm of other grain exporters to follow the American lead, it is very difficult for an exporter to determine the final destination of such an anonymous product as grain. However, the cutting off of grain supplies for political reasons—however understandable the American President's bitterness at discovering that his lifelong beliefs about Soviet intentions had been erroneous—is bound to affect the grain-buying policies of both the USSR and other countries. International territorial disputes are not unknown in the Third World, and many developing countries are bound to ask themselves if they can safely depend on supplies of American grain as part of their development strategy, or whether they should not aim for greater self-sufficiency. It seems quite likely that the USA has lost not only its biggest customer, but other trade as well. The consequences are likely to include lower world prices and increased expenditure on price support by the US Government. The USA is almost certain to remain the world's largest grain exporter, because it has the land, climate, organisation, and know-how, but the extreme predominance which has developed in recent years may be reduced.

Whatever happens as the result of these political developments, however, it seems reasonable to assume that, in the future as in the past, most of the world's population will have to be fed on food grown within national boundaries. International trade is important for some countries, but it would be unwise to assume that the countries with large and rapidly growing populations could obtain more than a small part of their food needs from imports.

Retrospect and Prospect
Before looking to prospects for the future, it may be illuminating to look back over the post-War period. In the 1950s, production throughout the world increased rapidly, and substantial stocks of cereals built up in the USA and

Canada. The USA used much of its grain surpluses as food aid, and in the early 1960s supplied some 15 million tons annually, enough to feed 100 million people. When the monsoon failed 2 years running in India in the 1960s, it was only this food aid which prevented a serious famine. On the other hand, it has been argued that food aid discouraged some countries from building up their own agriculture. At about this time, some very grim forecasts were made. One book, by W. P. and P. Paddock, published in the USA in 1967, was entitled *Famine 1975!*, and concluded 'It is already too late. By 1975 famine conditions will be world-wide'. (It is dangerous to put a date on one's prophecies of doom.) Other writers saw grounds for hope in the 'green revolution' which was raising yields in many countries. In 1973, however, the rise in oil and food prices caused difficulties for countries like India, and at the same time a more sober assessment began to be made of the 'green revolution'. It began to be realised that increasing agricultural output required a package of changes, of which improved plant strains were only one.

Even among respectable economists and agronomists, there is a considerable range of opinion about future prospects, from the fairly pessimistic to the highly optimistic. At the optimistic end of the spectrum one might mention Dr Colin Clark, a penetrating commentator on agricultural affairs, who maintains that it is the growth of population which forces mankind to seek new ways of increasing food production, that attempts to control population are unnecessary, and that food production can be increased to feed any possible population up to the stage where emigration to other planets becomes possible.[6] Similarly optimistic is the famous futurologist Mr Herbert Kahn, with agricultural colleagues, in a report in connection with his encouraging prognosis for the next two centuries.[7] An American agricultural economist, Professor Cochrane, takes a 'guardedly optimistic view'.[8] More pessimistic are two distinguished French agronomists, who indeed maintain that the world's greatest famine has already begun.[9]

In spite of this wide distribution of views, most students of the question are agreed on certain points. There are technical possibilities for considerable increases in production, but they involve social as well as technical changes in agricultural production, and raise complex and not always foreseeable environmental problems.[10] Food aid can play a role, but probably only a limited role; the main emphasis must be on increased production in the developing countries. The usefulness of food aid is for more specific purposes, such as guarding against famine and oiling the wheels of development projects.[11] World population must ultimately be stabilised—and the sooner the better—but, given effective action to transform traditional agriculture in tropical countries and energetic programmes to encourage family planning, the forecasts of massive famine may be belied, as they have in the past. However, as the Duke of Wellington said after the battle of Waterloo, it could well be 'a damn close-run thing'.

Summary
Ever since Robert Malthus raised the issue of the relation between food supply and population growth, it has given rise to controversy. The developing countries today are experiencing very high (although slightly falling) rates of population growth, which will necessitate something like a doubling of food production over the next 30 years in order to maintain even current *per capita* consumption—let alone improve it. Although the extent of world hunger is often exaggerated, diets are often inadequate. There are considerable technical opportunities for increasing food production, but they raise serious environmental and organisational problems and do not—most, although not all, economists believe—remove the need to stabilise world population as soon as possible.

Notes
1 *Scientific American*, August 1950.
2 Bennett, M. K., *The World's Food*, New York, 1954, p. 189ff.
3 Clark, Colin, *Starvation or Plenty*, London, 1970.
4 FAO, *Agricultural Commodity Projections 1975–1985*, Rome, 1979, Table I, p. 4.
5 Griffen, K., *The Political Economy of Agrarian Change*, London, 1974.

6 Clark, Colin, *Starvation and Plenty*, London, 1970, and *Population Growth and Land Use*, London, 1967.
7 Chou, M., Hansen, D. P., Kahn, H. and Wittwer, S. H., *World Food Prospects and Agricultural Potential*, New York, 1977, and Kahn, H., *The Next 200 Years*, New York, 1976.
8 Cochrane, Willard W., *The World Food Problem: A Guardedly Optimistic View*, New York, 1969.
9 Dumont, René and Rosier, Bernard, *The Hungry Future*, London, 1969.
10 Brown, Lester R. and Finsterbusch, G. W., *Food: Man and His Environment*, New York, 1972, and Brown, Lester R., *Man, Land and Food*, Washington, DC, 1965.
11 Food aid has been interestingly used as part of an American programme of agricultural development in Turkey. The traditional system was based on a cereal rotation using fallow and communal grazing on the hills. But the fallow system provided low yields, and over-grazing in Spring and Autumn was beginning to cause erosion on the common grazing (typical dilemmas of 'traditional' agriculture). The advisory team advocated the growing of legumes in place of fallow and an opening and closing date for communal grazing. Food aid was provided as a safety net, or bribe, to encourage the farmers to undertake this change.

Further Reading
Some of the best short studies in recent years have been published by the Worldwatch Institute, Washington DC, for example:
   Worldwatch Paper 8, *World Population: Signs of Stress, Signs of Hope*, 1976.
   Worldwatch Paper 9, *The Two Faces of Malnutrition*, 1976.

CHAPTER FOURTEEN

Agricultural Policy in Developing Countries

The countries of the world are often divided into three groups; the 'developed' countries (Western Europe, North America, Japan, Australia, New Zealand); the centrally planned or communist countries; and the rest, the remaining countries of Asia, Africa, and Latin America. These countries, sometimes known as 'The Third World' have been successively described as 'underdeveloped', 'less developed', 'developing', and 'late developing'. It can be argued that this euphemistic progression is misleading, because it suggests a uniformity which does not exist, and perhaps implies questionable assumptions about the nature of economic change. However, these countries do have some similarities: they are tropical or sub-tropical; most of them have a high proportion of the population in agriculture (often over 50 per cent); and they have relatively low incomes. (Figures of *per capita* income are notoriously misleading as indicators of living standards, but huge differences mean something.) It has recently been generally recognised, however, that there are large differences between the countries of the 'Third World', in natural endowments, the nature of their problems, and the level and rate of growth of real income. The UN statisticians now distinguish three levels of developing countries (plus the oil-exporting countries, and two levels of 'developed' countries).

The Rise, Fall, and Partial Recovery of Development Economics
The economic problems of the 'developing' countries have

led to the emergence, since the Second World War, of a branch of economics generally known as 'development economics'. However, in this branch of economics—or at least its most fashionable and influential school—an initial boom has been followed by an agonising re-appraisal, since the facts stubbornly refused to fit the theories. Only slowly is a new consensus beginning to emerge in which, among other things, agriculture and rural development receive a higher priority. Let us therefore briefly review the history of development economics before turning to the specific problems of agricultural policy.

In a sense, development economics is as old as economics itself. To the 'classical economists'—Smith, Ricardo, Malthus, Mill, and in Germany, List—economic development, or growth, was of central importance. These writers differed on some aspects of policy: Ricardo and Malthus feared that economic growth might be halted by diminishing returns in agriculture, whereas Smith, List, and Mill were more optimistic. List favoured protection for industry in 'less developed' countries like Germany, whereas the British political economist favoured free trade; but they had much in common. Smith and List, for example, postulated stages of development, by which a primarily agricultural country came to develop industry and commerce. Moreover Smith, Mill, and List laid great stress on the educational, social, and political prerequisites of development—a widespread level of basic education, free speech and liberal political institutions, law and order, and the removal of economic systems (such as 'servile' forms of agricultural tenancy) which discouraged economic growth. These factors played a vital role in the process by which the currently developed countries became developed. In countries as diverse as Great Britain, Denmark, Germany, and Japan, reasonably efficient legal, administrative, and educational systems were established throughout the country before modern industrialisation began. At the end of the eighteenth century, Great Britain had a literacy level of around 40 per cent—probably equal to that of the 'Third World' in the mid-1970s. Moreover, all these countries experienced an agricultural revolution before an industrial revolution, although (as explained below) the agricultural revolution took very different forms.

After the Second World War, a few historically minded economists stressed the need for balance between agriculture and industry, the creation of an efficient administrative system, investment in people as well as technology; walking before you run. But their voices were drowned by those of the impatient advocates of a 'big push'. It was often assumed that—given independence, expropriation of foreign firms, a 'national plan', and a programme of industrial investment by nationalised enterprises—a modern industrial economy would speedily be achieved. The idea of population control was often dismissed—a view sometimes influenced by Marx's denunciation of Malthus as 'a hired hack of the bourgeoisie'. It would, of course, be an over-simplification to suggest that these ideas were uniformly accepted by the leaders of the less developed countries, or that they were always based on economic theorising. However, such ideas were common, especially in the African countries, and they were implicitly or explicitly supported by a great deal of development economics—notable exceptions being Professors Arthur Lewis (in his books), Myint and Bauer.

Surplus Labour in Agriculture?
One influential idea in development economics was that of 'surplus labour' in agriculture, and the best-known model was put forward by Sir Arthur Lewis himself, in a paper which is not altogether in keeping with the more eclectic approach adopted in his classic book *The Theory of Economic Growth*.[1] This model was developed by other economists, and is often known as the 'Lewis–Fei–Ranis model'. Its main assumption is that there is an unlimited supply of labour moving out of agriculture, and available for industrial employment at wages only slightly above the agricultural level. Within the agricultural sector there is more labour than is needed; the marginal product of labour is zero or even negative; therefore the movement of labour out of agriculture will not reduce agricultural output. The implication for policy is that investment should be concentrated on investment in manufacturing industry, which would soak up the labour leaving the land, and set the mechanism of development in motion.

It soon became clear, however, that things were not

working out this way. There were often difficulties in raising food production sufficiently fast to keep up with the very high rates of population growth. Moreover, the rural–urban migration often overstrained the ability of cities to provide the basic infrastructure, or sufficient housing or employment. In most of the less developed countries, there is more 'surplus labour' in the towns than in the countryside. Finally, rural poverty and urban employment exist alongside an often ostentatious style of living by the new urban *élite* (the Mercedes syndrome). This gloomy catalogue conceals very considerable differences between countries. Nevertheless, the problems of lagging food production and urban unemployment in many countries caused growing criticism of the 'accepted' doctrines of post-War development economics.

The Counter-Revolution in Development Economics
The criticisms took several forms. From the beginning, a few economists had given different explanations of the development process. Economists like Myint, Schultz, and Mellor gave accounts of the progressive change from a low-productivity, subsistence agriculture to a high-productivity commercial agriculture which indicated why a movement of population out of agriculture *by itself* could well lead to problems of food supply. People engaged in a (largely) subsistence agricultural system at least ensure that they and their families get fed. If some of them move to the town, those who are left have to produce a surplus for the towns, which involves both increased output per agricultural worker and also changes in the production and distribution system. This can happen, and has happened both in the past and in some of the Third World today, but it involves considerable organisational, technical, and social changes. These changes will not necessarily take place *merely* because labour is being drawn away to the towns.

A sharper critique of accepted doctrines was provided by Professor Bauer[2] who argued that state planning and international aid were being used to impose socially divisive and economically harmful policies by governments which had not even fulfilled the basic 'duties of the sovereign' described by Adam Smith. Bauer drew the conclusion that *all* international aid was misguided—a view not shared by many who would accept his criticisms of the way aid has, in fact, often been used. Bauer's criticisms of the policies adopted in many less developed countries are from a 'liberal' standpoint. But the French agronomist René Dumont has made somewhat similar criticisms from a Marxist standpoint.[3] His targets include the self-aggrandisement of African ruling *élites*, the neglect of the countryside, and a misplaced enthusiasm by many socialists for large Russian-style farms and sophisticated farm machinery. Other economists, notably Michael Lipton, have argued that 'urban bias'—or its absence—cuts across ideological differences; China and Tanzania have given priority to rural development, but so have Malawi and Taiwan.[4]

The arguments for giving greater priority to rural development are based partly on the need to help the largest concentrations of poverty, partly on the impossibility of providing adequate living conditions in Third World cities growing at their present rate. Bodies like the World Bank have in recent years argued strongly that priority should be given to rural development—which embraces both agricultural policy and wider aspects of rural policy—health, education, services like electricity and water etc.[5] The rural–urban migration has as much to do with primitive living conditions, and the lure of the 'bright lights' as with the level of income, so that the provision of some urban facilities in the countryside may be expected to slow it down. It is unlikely to stop it; if people want to live in towns, governments will not stop them in the long run, and liberal economists, at least, would not wish to stop them. However, if the dice were weighted less heavily in favour of the cities, this could be expected to slow down the rate of migration, which would give the cities a chance to at least provide some of the basic facilities for civilised urban living which are at present lacking. A less break-neck pace of migration, in conjunction with appropriate regional policies, could also encourage a more dispersed pattern of urban settlement in large cities, medium-sized cities and small towns. Such a pattern—which is in line with that in the developed countries—would enable better living conditions to be provided than when, as at present, migration is towards one or two monster cities in each country. Thus rural development is not only concerned with increasing food production and alleviating rural poverty: it is also an essential element in solving urban problems.

Is 'Traditional' Economics Relevant?

Before going further, a word is needed on methodology. This book has used a type of economic analysis which Samuelson calls 'the neo-classical synthesis'[6]—in particular the interactions of supply and demand via the operation of prices—and has applied this analysis primarily to the 'developed' countries. When one turns to agricultural policy in 'less developed' countries, the question has to be asked: is this type of analysis relevant to their problems? It has often been argued that it is not, although for differing reasons. One view is that Third World 'peasants' do not respond to economic incentives in the way that farmers do in developed countries. As Schultz puts it: 'The niggardliness of agriculture in poor communities is frequently attributed to particular cultural values'.[7] But Schultz (and Myint) have argued cogently that this interpretation is at least exaggerated. A closer study of the constraint under which farmers in Africa, Asia, or Latin America operate suggests that there are good economic reasons why these farmers behave as they do.

A different criticism comes from the spectrum of socialist economists stretching from J. K. Galbraith through Joan Robinson to orthodox Marxists. These economists argue that traditional micro-economics is irrelevant both in developed and less developed countries. They tend to define terms like 'competition' and 'consumer sovereignty' in extremely restrictive ways, and then show that they do not exist. As Mr Todaro puts it: 'Consumers as a whole are rarely sovereign about anything . . . . The ideal of competition is typically just that—an idea with little relation to reality.'[8] The idea that markets and economic incentives do not work has dominated a great deal of development economics. However (as indicated in Chapters 5 and 10) many 'mainstream' economists, ranging from free-market advocates to market socialists, hold that markets do work, although sometimes imperfectly, while centrally planned systems also have imperfections. It is a question of comparing the imperfections of both, and choosing between them. To quote a very wise economist, the conflict between the socialist (or centrally planned) economies and the market-dominated economies is no longer really a controversy between advocates of planning and advocates of *laissez-faire*.

It is rather a controversy over the best methods of deciding, in the first place, which future, out of various alternative futures, the society wishes to move into and, in the second place, which means offer the best prospect of moving the society where it wants to go. On the whole, the socialist societies rely on the ideological dispositions of a small elite communist party to decide the first, whereas the market-type societies are more apt to rely on the broader wishes of the population. In regard to the second, the socialist societies tend to rely on hierarchical and often rather coercive organizations whereas the market-type societies rely more on "social agriculture", that is, using the forces of natural liberty but introducing new pressures, motivations, and rewards largely through the "grants economy", especially through government one-way transfers, so that the result is more to the political satisfaction of the total society. The socialist society is more like a factory and the capitalist society is more like a farm. This perhaps may account for the fact that agriculture is the great failure and the spectacular success of the two societies respectively. The so-called third world of the poor countries of the tropics unfortunately seems to have a remarkable capacity for falling between these two stools. These countries introduce enough intervention in the market, especially through quantitative controls, to destroy the operations of natural liberty and the invisible hand, or at least cut off some of its fingers! At the same time they do not substitute hierarchical centrally planned organizations.[9]

Economics or Political Economy?
Any discussion of 'traditional' or 'neo-classical' economics is complicated by the fact that these terms can be used in different ways. They have been applied by critics to the economics of (to quote the authors of some recommended books) Lewis, Myint, Kindleberger, and Boulding. The

approach of these economists is by no means uniform, but is in all cases very different from the kind of 'neo-classical' economics which consist of an elaborate structure of purely deductive reasoning, often making use of unsophisticated branches of mathematics such as the differential or integral calculus, but taking little account of institutional factors.

There are two criticisms of this type of economics, in its application to less developed countries. The first is that social, political and economic institutions—often closely intertwined—play a crucially important role in the rural economy of less developed countries. Professor Boulding cites development policy as one of the main failures of economics in the previous generation and writes:

The failure to provide poor countries with helpful advice is, I suspect, the result of the fact that economists have worked too narrowly within the confines of their own abstractions and their own discipline and have not recognized that a development process is something which involves the total society and that hence purely economic models have a very limited value.[10]

This criticism of academic over-specialisation is almost equally valid for developed countries, and reflects a weakness of 'modern' economics. Most of the 'classical' political economists such as Smith, Malthus, List, and Mill, and many later economists such as Marshall, devoted considerable attention to economic and social institutions. The concentration on purely theoretical models began in the 1930s, and has since come to dominate University economics. But there are still a few surviving practitioners of 'political economy', and some signs of a renewed interest in this 'dated' approach.

The second criticism of 'neo-classical' economics is that it is marginalist; 'the lore, of nicely calculated less or more'. This incremental approach is all very well in developed economies where there are no huge imbalances but is, it is argued, inappropriate in less developed countries, where 'quantum jumps' are taking place—or should take place—in the whole organisation of the economy. There is a valid distinction here. In Western Europe or North America, it is reasonable to assume that, for example, the price of land or labour roughly indicates its opportunity cost, and that farmers will combine inputs so as to produce at the point, more or less, where marginal cost equals price, which is some kind of economic optimum. Similarly, there will, in most cases, be a tendency for farms to move towards the optimum size (in spite of frictions, which can on occasion justify state intervention). But in the case of the Latin American latifundia discussed below there is no ground for any such belief. Changes which—most people would feel—are desirable both on economic and social grounds are unlikely to take place without a radical 'land reform'.

However, the quest for a 'new' kind of economics to deal with the problems of massive structural change can lead us back to some very old 'political economy'. The problems which less developed countries are experiencing today have considerable similarities with the problems of countries like Great Britain and Germany in the early nineteenth century, which provided the background to the writings of the classical economists—among whom one can include Karl Marx. Great Britain, in particular, was experiencing rapid population growth, massive rural–urban migration, a break-up of traditional village society, and a concentration of agricultural landownership. Thus it is not surprising that some 'classical' ideas have once more attracted interest; particularly Malthus's theory of population pressing on the means of subsistence, Ricardo's theory of land rents rising as the result of population pressure, and Marx's theories of 'polarisation' and class struggle. When these theories are stressed to the exclusion of all other considerations they can be misleading; indeed, as predictions they all proved erroneous for the countries in connection with which they were originally put forward. However, they raise important issues in the development process which receive little emphasis in one kind of 'neo-classical' economics which dates from the era of Victorian stability which followed the violent upheavals of the first four decades of the nineteenth century. It is unfortunate that most students (or even teachers) of economics do not nowadays read even extracts from the great economists of the past; without such a background one can easily become a prisoner of current economic fashion.[11]

'Classical' Economics

Two 'models' of the 'classical' economists are relevant to rural development in the Third World today. The first, developed by Malthus and Ricardo, postulates that population is increasing, while land resources are limited. As more labour is applied to a given area of land the marginal product, and hence the average product of labour, falls.[12] At the same time, the increased demand for food causes its price to rise and it becomes profitable to cultivate poorer, marginal land (if there is any). Land on the margin of cultivation will just cover its costs of production, but intra-marginal land will earn an increased 'economic rent'.[13] If the land is owned by owner-occupiers, the higher price will increase their incomes (assuming that they produce for sale, and that this gain is not offset by a fall in the size of holding). But if the land is owned by landlords, to whom the tenants pay a competitive cash rent, then rents and landlords' incomes will rise. (A rise in the food price from *a* to *b* in Fig. 47(b) will push back the margin of cultivation from *c* to *d* and increase total rent by the dotted area.) As J. S. Mill put it 'They [agricultural landlords] grow richer, as it were, in their sleep, without working, risking or economising.'[14]

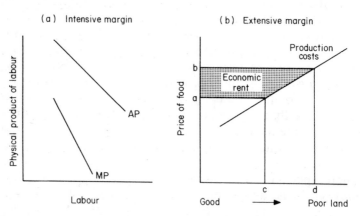

FIG. 47. Relationships between increases in labour, production, land-rent, and demand for food in Third World countries

At the very time that such ideas were becoming the 'conventional wisdom' (Mill's book became the standard economic textbook for a generation) they were ceasing to be valid. Food prices and rents had risen sharply over the period from about 1780 to 1859, but thereafter they fell (in both real and money terms). This fall resulted at first from the opening-up of new land in North America but later because technical improvements increased yields (thus raising the AP (Average Product) and MP (Marginal Product) curves. The weakness in the Ricardian model was its underestimate of the possibilities for technical improvements, and these possibilities have certainly not been exhausted in the Third World, even though the process is difficult and complex.

However, the Ricardian–Malthusian model can be applied to many Third World countries today (provided that one bears in mind how it ceased to apply in the countries which are now developed). In the densely populated countries of South and South-East Asia, increasing population has led to a fall in the size of holdings, which has not always been offset by increased yields. Moreover, when there is a tenancy system, landlords are able to benefit from high rents because of competition for land, in return for which they provide little in the way of services. There are often strong monopoly elements in the position of landlords (and moneylenders, who are frequently the same people) in these countries. The rationale of regulations limiting the extent of tenancy is the need to transfer monopoly gains from the landlord to the occupier, both to relieve poverty and also, hopefully, to put the occupier in the financial position where (given other prerequisites such as knowledge and ancillary services) he can achieve the take-off into higher-yielding agriculture. However, the problem is exacerbated by too many people trying to obtain land. Thus a solution requires changes outside the sphere of agricultural policy—the provision of more non-agricultural employment (hopefully not all in the big cities) and a reduction in the rate of population growth.

A different type of Malthusian dilemma is faced by Africans practising shifting agriculture, or nomadic agriculture, especially in the Sahel region south of the Sahara. Even though the population density is extremely low (less than 10 people per square mile) it is too high, given the prevailing technical and organisational system. The increase in human and animal populations has caused a decline in the length of fallow periods, of overgrazing, which is leading to a breakdown in the soil system and an extension of the desert. The marginal and average product curves are shifting *downwards*. The problem here arises from the absence of property rights. When land is communally owned but individually used, there is no incentive for an individual to carry out improvements, limit grazing etc., since the individual who did so would not benefit from doing so. This problem has come to the fore with the growth of population resulting from the application of modern medicine, but it goes back much further. Libya was once the granary of the Roman Empire, and its transition to desert seems to have been caused more by changes in agricultural systems than in the climate. In Roman times there was settled agriculture, in either latifundia or smallholdings given to retired soldiers.[15] But with the collapse of the Roman Empire, settled agriculture declined and was replaced by nomadism. To halt, and if possible reverse, the 'ecological disaster' in the Sahel region, requires a change to a system of settled agriculture, involving property rights. Whether these property rights should be exercised by family farms, collective farms, or other types of legal entity, is a different question.

Marx and Marxism
Marx is a better-known and more influential economist than Ricardo or Malthus primarily because (in theory at least) the world's most successful revolutionaries—Lenin and Mao-tse-tung—were Marxists. The collectivisation of Russian agriculture, however, owes little to Marx, or even Lenin, being solely the creation of Stalin, whose agricultural ideas still dominate thinking in the growing number of communist countries and 'one-party democracies'. Marx, however, possesses an importance in his own right; his analysis, for all its faults, was broader than that of his followers, and some of his ideas are

accepted by non-Marxists. Marx argued that technology determined social and political organisation. 'The hand mill creates a society with the feudal lord: the steam mill creates a society with the industrial capitalist.' Within this social and political organisation, different economic classes struggle for power; political and intellectual movements are solely the manifestation of economic class interests. However, the wide variety of classes which had previously existed was being polarised into two groups; the bourgeoisie and the proletariat. The bourgeoisie (which did not have the meaning of 'middle class' which it later acquired) was a small group which owned all the land and capital, and were getting steadily richer: the proletariat was the large group of labourers who owned no land or capital and were getting steadily poorer. This growing polarisation would eventually lead to the communist revolution, after which there would be no class conflicts.

Some of these ideas can be accepted, at least partially, by non-Marxists. Changing technology does bring social and political changes with it; different classes do sometimes have differing interests; political movements do sometimes have an economic basis. The economic interpretation of history is therefore illuminating. Non-Marxists differ from Marxists in not considering it a complete explanation; in not seeing all class struggle as between the bourgeoisie and the proletariat; and in not being convinced that communist revolutions have eliminated exploitation and class interest.

In his discussion of agricultural rent in *Capital* Marx, like Ricardo, assumed the existence of the prevailing British hierarchy of large landowners, tenant farmers and hired workers.[16] He was aware that this system was peculiar to Great Britain, but he assumed that this was the most advanced form of capitalist agriculture, and that all countries would inevitably move towards such a system. The large agriculture landlords would get richer and richer and the labourers poorer and poorer, until the communist revolution became inevitable. This is not what has happened. The predominant form of agriculture in the countries with the most efficient agriculture has been the family farm, mainly owner-occupied. Britain has experienced the same trend. The great estates have gone, or at least lost all the social and political power they once had, and the number of hired workers has declined enormously.

However, the kind of agrarian system which Marx analysed has parallels in some countries, especially those Latin American countries where the latifundia system prevails. In such a case there are indeed divergent interests between the latifundia owners and the rural proletariat. Indeed the extent of polarisation is greater, and the economic virtues are less, than in the case of the British nineteenth-century system. Similar clashes of class interest occurred in Latin American countries like Mexico, or Middle Eastern countries like Iran, Iraq or Egypt before land reform was carried out.

A rather more indirect parallel with Marx's theory of polarisation is the process whereby the change from a society based on status to one based on contract leads, in the first instance, to greater inequality; some farmers do well, while others do badly, or are forced to become labourers rather than independent farmers.[17] This has a close parallel in the changes which occurred in British agriculture from the fifteenth to the early nineteenth century. As a social historian puts it:

The bottom of the trouble lay deeper, in the growing pains of historic change. Society was passing from a system of wide distribution of land among the peasants at easy rents ... to a gradual abolition of peasant holdings and their consolidation into larger, highly rented farms. This implied a further reduction of mere 'subsistence agriculture' and a greater production for the market. It may or may not have been a change from a better form of life to a worse, but it was certainly a change from a poorer to a richer countryside.[18]

This growing inequality during the early stages of the transformation of traditional agriculture raises problems for agricultural policy. How can these growing pains of historic change be alleviated without sacrificing the benefits of the change?

Agrarian Problems of Africa, Asia, and Latin America
It is possible to draw certain distinctions between the agricultural problems of Africa, Asia, and Latin America.

In Africa (South of the Sahara) the traditional form of agriculture is 'shifting cultivation'. A piece of land is cleared and burned, leaving tree roots in the ground. It is planted with crops (using hand tools) and cropped for a couple of years. It is then allowed to lie fallow, and another area is cleared. This is a satisfactory method of cultivation, provided that population densities are low. But with the rapid increase in population of recent years this system is becoming inadequate and even pernicious. Not only do diminishing returns to labour set in, but the soil structure begins to break down as the fallow periods are reduced. Over-grazing by nomadic herdsmen has a similar consequence, and the two systems have led to the steady spread of the desert. A changeover to a form of settled agriculture which can maintain soil fertility is taking place, but one of the problems is that scientific investigation of tropical agriculture is still in its infancy. The natural conditions (e.g. alternate droughts and downpours) are different from those of temperate agriculture, and there is not the background of over a century of research on temperate agriculture.

Asia, on the other hand, has had settled agriculture for centuries and—notably in rice cultivation—has evolved sophisticated systems well suited to the natural environment. The problem is that the rise in population, given the inability of the cities to absorb the growth of rural population and the lack of virgin land, is resulting in a fall in the size of the cultivated area per person and an incipient Malthusian situation. The 'green revolution' is beginning to introduce higher-yielding systems, but it also gives rise to social problems; some farmers are successful while others are squeezed out.

Latin America, on the other hand, has a relatively low population density and bountiful gifts of Nature; the fact that it has not altogether fulfilled its promise lies in people and policies rather than in physical conditions. One unfortunate legacy of the Spanish colonial past is still the 'latifundia' system, consisting of large estates extensively cultivated and functioning more as a part of the political and social structure than as efficient economic units. 'Land reform' has often been advocated, and is beginning (although, as mentioned below, this provides no miracle cure). There are thus differences between Africa, Asia, and Latin America, but all face the problem of transforming traditional agriculture.

Transforming Traditional Agriculture

The man who farms as his forefathers did cannot produce much food no matter how rich the land or how hard he works. The farmers who has access to and knows how to use what science knows about soils, plants, animals, and machines can produce an abundance of food although the land be poor. Nor need he work nearly so hard and long.[19]

So begins an important book by a Nobel Prizewinner in Economics. It is a theme which has been documented in several more recent books (see Further Reading). Professor Mellor distinguishes three stages in agricultural development:

(1) *Traditional agriculture, mainly for subsistence*. This is technologically stagnant, using well-tried methods designed to minimise risk, and with little capital output. Increased output can be obtained by using more labour and land, but if the supply of land cannot be increased in the same proportion as the increase in population, sharply diminishing returns to labour set in.

(2) *Technologically dynamic agriculture; low capital technology*. This type of agriculture makes use of scientific discoveries to increase yields, but still uses substantial amounts of labour. It covers the rotational system introduced in eighteenth-century Britain to increase yields and provide more winter animal feed, as well as the techniques of rice farming pioneered in Japan in the twentieth century.

(3) *Technologically dynamic agriculture; high capital technology*. This is represented by the agriculture of, say, the USA, in which a great deal of machinery is needed, but little labour.

Some countries have gone direct from Stage 1 to Stage 3 (the USA, or even the Soviet Union). For the developing countries, however, there are great advantages in concentrating on Stage 2, using 'intermediate technology'. When a country has limited capital and abundant labour it is simple common sense—and orthodox neo-classical economics—to use techniques which use plenty of labour and little capital.[20]

One point stressed by all the economists who have written on the transformation of traditional agriculture is that scientific discoveries—the breeding of 'miracle' wheat strains, etc.—are only one facet of the process. The application of science to agriculture requires investment in people as well as things, and involves gradual, but ultimately far-reaching, changes in organisation. A traditional farmer, or a virtual serf who simple takes orders, has to evolve into an entrepreneurial farmer who combines inputs scientifically and makes use of an extensive back-up system for credit, equipment, know-how, and marketing.

If traditional agriculture is to be transformed, farmers must possess: (a) the motivation to achieve change; (b) the assurance that the change will benefit them; (c) access to ancillary services necessary to achieve the change and sufficient knowledge to use them. The motivation to achieve change usually takes the form of a desire for improved material well-being, although non-material considerations, such as nationalist or ideological fervour, have often played a role for a time. Regimes which allow no scope for personal advancement, however, rarely prove successful in the long run. This point is now accepted even by some communist governments.[21] The farmer also needs assurance that any improvements he makes will—at least in large part—benefit him and his family rather than, for example, a landlord or merchants or the government. Land tenure and marketing systems are thus important. Finally, the farmer needs a certain level of education and self-confidence, as well as access to services which he cannot provide himself, and which assume a growing importance as agriculture becomes more developed. For all these reasons, the institutional context is important in determining whether agriculture develops, and how it develops. From this point of view, the history of the countries which are now classified as 'developed' contains some useful lessons for the developing countries.

In the countries which are now developed, the industrial revolution was preceded by an agricultural revolution which raised yields, achieved higher output with less workers, and so provided food for the expanding cities. But this transformation of traditional agriculture took place in very different ways. In Great Britain, the reorganisation was largely carried out by a landowning class. The outcome was a pattern of consolidated holdings which, for the time, were large and used an advanced technology. Most of the farms were tenanted, and employed substantial amounts of hired labour. There was therefore a three-tiered pyramid-like social and economic structure. At the top were a few thousand large landowners. Under them were some 200,000 tenant farmers, and under them were a million agricultural labourers.

This structure had a considerable influence on Karl Marx's theory of capitalist development, based on the idea that society was becoming more and more polarised into a small land- and capital-owning class (the bourgeoisie) and a mass of workers who owned no land or capital (the proletariat). The third volume of *Capital* contains several references to the British system of agricultural landownership.[22] Marx was aware that this system was peculiar to Great Britain, but he assumed that it represented the most advanced form of capitalist agriculture. This proved not to be correct; other countries adapted a system based mainly on family farms (and Great Britain also moved in this direction).

Of the classical economists apart from Marx, several were highly critical of the English land-tenure system. Adam Smith argued that large landownership, as well as 'servile tenures' were discouragements to the natural progress of opulence. His complaint ·against large landowners was their 'conspicuous consumption'.

To improve land with profit, like all other commercial projects, requires an exact attention to small savings and small gains, of which a man born to great fortune, even though naturally frugal, is very seldom capable. The situation of such a person materially disposes him to attend rather to ornament which pleases his fancy than to profit for which he has so little occasion.[23]

This criticism applies even more to the kind of landowners who existed in the Middle East until very recently, and still exist in Latin America. These landowners have shown far less interest in agricultural improvement than eighteenth-century English landlords. (Nor have they built the fine country houses which, in historical retrospect, have perhaps been a better investment than Smith allowed.)

Smith's second point is that slavery and 'servile tenures' discourage improvement because the occupier lacks security.[24] A farmer is unlikely to invest time and money unless he knows that he, or his children, will gain the benefit. This criticism applied strongly to the Irish system of tenancy (as well as to some forms of tenancy which still prevail in Latin America). On the other hand, Smith pointed out that if a tenant had security of tenure, which was almost as good as freehold ownership, he would be ready to invest. This point about the economic desirability of secure legal titles is still relevant in many developing countries. However, the effects of any particular tenancy system can vary considerably according to the economic and social context in which the system is operated. For example, share-cropping has a bad name, being associated with an impoverished, downtrodden class of occupier; but in New Zealand, which has one of the most efficient and socially equitable agricultural systems in the world, share-cropping has none of these connotations; it is a useful stepping-stone to owning a farm.

In the middle of the nineteenth century, J. S. Mill went beyond Smith's criticisms, advocating 'a regime of peasant properties' in which 'the whole of the produce belongs to a simple owner, and the distinction between rent, profit, and wages does not exist'. He argued that there was no necessary connection between peasant proprietorship and 'an imperfect state of the arts of production', and that there were great social advantages.

No other existing state of agricultural economy has so beneficial an affect on the industry, the intelligence, the frugality and prudence of the population, nor tends on the whole so much to discourage an improvident increase in their numbers—and that no existing state therefore is on the whole so favourable, both to their moral and physical welfare. Compared with the English system of cultivation by hired labour, it must be regarded as eminently beneficial to the labouring class.[25]

These ideas were taken up in Denmark, the USA and other highly efficient agricultural countries. Denmark, for example, deliberately took a different course from England. It organised its enclosure movement so as to produce a system of family farms, originally of around 20 hectares, backed up by marketing, credit, and even advisory services organised by the farmers themselves. It is perhaps unfortunate that the Danes hardly ever advise developing countries, since their history—and that of Japan—has many lessons to teach. Miss Barbara Ward, writing of the way in which agricultural development can help to solve urban problems in developing countries, draws on these lessons. After mentioning (in 1969) the 'green revolution' of the 1960s, she writes:

A chance therefore exists that the critical increase in agricultural productivity which preceded industrialisation in the 18th and 19th centuries is now belatedly appearing all through the developing continents. There are choices to be made. Larger harvests and greater incomes may well be directly engrossed by feudal owners or enterprising farmers. Large holdings can be mechanised, smaller farms consolidated, increasing the gains of the fortunate and ruining the little man. As in east Prussia in the 19th century, a vast region also devoid of small diversified urban centres can be handed over to mass production largely for export on vast estates in which both direction and income are concentrated in a single hand. Or as in Denmark at a comparable period, small farmers can be given the benefits of credit and education, achieve the advantages of scale through co-operation, and use a network of small market towns where storage, administration, high schools and extension headquarters help to build up a lively population which in turn attracts traders and light industry.[26]

The USA also implemented a 'land reform' in the Great Plains region in the second half of the nineteenth century. The first settlers were large ranchers who employed 'cowboys' and carried on a very extensive type of agriculture (a brief era immortalised by the cinema). The ranchers were followed by family farmers encouraged by the Homestead Act of 1862. Professor J. K. Galbraith, a sound agricultural economist, points out that the USA's agricultural development called for:

a land policy which would get the land settled and ploughed, and a transportation system which would get the products to market. To this end the government surveyed the land, gave 160 acres to anyone who had proved his good intentions by farming it for a few months, and subsidised the building of railways. These essentials being provided, development proceeded with unexampled speed. It was our unquestioned fortune that community education experts, grain marketing analysists, home economists, vocational counsellors, communications specialists, or public safety advisers had not been invented.[27]

The large ranches gradually gave way to family farms, both because of government policy, but also because the family farms proved more efficient. The average size of holdings in the Western USA fell sharply between 1860 and 1900; later, in the 1940s, it began to rise, as mechanisation enabled a family to cope with a larger holding, and as a gradual process of amalgamation set in. This 'U curve' could well be followed in Latin American countries now engaging on land reform.

Japan offers an even more relevant example to the developing countries. After the opening up of the country in 1868, a land reform was initiated which eventually led to farmers either owning their land or possessing secure leases. At the same time, an intensive research programme was initiated to develop techniques suited to smallholdings; the result was a striking improvement in yields. Japanese farms are still small in terms of acreage, and they use small-scale machinery, but they have yields some three times those of some other Asian countries. In the early stages of its agricultural modernisation, Japan also relied heavily on a land tax to finance development. The virtue of a tax based on the area of a holding—as distinct from a tax on income—is that the marginal tax rate is zero. There is therefore not the same discouragement to increased output as there is with a tax on income, or even a tax on consumer goods.

The Russian Model

A very different influence in some developing countries has been that of the Russian (and more recently the Chinese) Revolution. In both cases, collectivisation was undertaken for political and economic reasons. A class of independent farmers is unattractive to a communist party, since it encourages 'bourgeois' attitudes, and poses a potential threat to the dominance of the party. If farming is organised in units employing large numbers of people, control over the rural population by party officials is facilitated. It was also argued that family farming was grossly inefficient, and that large units could make full use of modern machinery. However, the immediate effects of Russian collectivisation were extremely harmful. It produced a famine in which between 2 and 4 million people died (in addition to the 10–12 million killed in Stalin's 'purges') and grain production reached the 1928 level only in the early 1950s. Since then, agricultural production has increased, but has always caused problems. On the other hand, the state farms were used to bring about a large extension of the cultivated area, in the previously uncultivated Eastern areas. This opening-up (although not without failures, such as Khruschev's 'virgin lands' campaign) was necessary, and required some kind of state intervention. Perhaps state farms were appropriate for this type pf pioneering (although the USA and Canada show that it can be done in other ways). However, the consensus of agricultural economists is that the large Russian state and collective farms have not been a great success. The economies of scale in farming are exhausted at a very low number of workers per farm, while the managerial diseconomies rise sharply. The economies of scale lie in processing, marketing, and the supply of credit, fertilisers, etc.; it is possible to secure economies in these sectors e.g. by co-operative organisations) while obtaining the economic and—some would think—social advantages of family farming. This has indeed been the experience with some export crops originally grown in Asia and Africa on plantations. Although the plantations remain—sometimes suffering from a politicised system of nationalisation—smallholders supplying processing and marketing agencies have tended to increase in importance.

The Chinese Commune

In recent years Mao's China—with particular reference to the rural commune—has become the Utopia which, for many western intellectuals, Stalin's Russia represented in the 1930s. In his textbook, Mr Todaro writes that 'if the reports are to be believed' China has eliminated unemployment and inflation and established a regime based on social justice.[28] It is already clear that the reports were greatly exaggerated. (As a non-Sinologist, it seems to the author that, in a country in which, in 1976, an earthquake can kill half a million people without anyone outside the country hearing about it for a year, detailed accounts of the economic system deserve to be treated with some caution.) According to the present Chinese Government, and the slightly greater number of Chinese-speaking visitors, the cultural revolution was both a cultural and an economic disaster, which set China back a generation. However, the available information on the communes does suggest that they have, in some ways, been more successful than the Russian collective farms.[29] They have, in particular, displayed ingenuity in devising a low capital technology for agricultural production, and in developing simple manufacturing industry in the countryside, thus slowing, although not stopping, the flow of population to the big cities. The Chinese have also—if the reports are to be believed—had considerable success in reducing the rate of population growth, although by means of intervention in personal life which most societies would find unacceptable.[30] However, the more successful aspects of the communes are not all characteristically communist—although they may well be characteristically Chinese. The idea of using labour-intensive low-capital technology when labour is abundant and capital scarce, is fully in accord with neo-classical economics, as is the idea of developing small-scale manufacturing in the countryside, and discouraging a high rate of population growth. Moreover, the Chinese have been equally successful in agricultural production under a 'bourgeois' system in Taiwan, and in trade and commerce on a barren rock with no natural advantages whatever (Hong Kong), or on what could easily have been a decaying imperial fortress (Singapore). The Chinese seem to do well under any kind of regime which guarantees law and order and allows reasonable scope for enterprise. As Mr Todaro very sensibly concludes, other countries should not necessarily emulate the communist Chinese system but should learn from 'the lesson it provides about agricultural output and promoting rural industries through small-scale labour-intensive activities supported by publicly provided economic and social services'.

Land Reform

The term land reform is defined by a leading authority on the subject as 'the redistribution of property or rights in land for a benefit of small farmers and agricultural labourers'.[31] It has been carried out mainly in countries in the Middle East and Latin America which previously had a highly concentrated pattern of landownership (and in the case of some Latin American countries which still have). It is both a social/political change and also an economic one. The social/political aspect raises value judgements. The change has certainly been welcomed by those who benefit, and most 'liberal' commentators regard the consequent rise in the status of a previously depressed class as highly desirable. Marxists, on the other hand, are opposed to it as an end in itself, and support it only as a transitional step to collectivisation. On the economic side, there are two questions. First, has land reform facilitated the transformation of traditional agriculture and raised production? (One should really add 'compared with what production would have been in the absence of the change', but this creates difficulties.) Second, what are the associated policies, or the types of land reform, which cause production to rise further than it falls? There is now a fair amount of evidence on these questions. Some land reforms have been economically successful (in the sense of maintaining or raising production); some have been economically unsuccessful, at least for a decade or so.

Apart from the highly successful Japanese land reform, the first land reform in developing countries was instituted in Mexico during the revolution, with the slogan 'Land and Liberty'. This movement began in 1911 and continued until the 1930s. The immediate effects were disappointing; the production of corn (i.e. maize), the basic rural food, was much the same in 1940 as in 1910, although population had increased by 50 per cent (however, continuous violence can hardly have encouraged agricultural production). In the 1950s and 1960s, public investment in the breeding of new strains of cereals paid off; output rose by some 7 per cent a year—among the highest rates in the world, and well in excess of Mexico's very high rate of population growth. Mexican agriculture was—with some justification—held up as a success story. By the late 1970s, however, it became clear that the gains from this phase were being exhausted. Further expansion was hampered by poor transport and credit facilities, as well as natural limitations—primarily of water, a more severe constraint than land. Population is still doubling every generation, and family planning programmes have received little official support. In 1979, the Mexican President announced that priority was to be given to increasing production rather than to a further distribution of land which, if continued, would 'leave everyone with a piece of dirt'. The outlook for the 1980s is that sustained industrial growth, fuelled by oil revenues, will take place without a solid agricultural base. This is likely to strain the fabric of rural society, maintain the exodus to overcrowded cities, and force the expenditure of a substantial proportion of the oil revenues on food imports. The conclusion would seem to be that, after two decades, the land reform as such proved a success, but that Mexico is now suffering from a failure to invest sufficiently in the things which must accompany land reform—and from a failure to bring down its rate of population growth.

Some land reforms have been less (economically) successful than Mexico's; some more successful. The least successful were those in Bolivia after 1952 and in Iraq after the revolution of 1958; in both cases agricultural output fell by about half, and has been slow to recover. In Bolivia, the land was seized in a peasant uprising. In Iraq the impetus came from communists seeking to set up collective farms. These were not set up, but the disruption of the period had long-lasting effects. However, as one survey concludes:

The Bolivian and Iraqi reforms both stand as evidence of the high cost of postponed reform and unplanned implementation. Yet admitting the seriousness of the production declines, it is wrong to condemn the reforms on that ground alone. These countries have ended two of the world's worst neo-feudal oligarchies. This is no mean achievement.[32]

The Egyptian reform of 1952 was much more successful. It was carefully prepared and carried through, with apparently no adverse effects on production (although Egypt faces serious difficulties given its enormous population density in the Nile Valley, while the Aswan High Dam was not proved an unmixed blessing).[33] The Iranian land reform of 1962 has attracted very different verdicts. At the time, it was denounced by overseas students as a sham and by the mullahs as contrary to the Koran. Qualified observers judged it to be a genuine change, and socially desirable, but reserved judgement on how well it would be followed.[34] After the Islamic revolution of 1979, the leaders of the revolution complained that agriculture had been neglected under the Shah's regime, as demonstrated by the fact that Iran had changed from being a food exporter to being a food importer. There would appear to be some truth in this criticism; the old order appears to have been destroyed without sufficient effort devoted to putting something better in its place; e.g. irrigation has suffered from unclear divisions of responsibility. Nevertheless, it is estimated that output in the 1960s and 1970s rose by 2–3 per cent, which is quite respectable. Demand rose faster than food output, but much of this demand resulted from increased incomes and newly acquired tastes for expensive, non-traditional food.

These and other examples indicate that land reform can cause temporary disruption, and that there can, on occasion, be conflicts between social and economic objectives. On the other hand, land reform can be economically satisfactory, provided that the size of holdings is reasonable (given prevailing circumstances, the availability of irrigation, etc.) and provided that the land reform is accompanied by a continuing development of appropriate credit, marketing and extension services (and a system of local and regional political administration, which is often rudimentary). Moreover, it has to be recognised that the transition from serf to entrepreneurial farmer will not take place overnight. It will probably take more than one generation; it took centuries in Europe. Land reform is thus merely the beginning of a process.

Land tenure institutions define a farmer's status. They create the framework of expectations within which hopes and fears motivate him to economic activity.—Reform is sometimes dramatic but the slow evolutionary impacts of measures taken *after* the reform decide ultimate success or failure'.[35]

'Urban Bias'

In many developing countries agriculture, and more generally the countryside, has been neglected, and this situation to a large extent still prevails. Lipton (*op. cit.*) gives a wealth of examples of the low percentage of public investment going to agriculture, of governments mainly concerned to hold down food prices in the supposed interests of urban consumers, of enormous differences in the numbers of doctors or teachers per thousand people in the cities and the country, and of the low status and salaries of agricultural extension workers.

Correcting 'urban bias' is easier said than done, but at least the issues can be clarified. The main requirements can be listed as follows:

(a) Prices high enough to encourage production. On this point, 'traditional' development economics still raises the possibility of a 'backward sloping supply curve' and quotes the low price elasticities of supply calculated for some developing countries.[36] These calculations suffer from all the difficulties of supply elasticities (see Chapter 8), combined with the fact that there is often a subsistence sector, a mixed subsistence–commercial sector, and a mainly commercial sector, with a changing balance between them. The main point is that low prices in the end affect output by means of the effect on investment.

(b) A substantial share of national public investment for agriculture in particular, and for rural areas in general, and a high priority for the development and dissemination of appropriate agricultural technology.

(c) A pattern of financial and non-financial incentives which attracts people of sufficient calibre into ancillary services such as extension and marketing.

(d) A 'people-orientated' rural policy which is genuinely concerned with improving the ability of the rural population to earn higher incomes and also to enjoy the benefits of modern living conditions.

Summary

'Development economics' has tended to look on agriculture merely as a source of labour for the cities, and has in consequence been led to policy recommendations which are now widely regarded as having been mistaken. In the light of lagging food supplies and urban unemployment in many developing countries, current theory indicates the need for a higher priority for agriculture and rural development. Although the same basic economic concepts can be applied both to 'developing' and 'developed' economies, some aspects of economics are of particular relevance to the developing countries, including parts of the 'classical' economics of Ricardo, Malthus, and Marx. The main needs of the developing countries are simultaneously to reduce their very high rates of population growth and to achieve a transformation of 'traditional' agriculture. Technical progress is only one aspect of this transformation; both for economic and social reasons an appropriate pattern of farm tenure has to be encouraged by government policy. The economies of scale are more in processing and marketing than in production, so that it is possible to combine family farming with efficient ancillary services. The agrarian problems of Asia, Africa, and Latin America differ considerably, but many countries in all three areas suffer from 'urban bias'; more emphasis on both agriculture and rural industry is needed, both to increase food production and also to reduce the rate of rural–urban migration, which raises serious problems for the rapidly expanding cities.

Notes

1 Lewis, W. A., 'Economic development with unlimited supplies of labour', *Manchester School*, May 1954.

2 Bauer, P., *Dissent on Development*, London, 1972.
3 Dumont, R., *False Start in Africa*, 1966. Professor Dumont, who advised Fidel Castro on the collectivisation of Cuban agriculture, subsequently showed some disappointment with the practical implementation of socialism—or, rather, questioned whether it was 'real' socialism (*Is Cuba Socialist?* 1974). Professor Dumont's socialist attitude—as distinct from his agricultural knowledge—is widespread in intellectual circles. The agricultural ills of the Third World are attributed to Western neo-colonialism acting through multi-national corporations; see *How the Other Half Dies*, by Susan George (Penguin, London, 1976), an attack on 'agri-business' and export crop production, which forms the basis of a film, *Growing Dollars*, produced by UN–Habitat, Geneva. (The films on agricultural development available on loan from the UN–Habitat library can be strongly recommended for teaching purposes—provided they are taken with a pinch of salt. The reality is more complex. Export crop production, organised by foreign companies, can sometimes be disruptive, but many countries are better off producing crops for export than if they produced only domestic food crops.
4 Lipton, M., *Why Poor People Stay Poor*, London, 1977.
5 The World Bank, *The Assault on World Poverty*, Washington, DC, 1975.
6 Samuelson, P., *Economics: An Introductory Analysis*, Ch. 1.
7 Schultz, T. W., *Transforming Traditional Agriculture*, New York, 1964, p. 26.
8 Todaro, M. P., *Economic Development in the Third World*, London, 1977, p. 11. His analysis of rural problems, however, and his recommendations for policy, are in effect based on the kind of 'neo-classical' economics used by Myint.
9 Boulding, K. E., *Economics as a Science*, New York, 1970, p. 51.
10 *Ibid.*, p. 153.
11 Any reader who wishes to acquire some knowledge of the 'classical' economists can be recommended to start with *A History of Economic Doctrines* by C. Gide and C. Rist, which has the virtue of including extensive quotations. He might then compare two very different analyses published in the same year. *The Communist Manifesto* by Marx and Engels and the last chapter (Bk. V, Ch. XI) 'On the scope and limits of the laissez-faire or non-interference principle' in *The Principles of Political Economy*, by J. S. Mill.

12 Mellor, J. W., *The Role of Agriculture in Economic Development*, New York, 1966, p. 161ff.
13 Stonier, A. W. and Hague, D. C. *A Textbook of Economic Theory*, London, 1972, p. 276ff.
14 *Principles of Political Economy*, Bk. V, Ch. II, para. 5.
15 Burton, John, 'Externalities, property rights and public policy', in Cheung, Steven N. S. *et al.*, *The Myths of Social Cost* (Hobart Paper 82), Institute of Economic Affairs, London, 1978.
16 *Capital* (1909 edn.), Vol. III, p. 726ff.
17 The relevance of the Marxian/Ricardian type of analysis, in which one group gains at the expense of another, is explicitly maintained by Keith Griffen in *The Political Economy of Agrarian Change*, which tends to stress the unfortunate consequences of the 'green revolution'. But there is a danger of seeing only one side of the question. A reporter recently in Java puts the other side. 'Jakarta's anti-technology lobby, led by a few trendy foreigners filled with the stale, pre-cooked campus populism of the 1960s, tells you that all those new motorcycles (averaging 46 per village, and trucks, mini-buses and cars too) plus the 10–12 television sets per village and all the new brick houses replacing bamboo huts, don't mean anything because they belong to the naughty, selfish, landowning minority. The truth, as they tell it, is that the landless and nearly landless 40–70 per cent who count are getting nothing but poorer. The new rich technology is to blame; it has driven down wages, put field hands out of work, shattered village welfare institutions and led to land concentration. [This pessimism] is wildly unjustified. In four months visiting 35 villages scattered the length and breadth of Java, your correspondent found a few pockets of poverty. . . . With these very few exceptions, village Java has prospered dramatically in the past five years. When asked "Are you richer or poorer than you were 10 years ago?" every villager replied that he was better off'. *The Economist*, July 14, 1979, p. 48.
18 Trevelyan, G. M., *English Social History*, London, 1944, p. 119.
19 Schultz, J. W., *Transforming Traditional Agriculture*, New York, 1964, p. 3.
20 In his popular book *Small is Beautiful* the late Dr K Schumacher advocated the use of 'intermediate technology' especially for the developing countries but in some respects also for the developed (in order to economise on non-renewable resources and reduce pollution). He criticized

economics for supporting the introduction of inappropriate technology. But this criticism applies mainly to certain 'advanced' economists who have forgotten simple micro-economics. It does not apply to all mainstream economists; Professor K. Boulding, the author of a textbook of mainstream economic theory, has also coined the phrase 'spaceship earth' and written well on this theme. And the American agricultural economists who have concerned themselves with the developing countries have been strong advocates of 'intermediate technology'.

21 The author once attended a lecture at Cambridge by a visiting Hungarian economic planner, chaired by a Professor of Economics of a Marxist persuasion. The lecturer concentrated on the need to restore economic incentives in the Hungarian economy, which prompted expostulations from the chairperson. The tough communist official complained afterwards, 'That sort of thing is all right in theory but it isn't realistic. How can you expect people to work if they don't get anything out of it?'

22 *Capital* (1909 edn.), Vol. III, p. 726ff.

23 *The Wealth of Nations*, Bk. III, Ch. 11.

24 It is widely assumed in 'progressive' intellectual circles that slavery and the slave trade were the products of 'capitalism' and *laissez-faire*. In an undergraduate essay I have even had Adam Smith described as a 'supporter of a system based on slavery'. In the interest of more than merely historical accuracy, it should be pointed out that the period in which many British fortunes were made in the slave trade or the West Indian slave plantations—the 17th and 18th centuries—was one dominated by Mercantilist ideas that the state should exercise close control over commerce. Several Mercantilist writers held that the slave trade was good business for the country. Adam Smith's attack on 'the mercantile system', and on slavery, was part of a movement of ideas which led Britain to take the lead in banning the slave trade.

25 *Principles of Political Economy*, Bk. 1, Ch. IX, para. 4.

26 'The Poor World's Cities', *The Economist*, 6 December 1969, p. 56.

27 Galbraith, J. K., *Economic Development*, Oxford, 1964, p. 58.

28 *Economic Development in the Third World*, p. 229ff.

29 Clark, Colin, 'Economic development in Communist China', *Journal of Political Economy*, April 1976.

30 Aird, John S., 'Fertility decline and birth control in the People's Republic of China', *Population and Development*

Review, June 1978, p. 225. Also The Economist, 1–7 March 1980, p. 38.

31　Warriner, D., Land Reform in Theory and Practice, London, 1969, p. xiv.

32　Raup, M., 'Land reform and economic development', in Johnston, B. F. and Southworth, H. M., Agricultural Development and Economic Growth, New York, 1967.

33　Brown, L. R. and Finsterbusch, G. W., Food: Man and his Environment, New York, 1972.

34　Warriner, Land Reform in Theory and Practice, Ch. V. and Ann Lambton, The Persian Land Reform 1962–66, Oxford, 1969.

35　Raup, M., 'Land reform and economic development', p. 267.

36　Ghatak, S., Development Economics, London, 1978, p. 107ff.

Further Reading

The outstanding book on development economics is *The Theory of Economic Growth*, by W. A. Lewis; in its broad historical sweep, as well as its subject, it bears comparison with *The Wealth of Nations*. Probably the best textbook is *Development Economics* (third edition, New York, 1977), by C. P. Kindleberger and B. Herrick, although *Economic Development in the Third World* (London, 1977), by M. P. Todaro devotes more space to agricultural systems. *The Economics of the Less Developed Countries* by H. Myint (London, 1964) is a thoughtful essay which marked a turning-point in the subject.

The following deal specifically with agricultural policy in developing countries:

Dumont, René, *Types of Rural Economy*, London, 1970.

Hayami, Y. and Ruttan, V. W., *Agricultural Development: An International Perspective*, San Francisco, 1971.

Johnston, Bruce F. and Kirby, P., *Agriculture and Structural Transformation: Economic Strategies in Late Developing Countries*, London, 1975.

Mellor, J. W., *The Role of Agriculture in Economic Development*, New York, 1966.

Schultz, T. W., *Transforming Traditional Agriculture*, New York, 1964.

Warriner, Doreen, *Land Reform in Theory and Practice*, London, 1969

CHAPTER FIFTEEN

Agriculture and the European Economic Community

The problems of world agricultural trade and of agricultural price policy have been complicated in recent years by the development of regional economic groupings, in particular the European Economic Community. The Treaty of Rome (1958), by which the six nations of France, West Germany, Italy, Belgium, Holland and Luxembourg founded the EEC, laid down that the common market to be established between member states was to include agriculture and trade in agricultural products (Article 39). However, the introduction of a common agricultural policy has given rise to some of the greatest difficulties in the formation of the Community. It also became clear in the abortive negotiations over British membership in 1961–63, and the discussions leading up to British membership in 1973, that problems concerning agricultural policy and trade in temperate agricultural products presented some of the greatest difficulties in British accession to the Community. Moreover, the non-European exporters of temperate foodstuffs—the USA, Canada, Australia, New Zealand, Argentina as well as certain sugar-exporting countries—have been concerned at the effect of the adoption of a common agricultural policy on their exports.

Why, in view of all these problems, has the EEC laid such emphasis on establishing a common agricultural policy? The reason is partly that the founders of the Community, anxious to achieve, in the words of the Preamble to the Treaty of Rome, 'an ever closer union of the European peoples' by means of economic integration, felt that the Community would be incomplete and unsatisfactory if it excluded such an important economic sector as agriculture. But there were also narrower considerations of national self-interest. France saw in the Community an opportunity to expand its agricultural exports, mainly at the expense of suppliers outside the Community, and of thus helping to alleviate its agricultural problems.

The problems of introducing a common market in foodstuffs and a common agricultural policy in the EEC arise from the fact that member states over the years—often for good reasons—have adopted differing methods of price support or differing levels of guaranteed prices. Changes in methods of price support, or in price levels, necessitated by the introduction of a common policy can raise difficulties for both producers and consumers, especially if the changes have to be made over a short transitional period. The common policy can also be more protectionist *vis à vis* non-members than the aggregate of previous national policies.

Take the simplified case of two countries A and B; both protect their agriculture, but A has less efficient farm structure and a higher producer price level. If a customs union is now formed between the two countries, and a common agricultural policy introduced, a common price will have to be introduced (apart from regional differences based on location in relation to supplying and consuming areas). Taking the most likely limits, the common price can be either at the high level in A, or the low level in B, or some level in between. If the price is set at the lower level, farmers in A will suffer a loss of income, unless some compensating 'non-price subsidy' is introduced. If the price is set at the higher level, production will be stimulated in B, so that the net effect is to bring about a higher level of production in $A + B$, and a lower level of imports, than would have prevailed in the absence of the union. Even if a price mid-way between those of A and B is adopted, the effect may still be to increase production. Because of the irreversibility of agricultural supply, the increase in production in B may well be greater than the reduction in A, especially if B has a more elastic supply curve.

An example which comes close to this theoretical case is the wheat situation in France and West Germany. On the founding of the EEC, France had lower wheat prices than West Germany, together with lower yields and a significant acreage of potential wheat land. West Germany had a small acreage of wheat in upland areas which was marginally profitable, but otherwise wheat production was in areas where it would have been profitable even at lower prices. It might therefore be expected that a move to a common price lying between the French and German levels would stimulate production in France more than it would reduce it in Germany. This is, broadly speaking, what has happened. German production has increased slightly (because of the continuing rise in yields); French production has increased considerably. There has since been a steady rise in the degree of self-sufficiency of the Community, which by 1980 had become a net exporter of several products.

The Treaty of Rome
The difficulties in the introduction of a common agricultural policy were foreshadowed in the Rome Treaty; although it does not go into any detail, it lays down certain general principles. Article 39 lays down that a common agricultural policy shall be implemented in one of three ways:

(a) common rules concerning competition;
(b) compulsory co-ordination of the various national market organisations;
(c) European market organisation.

It goes on to refer to the need to take account of the particular character of agricultural activities, arising from the social structure of agriculture and from structural and natural disparities between the various agricultural regions', and to 'make the appropriate adjustments gradually'. It also authorises the granting of aids 'for the protection of enterprises handicapped by structural or natural conditions' (Article 42). In the main, however, the working-out of common agricultural policies was left to the Commission of the EEC.

The First Mansholt Plan

The Commision's initial proposals for agricultural policy, and its general agricultural philisophy, were given in the 'first Mansholt plan' of 1960 (named after the Dutch Vice-President of the Commission responsible for agriculture).[1] The aims of agricultural price policy were outlined as the maintenance of satisfactory farm incomes in the Community, while at the same time avoiding over-production and respecting traditional trade flows with non-members. Free trade in agricultural products within the Community is a requirement of the Rome Treaty, but the Commission rejected free trade between the Community and the rest of the world. It proposed that the price level in the Community should be stabilised, and held at a level above that on the world market, by a variable levy on imports, plus (although the Commission was originally a little shamefaced about this) a subsidy on exports to bridge the gap between the price inside the Community and on the world market. Quantitative restrictions on imports operated by national governments, and limitations on the level of production to which guaranteed prices applied, were to be abolished.

The protectionist price policy was justified on two grounds; firstly, that time must be allowed for a planned and orderly reorganisation of agricultural production; secondly, that prices on the world market were, it was alleged, kept artificially low by the actions of exporting countries. But the report did not merely use the imperfections of the world market to justify protection. It supported efforts to bring about 'normalisation of conditions on the world market' and also a policy of structural reform in the Community's agriculture, both of which would make possible freer agricultural trade between the Community and the rest of the world. It stated quite bluntly that the raising of agricultural incomes in the Community required, in addition to price support, a reduction in the numbers engaged in agriculture, the amalgamation of uneconomically small farms, and the withdrawal of the poorest land from cultivation. It referred favourably to the idea of subsidies to farmers in marginal farming as a means of relieving hardship without obscuring agricultural reorganisation.

The first Mansholt plan exemplified both the strength and weakness of much Continental thinking. It presented a coherent, and in many ways enlightened, long-term strategy for agricultural policy, for which one looked in vain in contemporary British offical publications. But the reliance on the setting of an appropriate common price as a means of achieving both the desired level of agricultural production and the desired level of farm income can be criticised as naive. When differing national prices are brought to a common level, and national limitations on production removed, there may not in fact be any common price which both avoids over-production and achieves the desired level of farm income. And in the tough political bargaining by which a common price must inevitably be decided, there are bound to be strong pressures for setting the price as high as possible. Moreover, the Commission under-estimated the difficulties of sweeping away the national agricultural policies based on conditions in the various member countries, or indeed the objections to doing so.

The Common Agricultural Policy
The policies proposed in the 'first Mansholt plan' were in many respects accepted by the Council of Ministers of the Community. In the setting of the common prices, however, an understanding political process resulted in prices being set above the level recommended by the Commission. The Commission's initial attempt in 1961 to bring about a slight reduction in the German cereal price (and an increase in the French cereal price) as a first step towards a common price level, brought violent protests from the German farm organisations. Protracted and often tense negotiations followed, and it was not till 1964 that an agreement on cereal prices was reached, to be effective from 1967. The cereal prices, especially the wheat price, were higher than that recommended by the Commission. Once this decision had been made, it was necessary to set the prices of livestock products at a correspondingly high level, in order to make livestock possible and prevent an undesirable switch to cereal production. Another change that occurred between the Commission's original proposals and the

political compromise eventually accepted was a reduced emphasis on structural reform.

The financing of the common agricultural policy (CAP) is through the European Guarantee and Guidance Fund, generally known as FEOGA from the initials of its French title 'Fonds Européen d'Orientation et de Garantie Agricole'. The Commission's original proposal—which, with certain modifications, has been accepted—was that import levies should be paid into this fund, which would then finance price support operations, e.g. support buying and export subsidies ('guarantee'), as well as measures of structural reform ('guidance'). This principle is one which favours food exporting countries at the expense of food importing countries, since the former will pay less import levies into the fund and receive more out of the fund for export subsidies. As the main food exporter in the Community, France thus stood to receive far more from the fund than she paid in. The French argument was that the arrangement simply put all member states on the same footing, by removing the advantages that any of them might gain from imports of cheap food. It is probably more realistic to see in the arrangement one which was attractive to the Commission because of its 'supranational' character; insisted on by France for the economic benefits she obtained; and accepted by the rest of the Six as part of the price for French participation.

The Levy System

Even in the 1960s the price support system actually introduced was not as clear-cut as that envisaged in the original Mansholt proposals. Quotas for sugar beet were retained (although increased) and it was found more satisfactory to use deficiency payments for olive oil and durum wheat. From the beginning, therefore—even before the complications caused by 'green' currencies and the enlargement of the Community—the CAP was more complex and less uniform than originally envisaged. Nevertheless, the general principle was implemented of free movement of agricultural products with a price level maintained—usually at a level well above that on world markets—by means of import levies, support buying, and export subsidies. For some commodities, such as cereals, the levy and support buying arrangements operated so as to ensure a guaranteed price to the farmer. For other products, such as fatstock, the support was of a more general type, which did not exclude considerable fluctuations.

The system for cereals was the first to be introduced, and the method adopted has been applied to a large extent to other products. There are three types of support price for cereals; the 'target price', the 'intervention price', and the 'threshold price'. The target price is the basic price, and represents the average price the system is designed to maintain. A main target price is set for the point of greatest cereal deficit in the Community, Duisburg in the Ruhr in Germany. On the basis of the main target price, regionally varied target prices are calculated which lie below the Duisburg price, according to transport costs to Duisburg. (This 'regionalisation' of the cereal price, has in practice given rise to considerable difficulties.) The intervention price is set 5–10 per cent below the target price, and is the price at which the official agency is ready to buy cereals in order to maintain prices; it is therefore the price that the farmer can be sure of getting. The threshold price is set for various import points at such levels that the target price is maintained in Duisburg. On the basis of the threshold price, the import levy is determined: it represents the difference between the lower c.i.f. import price at the frontier and the threshold price. However, the Commission has the power to decide what price is to be taken as the import price, which appears to give it some latitude to decide the levy. For processed cereal products, a range of levies are calculated on the basis of the cereal levy. Thus each week a range of different levies is calculated for noodles, spaghetti, etc., which seems a victory of consistency over common sense.

The price support system for pigmeat, eggs and poultry, does not provide for guaranteed prices or support buying, although prices are supported by minimum import prices, import levies and export subsidies. There is an elaborate system of import levies. Since two-thirds of the cost of these products is for feeding stuffs, the basic levy is based on the difference between the world market price of cereal feeding stuffs and the price inside the community, plus an amount designed to give protection to Community producers. In addition, a minimum import price ('sluice-gate price') is fixed, which is supposed to be based on the minimum of cost of production at world market feed prices. If the import price of the production falls below this level, a supplementary levy is imposed.

For fat cattle a 'guide price' is set, which is much the same as a target price, except that it relates to certain representative markets rather than the main deficit area. This guide price is maintained by means of import quotas, tariffs and levies, and by an intervention price set 4–6 per cent below the guide price. The market regulations for sugar are on the same lines as those for cereals, with the difference that the target price is set for the region of greatest surplus. Northern France: the target price will therefore be lower than prices in deficit regions. For fruit and vegetables, there are customs duties, backed up in some cases by variable levies. In addition, there is a scheme for the withdrawal of produce from the market when the price falls to a 'withdrawal' level fixed each year for each category of fruit and vegetables. The scheme is operated by producer groups which withdraw supplies from the market and are compensated by FEOGA—a system more likely to encourage over-production than the Dutch minimum price scheme discussed above.

In addition to the expenditure on agriculture by the Community, there was still in 1980 a substantial volume of national expenditure. This took the form of various concealed or overt aids to agricultural production and marketing which were hardly compatible with the spirit, or even the letter, of the Common Market. The Commission which was worried about the distorting effect on competition estimated that there are few such subsidies in the UK, but many in some other member countries.

For many types of agricultural produce, the introduction of the CAP has been followed by the emergence of unsaleable surpluses, the reduction of imports from outside suppliers and 'dumping' on world markets. Has the one caused the other? It does not necessarily follow that, because B follows A, it was caused by it; it has sometimes been argued that the problems of surplus would have arisen in any case. It is undoubtedly true that the problems of surplus arise from a wave of technical progress in European agriculture, at a time of fairly stable demand, and that these problems would to some extent have been experienced even if there had been no CAP. However, there are good reasons for thinking that the CAP has increased them. Firstly, the attempt to establish a common price has almost certainly led to higher prices in some member states than would have been accepted by national governments responsible for the costs of national policies. Secondly, some national controls on output were originally abolished (although this policy has now been partially reversed). Thirdly, it is in the nature of a customs union to divert trade from third parties. In the case of industrial products (in which the EEC has anyway followed a fairly liberal policy) there may be 'trade creating' effects which offset the 'trade diverting' effects but (because of the low income elasticities of demand) this does not apply to the same extent to foodstuffs.[2]

Is a Common Agricultural Policy Possible?
Looking back, from 1980, on the evolution of the EEC in general, and of the CAP in particular, one is struck by the infrequency—in political debate—of clear, radical analysis of the issues involved. Compared with, for example, the debate some two centuries earlier, on the proposed constitution of a United States of America (e.g. in *The Federalist*), incomparably more printed pages were produced, but their intellectual calibre compares unfavourably. It was rather glibly assumed that a customs union and a common agricultural policy, once implemented, would inevitably lead to a closer integration of economic and monetary policy, as well as foreign and defence policy. Little consideration was given to basic questions such as 'What type of union is envisaged?' 'In such a union, what powers need to reside with the Community, and what can be left to the nations (or regions or municipalities)?' 'What are the likely consequences of different possible divisions of power between the various organs of the Community?'
The discussion of agricultural policy has similarly tended

to skirt over the question whether a common policy—at least in the sense of a 'European market organisation'—is feasible or desirable, so long as economic sovereignty resides with the member states. It is one thing to have a common market organisation in, say, the USA, where there is a common currency and considerable uniformity in economic institutions. It is quite another in a union of states with separate currencies, liable to change their value in relation to each other; separate economic policies and institutions; and rates of inflation differing from (in 1979) under 5 per cent in West Germany to over 15 per cent in the UK and Italy. Economists began to turn their attention to these questions in the late 1960s. One British economist pointed out that divergences between countries could be divided into two categories: (a) differences in inflation rates; (b) differences in relative productivity growth in agriculture and industry.[3] Differences in inflation rates could, in theory, be compensated for by changes in exchange rates: indeed, according to the 'purchasing power parity' theory, this will tend to happen, without affecting incomes in agriculture and industry.[4] But differences in productivity growth between agriculture and industry were more problematical. If a country had an exceptionally high rate of productivity growth in industry, this would tend to hold up the exchange rate, and industrial incomes; agriculture would have to achieve a correspondingly high level of productivity growth, if it were not to experience an income 'squeeze'.

It is not impossible for agriculture to 'keep up' with industry. American agriculture has matched the (at least until recent years) high productivity of US industry, maintaining its relative income and its competitiveness on international markets. The price, however, has been a ruthless geographical concentration of production in the most suitable areas for particular crops, and the virtual abandonment of some marginal areas. British agriculture in the second half of the nineteenth century faced similar pressures; wheat production, for example, both fell and became concentrated in East Anglia. But many countries are unwilling to subject their agriculture to such pressures. For example, the high efficiency and reputation of German manufacturing can have an adverse effect on German agriculture, but Germany—on social grounds—is unwilling to allow too fierce a squeeze on its agriculture.[5] Hence the demand for protection of some kind against competitors in the rest of the EEC, let alone from outsiders. The converse situation, which should be ideal for agriculture, would be a country with a relatively efficient agriculture and a relatively inefficient industry. British agriculture ought therefore to be very happy. If it has not been so in recent years, this may be because (in addition to technical complaints about the calculations of Monetary Compensation Amounts—MCAs) the sterling exchange rate has been held up by North Sea Oil; moreover, some calculations suggest that the productivity of British agriculture, although higher than in many other EEC countries, is not as much higher as is sometimes believed (see Table 19).

Given, therefore, substantial differences between relative productivity growth in EEC member countries, and a political unwillingness to accept the consequences for prices and incomes, there would appear to be inherent contradictions in a truly common agricultural policy. Countries in the 'German' situation will press either for protection against other EEC countries, which is contrary to the idea of a CAP, or for a very high level of guaranteed prices which, if granted, will eventually lead to burdensome surpluses. On these grounds some basically 'pro-European' economists began to wonder, in the late 1960s, whether the objective of a common price level, except as a long-term goal, was feasible or desirable in an enlarged Community. More modest 'rules of the game' would, they began to feel, suffice to prevent disruptive clashes of national policy, while being less burdensome and wasteful.

The 'Second Mansholt Plan'

A different, although not necessarily contradictory aspect—the need for structural change—was stressed in a memorandum published by the Commissioner for Agriculture, Dr Mansholt, in 1968.[6] The memorandum stressed the need, in the light of growing self-sufficiency and rising support costs, to switch the emphasis from price support to structural change. The attempt to maintain the incomes of marginal farmers by means of price support could only aggravate the problems of surpluses, without solving income problems. The only solution was to encourage a reduction both in the agricultural acreage and the number of farmers, coping with the problem of hardship by generous cash payments to retiring farmers. These 'social' payments would enable prices of potentially surplus products to be reduced, thus balancing supply and demand. The memorandum envisaged a fall in the agricultural labour force in the 'Six' to 5 million in 1980 (compared with 15 million in 1960 and 10 million in 1970) and a reduction in the cultivated area of 7 per cent (5 million hectares out of 71). The area withdrawn from agriculture would be used for forestry and national parks. It was envisaged that grants would be used to encourage a concentration of farms into units of 80–120 hectares of cropland or 40–60 cows, and that the total number of dairy cows would be drastically reduced.

The 'Mansholt Plan' was strongly attacked by farm organisations throughout the Community. The French and German farmers' organisations were particularly critical, stressing the undesirable social consequences of such a drastic plan. These views were echoed by the French and German Governments. In both cases, however, the official government stance covered differences between Ministers, and between what was said and what was actually being done.[7] The French Government had, since the early 1960s, allowed and even encouraged a rapid rate of structural change, and some of the French young farmers' organisations realised that this was necessary to enable them to earn a decent living. In 1971, COPA (the association of national farmers' unions) organised demonstrations in Brussels which led to clashes with the police in which one person was killed and 160 injured. The proposals subsequently put forward by the Commissioner were turned down, and modified still more by the Council. In particular, all proposals to take land out of cultivation were dropped.

Ideas for encouraging structural change continued to be proposed by the Commission and were sometimes adopted, in particular a subsidy for slaughtering dairy cows. But the policies which emerged from the various pressures impinging on the Council of Ministers lacked the clear appreciation of the issues which characterised the Mansholt Plan. For example, farmers have been paid to slaughter dairy cows (with no certainty that they will not breed more) but, at the same time, grants have been made to farms to install equipment which enables them to expand their dairy production. However, in spite of ambivalence in Community policy, structural change has gone on, at a rapid rate. The agricultural area has declined, by nearly the amount envisaged in the Mansholt memorandum. Similarly, agricultural population in the 'Six' had fallen to 7 million by 1978, and the Mansholt target of 5 million by 1980 is likely to be reached before 1985. In a sense, therefore, the Mansholt proposals may have been too conservative.

The 'Mansholt Plan' was one of the last attempts by the Commission to act as a 'European Government'. In the 1970s it became clear that power resided with national governments, sometimes acting in common, more often pulling in different directions and papering over their differences with more or less satisfactory compromises. A CAP conceived on a centralised basis does not sit well with such a political background.

Green Currencies
In the 1970s the CAP has to some extent been undermined by a system of 'green currencies'. This arose almost by accident. The 'common prices' fixed for farm products each year by the Council are expressed in EUA (European Units of Account) based on a basket of currencies. As long as exchange rates are fixed, there is a direct relationship between these 'common prices' and the prices actually received by farmers, in national currencies. But with the breakdown of the Bretton Woods system and the change to floating rates in 1972 the prices in national currencies started to rise and fall with movements of the exchange rate. Such changes are really an inevitable accompaniment of floating rates. However, governments and farmers found them disturbing and agreed that, in order to 'stabilise' national support prices, the rate at which the Community

prices were translated into national currencies would not be the market rate, but an unchanging 'green' rate. This has the effect of causing national prices to diverge, and a system of levies and subsidies becomes necessary. For example, if the exchange value of the Dutch guilder rises in relation to the Belgian franc, the common price is translated into guilders at the old rate, the price in the Netherlands will rise above the price in Belgium, this difference will be maintained by a levy on exports from Belgium to the Netherlands and a subsidy on exports from the Netherlands to Belgium. The levies and subsidies are known as MCAs.

It seems to have been envisaged at first that the MCAs would merely compensate for exchange-rate 'wobbles'. But what happened was that currencies like the Deutsche Mark moved up, and currencies like the pound moved down, thus producing higher prices in Germany than in the UK. In other words, having achieved a common price level, after enormous negotiating effort, the Community abandoned it. There has not been a common market in the main foodstuffs in the Community in the late 1970s.

TABLE 38

Green Currencies

| Region | February 1979 | | February 1980 |
	MCAs (%)	National Price for 'common' price in ECUs of 100	MCAs (%)
West Germany	+10·8	110·8	+9·8
Belgium, Netherlands	− 3·3	96·7	+1·9
Denmark	Nil	100	Nil
Ireland	− 3·0	97·0	Nil
France	−10·6	89·4	−3·7
Italy	−17·7	82·3	−2·3
UK	−28·2	71·8	Nil

Source: EEC Commission.

There are two extreme views of the MCAs—which reflect differing views of the CAP in general. One view (shared by the Commission) is that the MCAs are economically harmful, and a block to the attainment of a common market which ought to be eliminated. At the other extreme is the view that—as Voltaire said about God—if the MCAs did not exist it would be necessary to invent them. They provide a face-saving way out of the impossibility of establishing a common price level when costs vary as much as they do and when national governments are unwilling to renounce their responsibility for the fate of their agricultural industries. An intermediate view is reached by a group of British and German agricultural economists.[8] They agree that a common price level is impossible in present circumstances, and that movement towards it should proceed at a rate which is tolerable for all the countries concerned, but insist that a common price level must remain a clear medium-term objective if the Community is to achieve its objectives.

Problems of the CAP
The problems of the CAP are both internal and external. The internal problems are: (a) the budgetary cost; (b) the cost in terms of food prices; (c) the complaints of some countries about the international allocation of costs and benefits. The financial cost of maintaining surplus stocks and disposing of them (e.g. by selling butter cheaply to the USSR) are considerable. The costs of the CAP account for 70 per cent of Community expenditure, and have been rising (even allowing for inflation). Moreover, three-quarters of expenditure on the CAP is for the disposal of surpluses. Agriculture Ministers tend to stress the value of guaranteed food supplies (although this argument is beginning to lose its force as the Community becomes a net exporter) but Finance Ministers in nearly all countries are becoming increasingly restive.

There is another cost, which does not appear as a cash expenditure, and that is the cost of higher food prices than would have prevailed in the absence of price support. This cannot be attributed solely to the CAP, since the member states would almost certainly maintain some form of price

TABLE 39

(a) Budgetary Cost of the CAP; billion EUAs (1 EUA = £0.65 in 1979)

1974	1975	1976	1977	1978	1979	1980
3·1	4·2	5·5	6·8	9·0	10·3*	10·9*

*Budgetary appropriations for Guarantee Section only.
Source: The Agricultural Situation in the Community, annually.

(b) Prices of EEC Products as a Percentage of World Prices

	1975–76	1976–77	1977–78
Soft wheat	124	204	216
Barley	117	147	206
Maize	128	163	203
Sugar	109	176	255
Beef	196	192	196
Pork	113	125	137
Butter	320	401	388

Source: Statistical Office of the European Communities, Yearbook of Agricultural Statistics 1974–1977, p. 266.

support in the absence of the CAP. It is not a cost which arouses such emotion as budgetary costs, and it is not easy to quantify, but it should enter into an economic assessment of any agricultural policy.

The external effects of the CAP concern its effects on food-exporting countries, and raise two issues: (a) moral responsibility; (b) the possibility of retaliation. For the most part, the effect of greater production in the Community is on countries (which are not developing countries) producing temperate agricultural products. The exception is sugar, a product which can be produced either in Europe from beet, or in the tropics from cane. The 'sugar islands' of the Caribbean (and Mauritius) are poor countries, which at the moment have little other than sugar to sell. The EEC's policy of expanding subsidised sugar production, and in recent years even subsidising exports, is inevitably harmful to these developing countries; such a policy is hard to reconcile with expressions of concern for the 'Third World'. Another country which, although not poor, is in an extremely vulnerable economic position, is New Zealand. It depends on agricultural products for three-quarters of its exports and in spite of strenuous efforts to diversify, has so far had only limited success either in expanding non-agricultural exports or in finding assured markets for the agricultural products it has sent to the UK for nearly a century. British Governments feel that, having benefited from cheap New Zealand butter and lamb for so long, and having had New Zealand support in two wars, they are under some obligation not to abandon her completely—a view which the other members of the Community do not, and cannot be expected to, share. The question—from the negotiations of 1961–63 to the present—has been whether the Community could accommodate these differences in attitudes.

TABLE 40

Self-sufficiency of the EEC

	1968/9	1976/7
Total cereals	86	87
Wheat	94	100
Barley	103	103
Maize	45	50
Sugar	82	111
Cheese	98	103
Butter	91	111
Beef and veal	94	104
Pigmeat	100	100
Poultry	101	104

Source: EEC, The Agricultural Situation in the Community 1979, p. 230.

The possibility of retaliation raises issues of *Realpolitik* rather then ethics. The USA, and Australia, have from the first been critical of the effect of the CAP on their exports, and suggested that they might be forced to take retaliatory action on EEC exports. This, indeed, happened in the 'chicken war' of 1961–63. In 1980, there were signs that the GATT approach was giving way to retaliatory protectionism, although mainly in sectors such as textiles and steel. There was, however, always the possibility that resentments arising from the CAP might add fuel to the flames. In 1980, the proposal to include a sheepmeat regime in the CAP led Australia to threaten to divert up to A$1 billion (£500 million) in trade away from the EEC.

One must finally add that one of the most striking characteristics of the CAP is its stupefying complexity, reminiscent of the eighteenth-century diplomatic problem of the Schleswig-Holstein succession, of which it was said that there was only one man in Europe who understood it, and he was a German Professor who had gone made. When it is virtually impossible for anyone who does not devote his life to the subject to understand the details of a policy, political discussion is likely to be even less well-formed than usual. In the spring of 1979 the European Parliament (the old nominated Parliament) passed a resolution which purported to be a demand for a rise of 3 per cent in agricultural prices. However, owing to a technical error in the unit of account used, the resolution actually called for a 17 per cent reduction! Even those who do not sympathise with the price-raising propensities of the old European Parliament (not originally shared by the new elected Parliament) can sympathise with its difficulties.

Reform of the CAP

The reform of the CAP has been discussed ever since the Mansholt Memorandum of 1968. Proposals on Mansholt lines have periodically been put forward by the Commission, although hardly with the *élan* of the 1960s.[9] More recently it has begun to be argued in some circles that—especially with the enlargement of the 'Six' to the 'Nine', and perhaps soon to the 'Twelve'—a reform of the CAP is only part of a wider re-assessment needed if the

Community is to function, and even survive. These issues have been clearly put by Professor Ralf Dahrendorf, a former Commissioner. In the 1979 Jean Monnet Lecture he was very candid:[10]

European union has been a remarkable political success, but an equally remarkable institutional failure. . . . So far as the substance of European cooperation is concerned, we have gone a long way forward; so far as the framework for taking common decisions is concerned, we have locked ourselves in to procedures and institutions which at times do more damage than good.

In its first twelve years, the EEC had a well-defined, important function which was the creation of a customs union in the widest sense of the term. The common agricultural policy had its origins in this context, although it came to serve other, partly unstated purposes.

He meant, presumably, that France should become the bread-basket of Western Europe.

Since the creation of the customs union, the Community has lost its way.

In the absence of clear and over-riding political purpose, the Commission has been floundering, at worst serving as a secretariat to the Council, at best inventing essentially arbitrary projects, the progress of which rarely went very far. The Council of Ministers has become largely technical. It has complicated an already virtually incomprehensible agricultural policy to the point at which this is little more than an instrument for Ministers of Agriculture to get for their farmers in Brussels and in the name of Europe what they would not get at their national Cabinet tables.

Professor Dahrendorf begins his reappraisal of Community policy by examining the common interests of the West European peoples which require common action. (His views may not be universally shared. The author—who does share them—would merely stress that a re-examination of the Community's structure should begin with fundamental issues of this type.) He lists four areas of common interest. The first concerns foreign policy, in particular relations with the USA and the USSR. The second concerns relations with the less developed countries, where Europe 'has a crucial role to play in setting up a more considered relationship'. The third concerns the preservation of a peaceful and liberal international trading order. The fourth concerns monetary stability—preferably on a world-wide basis but *faute de mieux* on a West European. He continues:

It would be possible to go on listing common European interests, though few others would be of similar importance but however long this list becomes, agricultural policy would not—or, to be exact, would no longer—figure in it. I am convinced that European union would not collapse if the Common Agricultural Policy collapsed. It had its place to cushion a massive migration from agriculture to industry. It may have served to balance French and German economic interests. It may even have been desirable in order to diminish the dependence of Europe on imports of foodstuffs. But today it has achieved all this. I have yet to see one single reason why a Common Agricultural Policy is indispensable today in order to advance the European construction.

This is a radical conclusion which, whether it is accepted or rejected, should not be dismissed as 'unthinkable'. It would involve a 're-nationalisation' of agricultural policy. Although having advantages from the point of view of manageability, comprehensibility, and cost, this might well open the door to reciprocal national protectionism (cf. the French embargo on British lamb in 1979). There are, however, intermediate possibilities. It might be possible to maintain a 'minimalist' common agricultural policy which would set minimum prices for intra-Community trade—at levels corresponding to the lower rather than the higher cost producers—while allowing national governments who wished to do so to give further assistance to their farmers from their own resources. The least disruptive method would be deficiency payments or payments per head of livestock (on the lines of the British Hill Cattle Subsidy). However, tariffs or levies (such as the French substituted for their ban in 1980) might perhaps be allowed in exceptional circumstances (under rules on GATT lines). After all, if the French wish to support a few thousand upland sheep farmers, it is hard to see that this threatens any vital European interest. Up till now (1980) most of the EEC members have been understandably reluctant to abandon the CAP devised after such anguish in the 1960s. Two circumstances, however, seem likely to force a reappraisal in the early 1980s. Firstly, the cost of the CAP is likely to exceed the 'Community's own resources' (from levies, tariffs and 1 per cent of VAT). Secondly, the enlargement of the Community to include Greece, Spain, and Portugal is likely to increase the strains in the Community; some pessimists would say, make it completely unworkable. It is also likely to give rise to the same problems with Mediterranean products which have been experienced with temperate products. If the example of the CAP is followed, there are likely to be even larger 'lakes' of wine and olive oil. It is probably only when crises of this sort have developed that a reform of the CAP will become politically possible.

The Control of Surpluses

Whether the CAP is reformed or abandoned, the farmers of agricultural policy will have to deal with the problems of surpluses. Even given the will to do this, there are differing views as to how it can be achieved. Methods that have been proposed include:

(a) *A reduction in support prices.* Farmers' representatives (and newspaper agricultural correspondents) reply that lower prices induce farmers to produce more, and that *higher* prices would tend to lower output. The issue is whether the supply curve is 'backward sloping' (see Chapter 8). It has been suggested above that there is a range of supply curves, but that, in the long run, the curve (even for agricultural products in general) is conventionally forward sloping, largely because of the effect on investment. On this analysis, some reduction in the degree of price support is necessary, but it will not produce quick results, and may have to be supplemented by physical controls in the short run.

(b) *Deficiency payments.* A change to this system might reduce the cost of the system of levies and support buying; it would certainly make the cost 'transparent'.

As far as production is concerned, however, it makes no difference whether a given price is supported by deficiency payments or levies. The main usefulness of deficiency payments (or payments based on acreage or livestock numbers) might rather be in giving support to some 'underprivileged' sectors (French lamb) without either imposing a massive administrative system on the whole Community or restricting intra-Community trade.

(c) *Production (or acreage) quotas*. This is the most effective way of controlling output in the short run. It is a system better suited to large than small producers, but it has always been used for sugar beet, and has been used in the UK for potatoes and hops. The objection is that if maintained for a long time, the system freezes the pattern of production. One way of meeting this objection is to make the quotas saleable, as has been done in the UK under the Hops Marketing Board. However, it would probably be better to regard quotas as a temporary expedient designed to hold the line while more fundamental measures, such as price reductions, work themselves out.

(d) *'Set aside'*. This is the American system of quantity control. If a farmer wishes to benefit from federal support buying he has to set aside, i.e. not use, a proportion of his farmland.

Some of these methods have begun to be at least considered. The Commission proposed in 1979 that quotas for sugar beet, which had been excessively raised after a short-lived rise in the world sugar price in 1974, should be reduced. One of the problems with such a policy is to allocate the cuts. In this case, the UK objected to any cut in its acreage on the reasonable ground that its self-sufficiency was less than that of other members, and the less convincing ground that the British climate was particularly well suited for growing a sun-loving plant like sugar beet. Other countries also objected, and the Commission's proposal was not accepted, for the 1980 crop.

The UK and the EEC
The UK, while supporting the movement for a European

union in the late 1940s and 1950s, never dreamed of joining it. On the Right, the view prevailed that the UK was a world power, while on the Left a common view was explained to the author as an undergraduate by a leading economist (and adherent of the Weberian concept of 'value-free' economics). 'Just look at the French; we don't want to get mixed up with people like that.' The UK thus sacrificed the opportunity to influence the agricultural policy of the EEC. The CAP developed primarily as a deal between France and Germany, and was largely based on the systems in force in those countries. If the UK (which was then more influential than today) had participated in the negotiations which led up to the Treaty of Rome, the CAP would have taken a different form. To accommodate the UK's greater reliance on food imports, and its deficiency payments system, the CAP would have been of a more eclectic, loose-knit type (which is perhaps what is needed today). When attention turned to the possibility of EEC membership in about 1960, the politicians were worried mainly about the possible effect on British farm incomes. Students of agricultural policy tended to discount this fear, on the ground that the British farm structure was better than that in most of the EEC and guaranteed prices generally lower; prices established for European farmers were likely to be profitable enough for British farmers.[11] Far more serious were the problems of:

(a) Reconciling a system based (mainly) on deficiency payments with one based mainly on the support of market prices.
(b) Retaining a quota of imports from traditional (and low-cost) suppliers, notably New Zealand and the 'sugar islands'.
(c) The balance of payments burden arising from the payment of levies and tariffs to Brussels. As a country importing substantial amounts of food from outside the Community, the UK would obviously pay more into the kitty than it drew out.

These problems were raised during the abortive negotiations of 1961–63 and again during the negotiations which led to accession in 1973. The Six for the most part maintained that 'New members have to accept the rules of the club', and the UK obtained few concessions, apart from the temporary import quotas for sugar and New Zealand produce.[12] The 'renegotiation' initiated by the Labour Government in 1975 brought little change, apart from a 'corrective mechanism' for limiting gross payments to the Community in certain circumstances.

In the late 1970s it became clear that the net payments from the UK to the Community were rising to a level which (especially after the ending in 1980 of a transitional arrangement, Article 131 of the Accession Agreement, which limited British payments) would make the UK by far the largest net contributor to the Community. There was some dispute over the figures, including an argument as to whether MCA subsidies should be regarded as benefits to the importing or the exporting country. On the hardly questionable assumption that, outside the Community, a country could obtain supplies at less than the cost in the higher-priced Community countries, the MCA subsidies should be regarded as a benefit to the exporting country (Column 1 in Table 41). British Governments began to argue that the UK was a poor country, and that it was unfair that it should be the largest net contributor. The French replied that the UK knew the rules before it joined, and that it had North Sea oil anyway. Other members of the Six were somewhat more sympathetic. This sort of debate is the stuff of international politics, which might be expected to lead to a compromise reflecting the bargaining strength of the participants. However, the Labour Government was divided between pro- and anti-Marketeers, which hardly facilitated the pursuit of a coherent policy. The following Conservative Government was very successful in obtaining short-term financial refunds, but at the cost of concessions on agricultural policy which are likely to aggravate the problems—for Britain and the Community as a whole—after 1982.

At the 1979 summit meeting in Dublin, the British Prime Minister, Mrs Thatcher, demanded financial rebates to give a 'rough balance' in British financial transactions with the Community. The other members offered a cut of £340 million in British contributions, through the 'corrective mechanism' devised in 1975. Mrs Thatcher rejected this

TABLE 41

EEC Net Budget Contributions and Receipts in 1978 in million European Units of Account
(1 EUA = £0·67)

	National Balances Reflecting Adjustments under Article 131*		Effect of the Ending of Article 131 Adjustment†
	1 MCAs Attributed to Exporting Countries	2 MCAs Attributed to Importing Country	
Germany	− 346·8	− 519·8	− 133·2
France	− 33·3	− 321·0	− 80·7
Italy	− 723·4	− 304·0	+ 50·5
Netherlands	+ 236·8	+ 57·0	− 28·6
Belgium/Lux.	+ 393·4	+ 350·3	− 22·0
UK	−1121·6	− 407·0	+302·3
Ireland	+ 530·5	+ 320·1	+ 12·7
Denmark	+ 620·4	+ 380·3	0

*Plus sign = net receipt; minus sign = net contribution.
†Plus sign indicates a rise in contributions.

Source: EEC Press Release, 9 April 1979.

'one-third of a loaf'. At the Luxembourg summit in April, 1980, she was offered 'two-thirds of a loaf' which she again rejected. At the end of May, however, after protracted negotiation, the British Government was offered marginally better terms, which were accepted. The agreement provided that the estimated net contribution by the UK of £1·08 billion in 1980 would be cut to £371 million, and a ceiling of £455 million placed on net contributions for 1981 and 1982.

The price of these short-term budgetary concessions was the virtual abandonment of any attempt to reform the CAP—the root cause of the British budgetary problem. Members of the Conservative Government had spoken of the need to reform the CAP but, from the beginning, their deeds had not altogether corresponded with their words. In May 1979 the UK raised no objection to what some observers considered excessive farm price rises, and later in the year it jointly vetoed a proposal from the European Parliament which would have cut the farm budget. While the size of the British 'loaf' was being acrimoniously and publicly debated in the early months of 1980, a 'package' on farm prices and sheepmeat was quietly being put together by national representatives in Brussels, for initialling when agreement on British contributions was reached. The price proposals represented an ignominious defeat for the Commission in its efforts to come to terms with the problems of mounting food surpluses and the rising costs of agricultural support. They provided for a doubling of the price rises originally proposed by the Commission for 1980, and the abandonment (at least temporarily) of proposals designed to curb the milk and sugar surpluses. The proposed 'super levy' on increased milk production was rejected, and the existing sugar beet quotas were retained. Commenting on the Commission's failure to obtain acceptance of its proposals, the Agricultural Commissioner, Mr Olav Grundelach, mentioned the lack of British support. 'The British could have fought on the farm spending issue but they chose to fight on the budget; they went for the money.' The British strategy seems to have based on the view, put foward by a senior Conservative Minister soon after taking office, that reform of the CAP would be a 'false trail', since it would not bring results within a reasonable period of time. Whether the British Government in fact chose the right trail in fighting ferociously for short-term concessions for the UK rather than choosing the 'long haul' of reforming the CAP and the *general* provisions for Community finance will be clearer in a few years.

Another part of the 1980 farm package was the British acceptance of a Community market regulation system for sheepmeat. There is to be intervention buying in France and a deficiency payments scheme in the UK. National prices are to be gradually 'harmonised' and export subsidies may, if necessary, be paid. A quota is to be instituted for New Zealand imports.

The sheepmeat agreement was defended by the British Government on several grounds: since the deficiency payments were being paid for out of Community funds, the UK would benefit financially; the use of deficiency payments rather than intervention buying would mean that farmers would benefit from higher prices, while retail prices would not rise, and a lamb mountain would not be possible. At the same time, the interests of New Zealand had been defended. On a longer view, however, the sheepmeat system could well open the door to problems similar to those experienced in other sectors. The proposal to harmonise guaranteed prices, and the acceptance in principle of export subsidies, recall the way in which similar agreements in the 1960s paved the way for current problems. And, once a quota has been set for New Zealand lamb, it can be reduced; New Zealand's fear that this is 'the thin end of the wedge' is not without justification.

Any serious attempt to reform the CAP was thus put off by the politicians in 1980. However, the issues have merely been postponed for a couple of years. In 1982, the British budgetary problems will almost certainly re-emerge, perhaps once more threatening the coherence of the Community; the cost of financing the CAP can be expected to rise until it exhausts the currently available cash resources; and the complaints of overseas producers against EEC policy can be expected to continue. Moreover, the enlargement of the Community will bring new problems.

Spain, Portugal and Greece are likely to echo the demands of Italy for a level of support for Mediterranean products corresponding to that given to temperate products, and the Community will face a choice between repeating the mistakes already made and reforming policy towards temperate products.

Summary

The European Community initiated a common agricultural policy in the 1960s, based on the principles of a common price set annually by the Council of Ministers and maintained by variable import levies, support buying and export subsidies. This system was to some extent undermined in the 1970s by the system of 'green currencies' and 'monetary compensation amounts' which allowed price differences between member countries. The introduction of the CAP has been accompanied by an increase in unsaleable surpluses and export 'dumping'. Although the basic cause has been an upsurge in the productivity of European agriculture, the CAP has probably caused higher prices and larger surpluses than would otherwise have prevailed. The cost of the CAP is giving rise to concern, and subsidised exports to the EEC are being criticised by other countries. With the enlargement of the Community to nine members in 1973, and the prospective accession of Spain, Portugal, and Greece, the strains on the CAP are likely to increase, probably leading either to radical reforms or to the break-up of the Community.

Notes

1 *Proposals for the Working-out and Putting into Effect of the Common Agricultural Policy in Application of Article 43 of the Treaty establishing the European Economic Community*, Brussels, 1960.
2 Kindleberger, C. F., *International Economics*, 1963, p. 324ff.
3 Hallett, G., 'The problem of agriculture in a European Union', *JAE*, vol. XX, no. 3, 1969, p. 317.
4 The purchasing power parity theory suggests that floating exchange rates will adjust themselves so that a bundle of (internationally traded) goods will cost the same in all countries. Thus if country A has an inflation rate 10 per cent

above that of country B, the exchange rate of its currency will fall by 10 per cent per annum in relation to B's currency. There is something in this theory, although it is not a complete explanation. 'Real' exchange rates (i.e. actual rates deflated by inflation rates) have shown a fairly stable trend in the 1970s, but with periodic 'peaks' and 'troughs'. An 'undervalued' currency tends to raise farm income.

5 Hallett, G., *The Social Economy of West Germany*, London, 1973, Ch. 4.

6 *Memorandum on Reform of Agriculture in the European Communities* ('Mansholt Plan'), European Communities Information Service, London, 1968.

7 Tracy, M. A., 'Fifty years of agricultural policy, *JAE*, Vol. XXVII, no. 3, 1976.

8 Heidhues, H. *et al.*, *Common Prices and Europe's Farm Policy*, Trade Policy Research Centre, London, 1978.

9 EEC Commission, *Improvement of the CAP*, 1973; *Stocktaking of the CAP*, 1975; and *The Agricultural Situation in the Community*, published annually.

10 'A Third Europe?' Jean Monnet Lecture delivered at the European University Institute, Florence, 26 November 1979 (mimeo).

11 A list of articles on British agriculture and the EEC is given in Cosgrove, Carol Ann, *A Reader's Guide to Britain and the European Communities* European Series 14), Chatham House/PEP, London, 1970. Perhaps the author may be permitted to mention that it does not go far enough back to include Hallett, G., 'British agriculture and Europe', Supplement to *Crossbow*, Spring 1961.

12 Young, Simon, *Terms of Entry: Britain's Negotiations with the European Communities 1970–1972*, London, 1973.

Further Reading

Camps, Miriam, *Britain and the European Community 1955–1963*, London, 1963.

Camps, Miriam, *European Unification in the Sixties*, London, 1967.

Fennel, Rosemary, *The Common Agricultural Policy of the European Community*, St Albans, 1979.

Marsh, John S. and Swanney, Pamela, J., *Agriculture and the European Community*, London, 1980.

Swann, D., *Economics of the Common Market*, fifth edition, 1980, Harmondsworth.

CHAPTER SIXTEEN

Problems of World Trade

For agricultural products of the temperate zone—such as cereals, meat and dairy products—there is for the most part no longer a single world market, in the sense that there was in the late nineteenth century. Prices in both importing and exporting countries are maintained by a varied range of import levies, controls and subsidies. Thus the 'world' prices at which agricultural products are bought and sold do not necessarily represent equilibrium prices determined by the range of world production costs in relation to demand. Trade in temperate agricultural products has not experienced the liberalisation that has taken place in trade in manufactured goods since the post-war period. Tropical products—which, with a few exceptions do not compete directly with the products of temperate agriculture—have not experienced nationalistic restrictions on trade to the same extent, although they also have their problems. Let us first examine trade in temperate products.

Export Subsidies and Import Levies
The growth of agricultural protection in importing countries has been paralleled by that of export subsidisation in the exporting countries. The parallel is not exact, since the export subsidies per unit are small in comparison with the import levies and subsidies of the importing countries; while some producers—e.g. Canadian Wheat farmers· and New Zealand dairy farmers—are primarily dependent on world market prices. In general, the 'traditional' exporters of temperate foodstuffs, the USA, Canada, Australia, New Zealand, Denmark, Argentine—are genuine low-cost producers (cf. the producer wheat prices in Table 42). Thus although it is undoubtedly true that world market prices are distorted,

TABLE 42

Support Prices for Wheat, 1978/9

	US $ per tonne
Switzerland	397·9
West Germany	199·8
UK	188·4
France	160·1
Argentine	108·3
USA	106·5
Canada	102·5

Source: International Wheat Council.

and do not represent true equilibrium prices, they may not be as much below true equilibrium prices, they may not be as much below true equilibrium prices as farmers in importing countries would like to think.

The effect of import levies and export subsidies on international trade and on prices is represented theoretically in Fig. 48. Let us assume that there are only two countries, which can be called 'America' and 'Europe'. The supply and demand curves intersect in 'America' at a lower price than in 'Europe', and these prices prevail when there is no trade between the two countries. If free trade is now established between the two countries, the price and level of production will rise in 'America' and fall in 'Europe' until an equilibrium price is established at which exports from 'America' are equal to imports into 'Europe' (P_1). (Transport costs can for simplicity be ignored; they have the same effect as an import levy.) If an import levy (or tariff) is now imposed by 'Europe', it has the effect of introducing a 'crank' into the price line. Prices will still have to be such that exports and imports are equal, but trade will be smaller. The 'world' price, corresponding to the American price, will be below the 'European' price by the amount of the levy, but will also be below the 'free trade' price, P_1. If 'America' now institutes an export subsidy, the effect is to introduce a 'crank' of a different type into the price line. The American price will be above

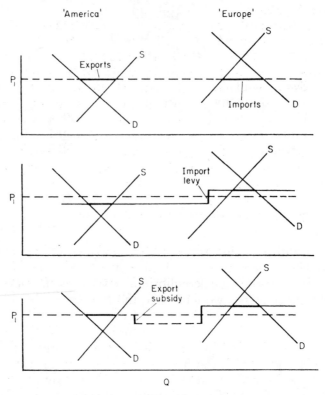

FIG. 48

the 'world' price by the amount of the export subsidy, and will rise slightly. The 'world' and 'European' prices will drop, and exports from 'America' to 'Europe' will rise.

This example assumes that the import levy and export subsidy are fixed. If, however, the levy is variable, and is adjusted so as to maintain a certain producer price, the 'European' price and the level of imports, will remain constant. The level of 'European' imports will determine the level of 'American' exports, and hence the 'American' price and production, unless the 'American' authorities accumulate stocks, divert supplies into non-commercial channels or restrict production by means of production controls. This theoretical example is not so far removed from what has actually happened in the world wheat trade in recent years.

'Food for Peace'

The agricultural price policies in exporting and—more particularly—importing countries, together with productivity changes largely independent of price policy, contributed to an inbalance in world trade in temperate agricultural products in the late 1950s and early 1960s. This was particularly marked in the case of cereals, production of which rose sharply in North America, while imports to the traditional West European markets remained fairly stable. There was in these circumstances a tendency, until the early 1960s, for stocks to build up in North America, and the USA instituted various programmes for restricting production. At the same time, it was obvious that many developing countries were short both of food and of foreign currency with which to buy it. This strange contrast between surplus and scarcity suggested to many people that the surplus countries should give their surplus to the less fortunate countries, and in accordance with this principle the US Congress passed Public Law 480, which authorises the Administration to, in effect, give away surplus foodstuffs. Technically, the food is sold for local currency, e.g. Indian rupees, which is then used to pay American advisers or given back in loans. The wheat programme grew to over 16 million tons in the 1960s but fell to under 10 million tons in the 1970s (see Table 43).

The principle of the 'Food for Peace' programme has not received undivided support among economists; it has been criticised on the grounds that it is a wasteful way of helping the developing countries, and harms commercial food exporters. The economist critics have argued that the developing countries must develop their own agriculture, and that if the developed countries wish to help them they should simply give economic aid. The developing countries could then, if they considered it desirable, use this aid to buy food, and they could buy it from the cheapest sources.

These criticisms do not always apply. Food disposal programmes will only harm commercial exports if they replace food which would otherwise have been bought in the commercial market. If, on the other hand, food delivered under disposal programmes is used to feed people

TABLE 43

World Exports and Imports of Wheat and Wheat Flour

	Average 1949/50– 1953/4	Average 1959/60– 1963/4	1976/7
	million metric tons		
Exports			
USA	9·3	18·4	26·4
(Concessional)	—	(12·6)	(c9·0)
Canada	8·0	10·2	12·9
Australia	2·8	5·4	8·3
France	0·7	2·2	6·8
Others	4·7	9·2	7·4
Total	25·5	45·4	61·8
(Concessional)	—	(16·0)	(c9·5)
Imports			
Developed countries	16·6	15·1	12·0
Communist countries	0·1	10·5	16·1
Developing countries	9·4	18·3	33·7
	25·5	45·4	61·8

Source: International Wheat Council.

who would otherwise have gone hungry, it will not harm commercial exports. It can also be argued that it is a counsel of perfection to say that aid should be given solely in the form of money. Most countries are reluctant to give more than a limited amount of financial aid to developing countries. However, when the question is of disposing of burdensome food surpluses—which the farm vote can be expected to support—legislators are inclined to take a more favourable view.

On this contentious question of food aid the author must also admit to having moved from an attitude critical of food aid programmes to a belief when the first edition of this book was published, that they were essential to resolve the food shortages in the developing countries; he has now moved slightly back, believing that food aid has an important, limited role—in relieving famine and in providing a 'back-up' to agriculture changes—but that the emphasis must be placed on increasing agricultural production in the developing countries. This is now the consensus among agricultural economists. It is also generally agreed that stimulating the production of unsaleable surpluses in the developed countries, in the hope that they will be used for food aid, is not an effective way of helping developing countries.

GATT and World Trade in Temperate Foodstuffs
Since the early 1950s, there has been a notable freeing of world trade in manufactured goods, which has taken place as a result of international agreements reached through GATT (General Agreement on Tariffs and Trade). But the GATT approach, based on lowering tariffs, has been hardly relevant to agricultural commodities, for which devices such as variable import levies and deficiency payments have been employed. The GATT procedure of agreeing not to raise tariff rates, and of bargaining for their mutual reduction, cannot apply when there are no fixed tariff rates.

Agricultural protection in importing countries has created problems for some exporters of temperate agricultural products, and the formation of the European Economic Community has made these problems more acute. But even if there is a decline in the imports of temperate agricultural products into Western Europe, there is no need to view this development as apocalyptically as it is sometimes viewed in English-speaking countries. When the development of world trade in temperate foodstuffs over the last half century is studied, the most striking impression is of the tremendous changes that have taken place in the distribution of exports and imports between countries. In the world wheat trade, for example, there has been a phenomenal increase in exports from North America since the pre-1939 period, and total world trade has more than trebled (Table 44). Whereas imports into the UK and Western Europe as a whole have tended

TABLE 44

World Trade in Wheat and Flour (000 long tons wheat equivalent).

Exports

	Average 1937–39	1976
Canada	3,871	12,904
Argentina	3,595	5,584
Australia	2,790	8,357
USA	2,357	26,395
USSR	1,104	1,400
France	—	6,811
Total*	18,030	61,795

Imports

	Average 1937–39	1967	1976
UK	5,076	3,867	3,422
West Germany	1,224	1,816	1,418
East Germany		1,165	1,670
Italy	852	833	2,428
Brazil	963	2,431	3,504
India	87	7,154	3,859
Pakistan		2,160	355
USSR	—	2,005	4,559
Japan	94	4,064	5,522
China	47	4,006	—
Egypt	2	2,354	3,956

*Includes others.

Source: International Wheat Council.

to decline, there has been a sharp rise in imports into Japan, the Communist countries, and many developing countries.

There are two extreme approaches to international trade in temperate products. One is a policy of complete free trade. It has, for example, been proposed that exporting and importing countries should abandon price support in a kind of 'multilateral disarmament'. This would result in a fall in prices in European countries, which could be allocated by transitional payments to support farm income. There is much to be said for such policies, but experience does not suggest that they are politically feasible. However, as the period of rapid structural change in European agriculture draws to a close, a move towards a more liberal trading system may gain increasing support.

The second 'extreme' policy is for the importing countries to be utterly 'inward-looking', set 'political' farm prices, subsidise exports if production exceeds domestic production, and ignore the effect on other exporters. Such a policy—besides being arguably against the interests of importing countries—can invite retaliation.

In between these two extremes lie various policies—on broadly 'GATT' lines—for limiting national powers by accepting certain general rules on production, undertaking joing buffer stock schemes, and generally seeking to prevent divergent policies from reaching a level where they threatened to cause widespread harm to the international economy. Ideas of this sort were raised in the 'Kennedy Round' GATT negotiations of 1964–67; in particular, international schemes for maintaining food stocks and agreements to ascertain the protective margins for the main foodstuffs in each country and agree not to increase them. In the event, only a limited agreement on international food aid was reached, but it was hoped that this agreement might be the forerunner of others. Any moves in this direction, however, were swept away by the commodity price explosion of 1972/3. At a time of scarcity and high prices, plans based on the danger of surplus were shelved; in the EEC, those who argued that higher guaranteed prices were needed to ensure adequate food supplies seemed to have been vindicated. In the event, prices fell and the late 1970s have seen a restoration of the kind of precarious balance in the international food market which prevailed in the late 1960s. The idea of in some way extending GATT principles to agricultural trade, however, received a set-back, and proposals to establish international food reserves and restrain the more disruptive types of agricultural policies have made slow progress in the late 1970s.

Tropical Agricultural Products
The exporters of tropical agricultural products are often dissatisfied with existing arrangements for world trade, although in their case they cannot justifiably blame agricultural protection in the importing countries for their problems. Tropical or semi-tropical products such as coffee, cocoa, cotton, rubber, tea, bananas, do not compete with temperate foodstuffs, and, with a few exceptions, do not suffer significantly from agricultural protection in the temperate developed areas. The exceptions are sugar and, to a lesser extent, oilseeds. Sugar can be produced either from cane in tropical or from beet in temperate countries, and the tropical sugar producing countries have undoubtedly suffered from the protection of sugar beet production in Europe and North America. Vegetable oils are a somewhat similar case, in that tropical oils such as ground nut oil compete with olive oil and rape seed oil and, *via* margarine, with butter. The competition of temperate products is less serious, however, for oilseeds than for sugar. Thus it is incorrect to say, as many economists persist in doing, that a reduction in agricultural protection in the developed countries would in general help the developing countries.

As far as the tropical non-food agricultural products are concerned—rubber, cotton, sisal, jute, etc. (and the temperate product wool) the competition they face is not from agriculture in the developed countries but from industry, which produces synthetic rubber and synthetic fibres. Restricting the development of these synthetic substitutes would help some of the developing countries, but it would be hard to implement such a policy, even if it were considered right to do so. The most that can probably be expected in this direction is that the governments of developed countries refrain from subsidising the production of synthetic commodities.

Some importing countries impose excise taxes on coffee and tea; however, the main issue here is not the effect on demand—which according to most of the studies that have been made is small—but the fact that these duties are used to give preference to certain countries. The EEC, for example, allows free entry to imports from its African associates but imposes taxes on produce from other countries, which has given rise to concern among competing suppliers that are not EEC associates. The problem is thus more one of relative benefits between supplying countries than of the effect on supplying countries as a whole. Nevertheless, these taxes naturally have some restrictive effect on consumption, however slight, and probably ought to be abolished (except perhaps for tobacco!).

The exporters of tropical products face the two problems: price instability, and a level of prices often considered to be inadequate. Price fluctuations are particularly large for two reasons: the producing countries have not followed the type of storage policy followed in the USA and Canada; and the price elasticity of demand for these products is low. Thus if supplies increase more rapidly than demand, prices drop sharply. The trend of world demand for tropical products is upwards—at least for the consumable products such as coffee, cocoa, tea and sugar—but, in any one period, production can outstrip demand and lead to a sharp drop in prices and receipts. One extreme case is cocoa. As a result of improved methods of pest control, production rose sharply in the late 1950s; world exports nearly doubled between 1957 and 1961, but the price fell as a result by nearly half, so that receipts remained virtually constant. Throughout the 1960s and 1970s cocoa has continued to experience successive booms and slumps.

International Commodity Agreements
Because of these large fluctuations, attempts have been made to 'stabilise' the prices of tropical products by

international commodity agreements. It has not always been clear, however, whether the aim was to stabilise or to raise the price level. Raising the general level can indeed be defended as a means of helping poor countries which export the commodity, but it runs the risk of causing the breakdown of any agreement, in particular by stimulating production in countries which are either not party to the agreement or do not, in practice, observe it. Moreover, in the case of products facing competition from synthetics, raising the price above a certain level is likely to cause a switch in demand away from the natural product.

For these reasons, and also because of the difficulties of getting countries to agree to a scheme, the history of international commodity agreements has been chequered. In the 1920s there was a rubber agreement, which broke down because of the expansion of production in non-member countries. At subsequent times before and after the War, schemes have been introduced for cocoa, coffee, sugar, wheat, olive oil and sultanas. But none has had a continuous history. When agreements periodically expired, there have often been disagreements between producing and conserving countries which have prevented a new agreement being reached. For example, if prices are high, producing countries are reluctant to enter a new agreement, whereas if prices are low, consuming countries are reluctant.

In principle, there are two main ways in which an international commodity agreement can function. It can be based on:

(a) a buffer stock;
(b) export quotas for individual countries.

Under a buffer stock scheme, an international authority is financed by member countries and empowered to buy on the world market when prices fall below some agreed 'floor' price, and to sell when they rise above an agreed 'ceiling' price. The buying and selling prices can be periodically revised, or set by reference to a 'moving average' of market prices. The theoretical attractions of such a scheme are considerable. It does not involve any interference with marketing channels or with individual countries' policies, and it provides stability without affecting the long run trend of prices. But in fact the only international buffer stock agreement that has ever functioned is that for tin; no agreement has ever been reached for agricultural products. The reason is basically that rivalries, animosities and clashes of interest between nations—not only between importers on the one hand and exporters on the other, but also within these groups—combined with the technical problems of deciding the right buying and selling prices have been so great that the nations have been unable to agree to the joint financing and operation of a buffer stock.

The method that has therefore been adopted has been that of export quotas. Each exporting country is given a quota of exports, which is increased or suspended when prices are high, but imposed when they are low. This method also raises several administrative problems. In the first place, there is the problem of ensuring that all exporting countries keep to their export quotas. Produce can be smuggled out, or even shipped out in the normal way, if national authorities are prepared to turn a blind eye; if 'cheating' of this type becomes too extensive, the agreement will break down. There is the further problem of implementing export quotas. A state export monopoly can keep exports down by building up stocks, but the countries concerned often lack the financial and technical resources to hold large stocks. If production increases too much, it may be necessary to seek to limit it, either by production controls, which are very difficult to administer, or by lowering the producer price. As far as the individual producer is concerned, a price reduction removes the point of the scheme; the country, however, may still benefit, in that the state trading board will earn surpluses which can be used for economic development.

Because of these difficulties the principle of 'compensatory financing' has been increasingly adopted in recent years. The purpose of supporting world prices when they are low is essentially to make the importing countries pay more than they would otherwise have done, and to maintain the foreign exchange earnings of the exporting countries. The same result can therefore be achieved by payments from importing countries to exporting countries when prices are low, and *vice versa* when prices are high. This principle has been adopted in the export stabilisation (Stabex) scheme, which is part of the Lomé Convention between the EEC and the associated African and Caribbean countries. The International Monetary Fund operates a scheme on similar lines, by lending money to primary exporting countries when prices are low, which is repaid when prices recover.

The most durable of the international commodity agreements (apart from the Tin Agreement) was the International Wheat Agreement which lasted from just after the War to 1972, when it was replaced by a food aid convention, and a trade convention providing for a regular exchange of views and information. The IWA provided for a wheat price between a 'floor' and a 'ceiling'. However, this stabilisation was largely achieved by the stockholding policies of the USA and Canada, together with the US acreage controls and food aid programme; thus the IWA mainly sanctioned a stabilisation which would have occurred in any case. However, the organisation set up to implement it—the International Wheat Council—served a useful purpose by acting as a forum in which trading countries could meet, obtain the best market data, review problems and exchange ideas and criticisms. It continues to serve this function, even though there is at the moment no Agreement of the usual kind. This 'educational' aspect of international commodity agreements is of considerable importance.

Cartels
International commodity agreements which rely on supply controls have elements of a cartel (or 'federated monopoly'). In its modern international form, this is an association of countries which agree to limit output in order to raise prices. The most famous cartel of recent years has been OPEC (Organsiation of Oil Producing Countries) although there is ground for argument whether it can really be classified as a cartel, since it has not reached explicit agreements to limit production. Proposals have been made

that the producers of other commodities should band together in the hope of achieving for their products the kind of price rise experienced in oil.

The conditions favouring the success of international cartels are:

(1) a small number of producers, with a high degree of co-operation;
(2) high costs for potential new producers;
(3) a low price elasticity of demand, and a high income elasticity of demand for the product;
(4) moderate price policies, implicitly accepted by importing countries.

On these grounds, oil is particularly suitable for the formation of a cartel; for other commodities, conditions are less favourable. The effectiveness of a cartel can easily break down because some countries remain outside it, or because some countries cheat, or because smuggling is stimulated. Cartels are, in the long run, less effective than might be thought.

New International Economic Order
This is a phrase coined in UN circles in the 1960s to symbolise the efforts of the developing countries to obtain more advantageous trading arrangements. It has been mainly associated with commodity price arrangements, embodied in the 'common fund'; however, wider, and perhaps more promising, arrangements include (a) debt relief; (b) transfer of technology; (c) aid; (d) access for manufactured and semi-manufactured goods from developing countries in 'developed' markets.

The term 'new international order' originated in the theory put forward by Dr Prebisch and others that, because of inherent flaws in a largely market-orientated trade international system, the price of commodities would always fall in relation to the price of manufactured goods (see Chapter 3). It was assumed that developed countries exported manufactures, while developing countries exported commodities; therefore the terms of trade would, in the absence of some drastic change in the international trade system, always move against the developing countries. The conclusion was that all world trade should be controlled by a UN organisation which would ensure a better deal for developing countries. These views gained increasing acceptance in the 1960s, in spite of criticisms by some economists. In 1967, UNCTAD (United Nations Conference on Trade and Development) was founded; it acts as a secretariat on questions of trade which concern developing countries, and is associated with the ideas outlined above. In its early days, it sponsored a book by the late Professor Harry Johnson on *Economic Policies towards Less Developed Countries*.

The book which Professor Johnson wrote with his characteristic lucidity is arguably the best textbook on the subject, but it is critical of many of the ideas with which UNCTAD is associated. Professor Johnson supported increased monetary aid from the developed to the less developed countries, and argued strongly that the developed countries should open their markets to manufactured goods from the less developed countries; he also criticised agricultural protection in the developed countries. But he did not accept the argument that a new, centrally controlled trading system should be instituted in order to raise commodity prices, on several grounds. Firstly, there was no evidence of a long-term movement of the terms of trade against commodities; even if there was such a trend, this did not necessarily indicate that commodity exporters were becoming poorer in relation to exporters of manufactured goods, since productivity growth had to be taken into account. Secondly, even if commodity prices could be raised, this was an inefficient means of transferring income. It led to black markets and the development of substitutes. Direct money transfers were preferable. Thirdly, it was not true that the poorest countries depended heavily on commodity exports. Many countries which depended heavily on commodity exports—Zambia, Chile, Malaysia—were at the top of the league of developing countries, whereas the poorest and most populous countries—notably India and Pakistan—exported mainly simple manufactured products. These countries—representing the real problem of Third World poverty—were not poor because they received low prices for their exports, but because their productivity was low; the emphasis should therefore be on economic development.

Other economists put forward wider criticisms of the proposed New International Economic Order. Mr Samuel Brittan, the distinguished economic commentator of the *Financial Times*, suggested—paraphrasing Voltaire's comment on the Holy Roman Empire—that the proposed New International Economic Order was neither new, international, economic, nor an order. It was not new because it was a variant of the Mercantilist system of the seventeenth and eighteenth centuries, under which trade was strictly controlled by the state. It was not international because, when trade is purely a political matter, there are always differences of national interest which lead to clashes; wars were fought throughout the seventeenth and early eighteenth centuries to further national trading interests. It was not economic because it was political, and it was not an order because politicised trade relationships are notoriously abrasive, and liable to periodic disruption.

Criticisms of this sort tended to be dismissed rather than discussed. Some of the leading members of the 'Group of 77'—representing developing countries, originally of this number, now more—had become firmly attached to the New International Economic Order, even though its implications had not been thought out very carefully. The leaders of the OECD countries, on the other hand, wished to show sympathy with the general idea of helping the developing countries, and felt that one should not begin by carping about economic technicalities. In 1974 the UN Assembly, with general support, passed a resolution proposing a New International Economic Order, and negotiations began under the auspices of UNCTAD which became known as the North–South dialogue.

The Group of 77 proposed that a common fund should be established, with money put up by the developed countries, to finance trade organisation elected on a 'one country, one vote' system. This 'common fund' would have extensive powers to maintain buffer stocks, control supplies, and 'stabilise' prices. The fund would have what became known as a 'second window', which would finance improvements in marketing and production methods. The products in which the fund would be empowered to operate would cover ten 'core' commodities (cocoa, coffee, tea, sugar, copper, tin, rubber, cotton, jute, and hard fibres) and eight other commodities (bananas, vegetable oil, meat, tropical timber, iron ore, bauxite, manganese, and phosphates).

At this stage, the OECD countries began to examine the practicalities of international commodity schemes, and soon came up with a number of objections. Firstly, it was not sensible to set up a fund, with a large capital and undefined powers, before deciding how the money was to be spent for particular commodities. It was necessary, first, to frame agreements for cocoa, coffee, and other commodities with price ranges, details of intervention methods, etc. Having reached such agreements, the Common Fund could act as a banker. But it was necessary to tailor agreements to individual commodities, since conditions varied from commodity to commodity, e.g. buffer stocks were practicable for, at most, tin, rubber, coffee, cocoa, and copper. Secondly, they were not convinced, on reflection, that the 'UN system' of 'one country, one vote' irrespective of whether the country even produced the commodity, would lead to harmony and efficiency, or a reasonable representation for consumers. Thirdly, the 'second window' duplicated aid through the World Bank and other international organisations.

The Group of 77 replied that the founding of the Common Fund was a test of good faith by the OECD countries, which had accepted the validity of the principle and were now seeking to evade this commitment. There followed several years of slow negotiation, in the course of which the Group of 77 began to realise that they had hoped for more than could be got from a reorganisation of commodity trade. But the OECD countries also had to give ground. In the Spring of 1979 a modest measure of agreement was reached on a Common Fund, comprising three points.

(1) The fund is to act as banker for agreements on individual commodities, and limited to suitable

commodities, initially sugar, coffee, cocoa, and rubber. This might be considered a win for the 'North'.

(2) The voting procedures give a slight predominance to the developing countries but expenditure decisions require a three-quarters majority. This might be considered a 'draw'.

(3) The 'second window' is to be established. This might be considered a win for the 'South'.

It is not difficult to predict that the effects of the Common Fund will be limited. Prices will continue to be set primarily by supply and demand, with intervention at best providing some increased stability, and facing all the difficulties of predicting prices and reconciling the interests of producers and consumers which commodity agreements have experienced for over half-a-century. There will be an extension of the UN bureaucracy, of possibly questionable cost-effectiveness.

And yet it would be wrong to dismiss this type of international organisation as merely an expensive irrelevancy. Producers and consumers do have an interest in establishing 'rules of the game' in international trade; 'jaw jaw' can be better than some alternatives. If individual countries or groups of countries simply give up talking to trading partners and pursue national goals by political fiat, the outcome can be a disruption of international trade which harms everyone. This danger has by no means been eliminated, but the modest agreement on a 'common fund' has at least defused some of the passions which had been building up on the subject. It is hoped that attention will now turn to other aspects of international economic relations, which are in many ways more important for the future of the developing countries—trade, aid, technology, the role of international corporations.

The 'New International Economic Order', with reference to commodity trade, can now be seen in something approaching a historical perspective; neither politicians nor UN economists come out of it very well. Even in the 1960s, there was considerable experience of international commodity schemes, and considerable knowledge about commodity price movements over more than a century.

Moreover, no very lengthy study was needed to show that raising the prices of internationally traded commodities was not going to help the large concentrations of the world's poor. And yet the ideas promulgated by UNCTAD and seized on by politicians ignored this evidence. There has been a falling off under UNCTAD from the high standard of, for example, the Commodity Policy Studies produced by the FAO in the 1950s and 1960s.

UNCTAD symbolises a shift in power away from the Western countries, as 'non-aligned' countries obtain the power and influence to match their population, resources and, in some cases, military power. It is in the interests of the Western countries to allow this shift of power to take place within a framework of civilised international relations. But the fact that some countries are becoming more powerful says nothing about the intellectual or moral calibre of their leaders' economic philosophies. The fact that neo-Mercantilist policies are put forward forcefully by the leaders of some emerging countries does not prove that these policies are in the interests of their people, or other peoples. There is a strong case—on the basis of government policy and international trade over the past four centuries—that the peoples of the world can benefit reciprocally from harmonious and reasonably unrestricted international trade.

Summary
International trade in the products of temperate agriculture has become considerably restricted by the protectionist policies adopted in some countries and groups of countries, notably the EEC. Although most countries have learned to live with this situation, resentments arising from it could exacerbate what seem to be the growing dangers of mutually damaging trade wars. The basic principles of GATT were never really extended to agricultural products, but some 'rules of the game' are in the interest of all parties. The prices of tropical agricultural products are subject to considerable fluctuation, and attempts have been made since the 1920s to stabilise them through international commodity agreements. These attempts have indicated the difficulties involved, especially when

'stabilising' is interpreted as 'raising'. The 'New International Economic Order' proposed for commodity trade was not well thought out, and the 'Common Fund' which has resulted from it is likely to have only limited results. Nevertheless, the need for a continuing dialogue between producers and consumers, and agreed 'rules of the game' is just as great as in the case of temperate products.

Further Reading

Bhagwati, J. N. (ed.), *The New International Economic Order*, London, 1977.

Caine, Sydney, *Prices for Primary Producers* (Hobart Paper 24), Institute of Economic Affairs, London, 1963.

Coppock, J. O., *North Atlantic Policy: the Agricultural Gap*, New York, 1963.

Corbet, H., *Raw Materials—Beyond the Rhetoric of Commodity Power*, London, 1975.

FAO, Commodity Policy Studies, 1952 onwards.

FAO, *The State of Food and Agriculture*, published annually.

Heidhues, T., *World Food—Interdependence of Farm and Food Policies*, London, 1977.

Johnson, Gale, *World Agriculture in Disarray*, London, 1973.

Johnson, H. G., *Economic Policy towards Less Developed Countries*, London, 1967.

Little, I. M. D., 'Economic relations with the Third World—old myths and new prospects', *Scottish Journal of Political Economy*, 1975.

Morgan, Don, *Merchants of Grain*, London, 1979.

Nagle, J. C., *Agricultural Trade Policies*, Farnborough, 1976.

Payer, C., *Commodity Trade of the Third World*, London, 1976.

Prebisch, P., *Towards a New Trade Policy for Development*, UN, New York, 1964.

Rowe, J. W. F., *Primary Commodities in International Trade*, Cambridge, 1965, Pt. IV.

UNCTAD, *Integrated Programme for Commodities*, 1976.

Yates, Lamartine, *Commodity Control*, London, 1943.

Index